Introduction to *Parallel Programming*

Introduction to *Parallel Programming*

STEVEN BRAWER

Encore Computer Corporation
Marlborough, Massachusetts

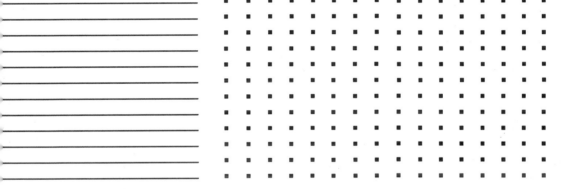

ACADEMIC PRESS, INC.

Harcourt Brace Jovanovich, Publishers

Boston   San Diego   New York
Berkeley   London   Sydney
Tokyo   Toronto

ACADEMIC PRESS, INC.
1250 Sixth Avenue, San Diego, CA 92101

United Kingdom Edition published by
ACADEMIC PRESS INC. (LONDON) LTD.
24–28 Oval Road, London NW1 7DX

Library of Congress Cataloging-in-Publication Data

Brawer, Steven, Date–
    Introduction to parallel programming.

    Bibliography: p.
    Includes index.
    1. Parallel programming (Computer science)
I. Title.
QA76.6.B716   1989   004'.35   88-35104
ISBN 0-12-128470-0

Printed in the United States of America
89 90 91 92   9 8 7 6 5 4 3 2 1

To Kathy

Contents

CHAPTER 1

Introduction

1.1 Who Should Read This Book

This book offers practical instruction in the art and science of parallel programming—creating a single computer program in such a way that it can be executed by more than one processor simultaneously. The book is intended for the applications programmer who is conversant with at least one algorithmic computer language, such as Basic, Fortran, C, Ada, or Pascal, but who has had no exposure to parallel programming. This book does not presume any familiarity with the formal concepts or terminology of computer science, nor does it make use of that terminology. Apart from several sections of Chapter 10, the mathematics is at the level of high-school algebra. The treatment of parallel programming is practical rather than theoretical, with all concepts illustrated by numerous examples. After reading the first six chapters of this book, the reader should be able to create his own parallel programs.

The parallel programming techniques described here are for a *shared-memory multiprocessor computer*. This is a computer with many central processing units (CPUs), all of which have equal access to a common pool of main memory. However, *it is not necessary to have a multiprocessor computer to create and run the parallel programs described in this book. It is quite sensible to run these programs on a uniprocessor (one CPU)*. (This book contains instructions on how to do this.) Many important conceptual problems of parallel programming, such as scheduling, data dependencies, contention, and race conditions—all described in this book—are encountered when parallel programs are run on a uniprocessor. These problems are inherent in the nature of parallelism and exist independently of the hardware.

All that is required to run the programs on a uniprocessor is operating system support of the appropriate kind. Appendix 3 shows how to create and run any of the parallel programs of this book on a uniprocessor computer with Unix.

1.2　Brief Introduction to Parallel Programming

The type of hardware for which the parallel programs of this text will derive the full performance benefit is a *shared-memory multiprocessor* computer. This is a single computer with two or more central processing units (CPUs). All the CPUs share a single pool of memory, and every processor can access any byte of memory in the same amount of time. At present, several general-purpose, shared-memory multiprocessors with more than ten CPUs are available. The operation of such systems is discussed in Chapter 3.

Multiprocessor computers can be used for general-purpose time-sharing as well as for compute-intensive applications. If a user only runs "canned" programs, or creates only single-stream (i.e., nonparallelized, programs that make use of only a single CPU at a time) applications, then a multiprocessor will not be any more or less difficult to use than a uniprocessor. When single-stream programs are used on a multiprocessor computer, each program runs on its own processor, if possible. If the number of programs becomes greater than the number of processors, then effectively each processor shares a smaller number of programs than would be the case on a uniprocessor.

In addition to running completely isolated programs, parallel processing is useful for calculations involving a number of nearly independent but communicating calculations. Examples include independent compilation of files, Monte Carlo simulations of trajectories, database management systems, sorting, enumerating relatively independent paths, exploring a maze, and parallel I/O.

A different kind of parallelism involves apportioning what is normally thought of as an indivisible calculation among many processors. To illustrate the general idea, consider a program which contains a loop over a variable i, in which the statement

```
x(i) = a(i) + b(i)
```

is executed within the loop. If this program were written in a way suitable for parallel processing, then one of the processors might execute the statement

```
x(1) = a(1) + b(1)
```

while, *at the same time*, another may do

```
x(2) = a(2) + b(2)
```

a third might do x(3), and so forth. Because different iterations of the loop are executed simultaneously, the work can be completed more rapidly than if it were done by a single CPU.

The type of parallelism that involves nearly independent tasks, such as database management, parallel I/O, and Monte Carlo simulations of trajectories, are examples of *coarse-grained* parallelism. On the other hand, the example in which different iterations of a loop are executed by different processors is called *fine-grained* parallelism. In coarse-grained parallelism, each calculation is conceptually nearly independent of the others and normally involves relatively infrequent communication among the individual calculations. In fine-grained parallelism, what is normally thought of as a single, indivisible calculation is partitioned among processors. This commonly (but not always) involves subdividing a loop and requires either relatively frequent communication between programs running on different CPUs or else a clever, noninteractive way of apportioning the work among the different processors. Fine-grained parallel programming is generally more difficult to do than coarse-grained parallel programming, although both types depend on exactly the same principles.

1.3   About the Text

The discussion in this book concentrates on the fine-grained applications, although techniques for coarse-grained parallelism are also discussed. There are few general principles for parallelizing such applications, and there is abundant opportunity for the programmer to demonstrate cunning, shrewdness, and intelligence. In many cases, determining the best way to parallelize on the fine-grained scale is an art, and examples are given in the text for which there is room for improvement.

This text stresses simplicity and focuses on fundamentals. As will be seen, it is possible to create a tremendous variety of parallel programs with just five library functions—one for sharing memory, one for creating processes, one for destroying processes, and two for interprocess synchronization (locks and barriers). This entire book, except for Chapter 13, utilizes only these primitives. The challenge of parallel programming arises from the extraordinarily complex interaction of these primitives with each other in any real application. In an appendix, we show how these primitives may be constructed from Unix[1] system calls.

The text is organized as follows. Chapters 3–6 provide an introduction to the basics of parallel programming. In these chapters, the programming model is presented, and the function calls which enable parallelism are described. These include forks (creating parallel processes), joins (destroying them), sharing memory, locks, and barriers (which are used to synchronize parallel programs). Simple scheduling techniques, as well as the subjects of contention and race conditions, are introduced. By the end of Chapter 6, the reader should be able to write a variety of parallel programs.

Chapters 7–10 elaborate on two important concepts of parallel programming: (1) scheduling, or partitioning the work to be done in parallel, and (2) data dependencies, which serve to limit parallelism. Chapter 9 presents a summary of scheduling techniques. Chapter 10 is a detailed treatment of the parallelization of linear recurrence relations, which illustrates how to overcome certain kinds of data dependencies by creating new algorithms. Chapter 10 requires familiarity with elementary matrix manipulations.

Chapter 11 discusses performance and programming issues, including threads, the structure of parallel programs, and caching.

Chapters 12 and 13 present a number of parallelized applications. Chapter 12, which describes a discrete event, discrete time simulator, is perhaps the most difficult chapter of the book. Discrete event simulation is an important area of computing, and, except for special cases, parallel programming is the only technique which has a hope of speeding up such calculations. (Vector processors are normally unsuitable for the considerable amount of logic involved.) As part of Chapter 12, parallel manipulation of linked lists is discussed. In Chapter 13, some additional applications are presented. Included in Chapter 13 is a parallel version of Gaussian elimination.

Chapter 14 discusses events and semaphores. These traditional topics are,

[1] Unix is a registered trademark of AT&T.

in fact, examples of the complex functionality that can be achieved with locks.

Appendix 3 shows how the parallel programs in this book may be run on a uniprocessor running the Unix V operating system or its equivalent.

Problems are interspersed in the text. In some cases, especially in the earlier chapters, the answers to the problems are provided. It is recommended that the reader try to work out the problems himself, before reading the answers. Parallel programming can be tricky, and there are traps which the reader should be aware of. Many of these are introduced in the problems. Many chapters have additional problems at the end. The answers to these are not provided. In Chapter 15, a number of programming projects are described.

The examples in this book use a stripped-down version of Fortran. The resultant language is simple and is virtually a subset of any algorithmic programming language. The constructs of the language are described in Chapter 2, and Appendix 1 compares similar structures in Fortran and C, for the convenience of the C programmer. The parallel programming examples are kept relatively simple so that the concepts and fine points of parallel programming are emphasized rather than the development of commercial quality code. It would be a simple matter to translate the examples into C, Pascal, or any other algorithmic language.

It is possible to implement parallel programming functionality by means of libraries, which provide subroutines that can be called from a program in a conventional language. Parallel programming functionality can also be invoked from a language in which parallel processing has been explicitly incorporated, in the form of language statements. An example of such a language is Ada. In an appendix, the parallel programming language EPF—Encore Parallel Fortran—is described, which is Fortran77 enhanced to include parallel programming language structures. This language is commercially available.

This book takes the library approach. There are several advantages to this. First, the user does not have to learn a new computer language. If the examples were written using a parallel programming language, it almost certainly wouldn't be one a user would either be familiar with or would use elsewhere, since no parallel programming language is either a standard or is widespread.

In addition, the library functions explicitly implement the basic concepts of parallel programming. Generally, a language implementation will stress one or another of the constructs, or even more likely, combine some and leave out others. It is useful to work with the elementary concepts, especially if one is just learning, as one then develops an appreciation of the different classes of situations and how to handle them. Furthermore, with this approach the user can do parallel programming on any computer with a multiprocessing operating system which provides shared memory, a lock, and support for creating and destroying processes.

1.4 The Context of This Book

The discussion in this text does not assume a knowledge of any particular operating system, and all the required concepts are explained. The operating system concepts are modeled after those of Unix. At the time of this writing, the important commercial multiple-processor computers offer Unix, and Unix is at present the most widely used operating system for technical computing.

For those readers who are familiar with Unix or with some other multiprocessing operating system, it might be helpful to distinguish between the fine-grained parallelism, which is covered in this book, and what has traditionally been considered multiprocessing system programming on a uniprocessor. In Unix, there are typically a large number of separate, weakly interacting "programs" (called *processes*) which exist at the same time and which carry out the tasks of the operating system. These processes can either run on separate processors, if they are available, or else they are time-shared with the users' programs on a single processor. The operating system processes coincide, in general, with a logical division of the system work into a number of nearly separate tasks, which transfer information to each other or to shared memory. The nature of the separate tasks generally reflects the underlying design of the operating system. This is a kind of coarse-grained parallel programming, sometimes referred to as *functional parallelism*.

The important point is that time-sharing operating systems have used multiple, nearly independent processes for almost 20 years, even though they have been running on uniprocessor computers. The multiple processes represent a logical subdivision of the tasks of the operating system. Using separate processes, even though running on a uniprocessor, allows the operating system to have great flexibility while keeping the design simple. Simplicity has often been stated as an explicit design goal of Unix.

Operating-system parallel programming, then, normally involves creating processes that communicate infrequently with each other. On the other hand, the applications described in this text are fine-grained. There is normally no performance advantage in running fine-gained parallel programs on a uniprocessor. Apart from some simple cases, fine-grained parallel programs are more complex than their uniprocessor counterparts. In fact, certain problems have yet to be formulated in a way suitable for parallel processing, and parallel programming is still a research topic at many universities. Moreover, fine-grained parallel programs will normally run slower on a uniprocessor than the nonparallel version of the program, because of the overhead of creating processes and the overhead of the required synchronization. One can learn parallel programming quite well on a uniprocessor, but for performance advantages, the programs are meant for the multiprocessor hardware.

1.5 Add-Ons

The author has made every effort to ensure that the parallel programs in this book are error free. Every program has been run on the Encore Multimax multiprocessor computer, using the library calls appropriate to that system. Nonetheless, there is abundant opportunity for error to enter the text between the program and the final book. Therefore, the author and the publisher assume no responsibility for errors or omissions. No liability is assumed for damage resulting from the use of information and programs in this book. Nor is it implied or stated that the programs meet any standard of reliability, structure, maintainability, or correctness. These programs and information should not be used in situations where physical damage or bodily injury can occur. Nor should they be used in applications for which the user has a formal responsibility. You must use the information and programs in this book at your own risk.

Having said that, the programs in this book are available on floppy disk in the Fortran version or in an equivalent C version. Use the coupon at the end of the book to order.

CHAPTER 2

Tiny Fortran

2.1 Introduction

This chapter presents the "Tiny Fortran" language which will be used in the examples in the text. Tiny Fortran is a proper subset of Fortran77, incorporating just enough features to enable the creation of parallel programs. (There is one small exception in that identifiers can be arbitrarily large in Tiny Fortran, as discussed below.) Tiny Fortran does not include any constructs which are not a part of Fortran77. In addition, it includes only those features which are common to all algorithmic languages, such as C, Basic, Modula-2, Pascal, and Ada. Tiny Fortran should be readily comprehensible to anyone with a working knowledge of one of those languages. The reader who knows Fortran may skip this chapter.

Appendix 1 presents a comparison of Tiny Fortran with the equivalent statements in C.

In order to carve Tiny Fortran from Fortran77, a great deal of Fortran77 was eliminated. The details of Tiny Fortran are given in the next sections. Below is a general description of what is present and what is absent.

- All I/O has been eliminated except for a simple, unformatted read and write to the monitor. There is no disk I/O. There are no format statements.

- *There are no global variables*. In Fortran77, global variables are specified in *common* statements. This mechanism is so different from what is used in other languages that the *common* statement, and global variables, are not used in any examples in this book. There is no *equivalence* statement.
- The only data types are reals and integers. There are no logical, character, double-precision, or complex variables.
- The control structures are limited to do-loops, unrestricted gotos, and if-then-else-endif blocks. There are no computed gotos, jumps from subroutine arguments, or multiple subroutine entry points.
- Both subroutine calls and function "calls" have been retained. A function is a module that returns a value (real or integer for Tiny Fortran). A subroutine is called by prefacing the module name with the word "call." Values are not returned by subroutines.
- Except for one application, it is assumed that the language is not recursive. The Fortran77 standard states that Fortran is nonrecursive, and while some implementations of Fortran and Basic do allow recursion, it was felt that nonrecursion is the lowest common denominator. (It is probable that the next, updated Fortran standard will allow recursion.)
- *There is no default typing*. In standard Fortran, variables whose names start with the letters i–n are integers, unless the variables are explicitly typed. A stronger connection with other languages can be made if default typing is not allowed. Most Fortran compilers include an option which turns off default typing. The author, who has confronted the perils of typing mistakes in Fortran programs for many years, strongly recommends use of this option.
- One liberty with the Fortran standard has been taken. The names of identifiers (variables and modules) are allowed to be any length. This is done so that the names used in the examples are informative and self-documenting. In standard Fortran77, names can consist of up to six characters. Many Fortran implementations allow identifiers to have more than six characters.
- Most Fortran keywords are not used in Tiny Fortran, such as assign, data, block data, implicit, dimension, internal, external, statement function, entry, and rewind.

2.2   Program Structure

A Fortran program is made up of a single main program and any number of subroutines and functions. (The main and each function or subroutine is a *module*.) Modules can be arbitrarily distributed among files, and all files may be compiled separately. There is no need to explicitly define or declare functions and subroutines earlier in a file which contains modules that invoke them (as must be done in C, for example). However, function names must be typed.

Each module has the following structure:

module name (if not main)
declarations
executable statements
return (if not main)
end

Fortran is line-oriented, which means that all executable statements are on a single line unless the statement is explicitly continued onto the next line or lines. Comment lines have a c in the first column, in which case the remainder of the line is ignored by the compiler. Otherwise, all statements must be indented at least seven spaces. Any statement may have a *label*, which is a nonzero integer, and labels are put anywhere in columns 1–5. Any symbol in column 6 of a line indicates that the line is a continuation of the statement in the closest previous noncomment line.

An example of a module which computes the maximum value of an array, and which has all the sections listed above, is

```
c       module name
        subroutine find_max_value(a,n,amax)

c       declarations
        real a(n),amax
        integer n,i
c       find maximum value of a(i),1 <= i <= n.
c       amax is maximum value.

c       executable statements. Note indentation for clarity.
        amax = a(1)
        do 1 i = 2,n
            if (a(i) .gt. amax) then
c           the following statement is continued to
c           the next line for purposes of illustration.
            amax =
     s                          a(i)
            endif
  1     continue
```

```
return
end
```

In Fortran, spaces are meaningless, so that, for example, the following statements (which appear in the previous module) are valid:

```
integern,i
doli=1,n
reala(n),amax
```

A common programming error is to omit the comma from a do-statement, so that the statement

```
do 1 i = k j
```

is actually compiled as

```
doli = kj
```

that is, the variable `doli` is set equal to the value of the variable `kj`. (The comma should appear between k and j.)

2.3   Identifiers

An identifier is a name, either of a variable or a module. In standard Fortran77, identifiers must have six characters or less. This constraint is relaxed in Tiny Fortran, so that identifiers can have any number of characters. The characters allowed in identifiers are small and capital letters (which are regarded as the same), numbers, and underscores. Every identifier must begin with a letter.

Valid identifiers are

```
x10
variable_which_holds_temporary_result
thisisalongnamewithoutunderscores
w123456789000007811
```

Spaces are meaningless, so that the statement

```
spin lock variable = 20
```

will be compiled as if it had been written

```
spinlockvariable = 20.
```

2.4   Declarations: Scalars and Arrays

Types are integer or real (floating point). For simplicity, only a single float-ing-point type is used. Every variable must be declared. Declarations have the following form:

type var [*var,var, . . .*]

where *type* is one of the keywords `real` or `integer`. Any number of iden-tifiers may be declared in the same statement. The term *var* is the name of a scalar, array, or function. Declarations may be continued onto any number of lines. If the variable is an array, its declaration must include the dimen-sion.
 A variable is either a scalar or an array. Arrays must be declared in main with their full dimensions. Arrays may be declared with their starting and ending dimension, thus,

```
real a(0:20),b(22:101)
```

This notation means that the index of a can take on any value between 0 and 20 inclusive, while the index of b can be between 22 and 101 inclusive. Thus,

```
i = 30
a(i) = 10.0
```

is an error, as is

```
i = 1
x = b(i)
```

If an array is dimensioned with only a single number, it is assumed that the leading index is 1. Thus

```
real array(80)
```

is equivalent to

```
real array(1:80).
```

This notation is generalized for multidimensional arrays. Thus

```
integer multi_dim_array(20,-8:44,0:3,16)
```

declares that `multi_dim_array` is a four-dimensional array, in which
the index of the first dimension can be between 1 and 20 inclusive, the index
of the second dimension is between −8 and 44 inclusive, the index of the
third dimension is between 0 and 3 inclusive, and the index of the fourth
dimension is between 1 and 16 inclusive.

The names of functions which are called in the module must also be declared as real or integer. For example,

```
integer find_a_number,a(10),k
  .
  .
  .
k = find_a_number(a)
```

(where the vertical ellipses mean any number of declarations and/or executable statements). The compiler "knows" that `find_a_number` is a function because it is followed by a pair of parentheses and because it was not
declared as an array.

2.5   I/O

The only I/O is unformatted I/O to the terminal. The statements are illustrated below:

```
      integer i,j,nproc
      real a(10)

      print *,'i = ',i,'j = ',j
      do 1 i = 1,10
         print *,'i a(i) = ',i,a(i)
 1    continue
      read *,nproc
```

The first print statement prints the values of i and j. The second prints i and a(i). The read statement assigns what the user enters to the variable nproc.

2.6   Array Storage

Many of the examples of this book make use of the fact that arrays are stored in column order. That is, for a multidimensional array, *the leftmost index varies most rapidly*. For example, the array a which is dimensioned a(4,3) is stored in the following order:

```
a(1,1),a(2,1),a(3,1),a(4,1),a(1,2),a(2,2),a(3,2),a(4,2),
a(1,3),a(2,3),a(3,3),a(4,3).
```

The usefulness of this storage scheme will become apparent when we discuss the manner in which variables are passed as arguments.

2.7   Assignment

Assignments are as in any language. Thus

```
real x,y
integer i

x = 10.0
```

means replace the current contents of (the memory location represented by) x with 10.0.

There is automatic coercion. Thus,

```
y = i
```

first converts the value of i to floating point, then stores the result in y.

2.8   Arithmetic Expressions

Arithmetic expressions are constructed in the conventional manner from the operators:

+   add

  −   subtract or unary minus
*   multiply
/   divide
**   exponentiation

The priority of operators is

    ** > *,/ > +,−.

In the examples in this book, parentheses are used where any possible ambiguity can exist.

Examples of arithmetic expressions are

```
i * j + 3              (the same as (i * j) + 3)
sqrt(x**2 + y**2)   (same as sqrt((x**2) + (y**2))
```

Conversions from integer to real is as in all languages and will not be discussed here. (The expressions in this book will not depend upon automatic conversions.)

Fortran has built in functions, which must be declared in the same manner as user-written functions. The built-in functions include

```
        real x,y,sqrt,float
        integer i,j,k,mod,int,min,max,a(100)

c       return the square root of x
            y = sqrt(x)
c       convert x to an integer.
            i = int(x)
c       convert i to a floating-point number.
            x = float(i)
c       return j modulo k.
            i = mod(j,k)
c       return min of a(j) and 50
            i = min(a(j),50)
c       return the maximum of j and 0
            i = max(j,0)
```

There are also the standard trigonometric, exponential, and logarithmic functions.

2.9   If-then-else-endif Blocks

The only conditional in Tiny Fortran is the if-then-else block. Its form is

> *if logical_exp then*
>   (statements)
> [*elseif logical_exp then*
>   (statements)
> [*elseif logical_exp then*
> .
> .
> .
> [*else*
>   (statements)] . . .]
> *endif*

Here, `logical_exp` means any logical expression. One kind of logical_expression is a `simple_logical_expression`

> `simple_logical_expression = (arith_exp op arith_exp)`

where `arith_exp` is an arithmetic expression and `op` is a logical operator. The logical operators are

`.eq.`   equal to
`.ne.`   not equal to
`.lt.`   less than
`.gt.`   greater than
`.le.`   less than or equal to
`.ge.`   greater than or equal to

Examples of `simple_logical_expressions` are

> `(x .eq. y(-3))`
> `(2 * sqrt(x**2 + y**2) .ge. float(i))`

A `logical_exp` is in general made up of `simple_logical_expressions` and the connectives `.and.` and `.or.`.

> `logical_exp = sle [{.and.:.or.} sle [{.and.:.or.} sle...]]`

where `sle` is any `simple_logical_expression`. Examples of logical expressions are

```
(x .gt. 0) .and. (x .le. 10)
```

which means that x must be between 1 and 10 inclusive, or

```
(y(i) .lt. x(i)) .or. (y(i) .lt. z(i))
```

which means that y(i) is less than either x(i) or z(i).

The `sle` may be evaluated in any order (as opposed to C, where they are evaluated left to right). The expression,

```
if ((x .ne. 0) .and. (a/x .gt. 0)) then
    .
    .
    .
```

may not work correctly if the second simple logical expression, containing a/x, is evaluated first.

Examples of if-then-else blocks are

```
if (a(i) .gt. amax) then
      amax = a(i)
endif
```

If a(i) is less than or equal to amax, then execution continues with the statement following endif. On the other hand, if a(i) is greater than amax, the statement in the if-block is executed, and then control passes to the statement following endif.

This can be written as

```
if (a(i) .gt. amax) amax = a(i)
```

Another example is

```
if (x .lt. 1) then
      z = 1
else
      z = 2
endif
```

In this case, if x is less than 1, z is set equal to 1 and execution continues with the statement following endif. On the other hand, if x is greater than or equal to 1, z is set equal to 2 and execution continues with the statement following endif.

For a final example, consider

```
if ((w .lt. x) .and. (x .lt. y)) then
      z = 1
elseif (w .gt. 5) then
      z = 2
elseif (w .eq. 22.3) then
      z = 3
else
      z = 4
endif
```

If w is less than x and less than y, then z is set equal to 1 and execution continues with the statement following endif. If this is not the case, but if w is greater than 5, then z is set equal to 2 and execution continues with the statement following endif. If neither of these conditions is true, but if w equals 22.3, then z is set equal to 3 and execution continues with the statement following endif. If none of these conditions is valid, then z is set equal to 4 and execution continues with the statement following endif.

2.10 Loops

The only looping construct in Fortran77 is the do-loop. The general form of the do loop is

```
do lab var = exp1, exp2, exp3
      .
      .
      .
          (statements)
lab continue
```

Here, lab is a label, meaning a positive integer. The variable var is any nonarray variable, real or integer. The arithmetic expressions exp1, exp2, and exp3 are any arithmetic expressions, which can evaluate to reals or integers.

When the do-loop is first encountered, the expressions exp1, exp2, and exp3 are all evaluated and converted to the same type as var, if the types are inconsistent. (Each expression may be real or integer, separately.) The variable var is then set equal to the value of exp1 (the converted value is used). If exp3 is positive, then if, initially,

```
var > exp2,
```

the loop is not done at all, and control passes to the first executable statement following the

```
lab continue
```

statement. On the other hand, if

```
var <= exp2,
```

then the statements within the loop (which can contain nested loops) are executed with the value of var set equal to exp1. After the statements are executed, the variable var is incremented by exp3. The variable var is then tested against exp2 again, and if it is less than or equal to exp2, the statements within the loop are done again, this time with var equal to exp1 + exp3. This process continues until var becomes greater than exp2, at which time the statements within the loop are not executed and control passes to the first executable statement after the loop.

If exp3 is negative, a similar procedure occurs, except that now the test is var less than exp2 (so that exp2 is the minimum value the loop variable can take).

Note that a do-loop need not be executed at all (in contrast to earlier versions of Fortran, where a loop was always executed at least once.)

Examples of do-loops are

```
      integer sum, i
      sum = 0
      do 1 i = 1,10
          sum = sum + 1
   1    continue
```

The statement

```
sum = sum+1
```

is executed ten times, for which i successively takes on the values 1, 2, 3,
..., 10, and at the end of the loop, sum will have the value 10.

```
integer i,j,sum,a(10)
k = 3
j = 12
sum = 0
do 2 i = 2 * k,mod(j,3),2
      sum = sum + a(i)
2    continue
```

The do-statement is equivalent to

```
do 2 i = 6,0,2
```

and the loop will not be executed even once.
    The final example is

```
integer i, ...
do 1 i = 10,1,-2
         .
         .
         .
1    continue
```

The loop will be executed five times, with i successively taking the values
10, 8, 6, 4, and 2.

2.11   Function/Subroutine Calls

Function names must be typed, like other variable names. Subroutine names
are not typed. When typing a function name, leave off the parentheses. Functions and subroutines may be called with no arguments. Parentheses must
be included for function calls with no arguments as this is the only way the
compiler "knows" that the name refers to a function rather than to a variable. When calling a subroutine with no arguments, use of parentheses is
optional. Examples are

```
real float,x,y,do_it
integer proc_id,fork
x = float(y)
```

```
x = do_it()
proc_id = fork()
call join()
call join
```

Functions return values and subroutines do not. To create a module, the function and subroutine definitions are

```
subroutine foo[(...)]
integer function foo(...)
real function foo(...)
```

2.12   Passing Arguments in Function/Subroutine Calls

It is common in Fortran to dimension arrays in function and subroutines as follows:

```
integer a(10),b(0:20)
.
.
.
call funct(a,b)
.
.
.
end

subroutine funct(x,y)
integer a(1),b(0:1)
.
.
.
return
end
```

In subroutine `funct`, the variable a is declared as an array of dimension 1, while the variable b has been declared an array of dimension 2, for which the lowest value of the index is 0. It is essential that the lowest value of the subscript be provided, but unless run-time checking of array indexes is performed, it is not necessary to inform the routine of the upper limit of the array index. The notation

```
a(1)
```

informs the compiler that a will be used as an array in the subroutine `funct`, and not as a function, and that the lower index is 1, and similarly for b.

The most important point about passing arguments in functions is that *all arguments are passed by reference*. That is, all variables are passed as pointers, not as the value. Changes made to arguments in subroutines are then visible to the caller. For example,

```
integer i
i = 20
call funct(i)
print *,'i = ',i
end

subroutine funct(x)
integer x
x = 0
return
end
```

The output of this program will be

```
i = 0
```

This is referred to as a *hidden change* of the variable i. Because i is passed by reference from the main to the subroutine `funct`, when it is altered in the subroutine, the alteration is also visible in main.

As a more complex example, consider the following:

```
integer a(10),i
do 1 i = 1,10
    a(i) = 2 * i
1    continue
call alter_array(a(3))
print *, 'a(3) = ',a(3)
print *, 'a(4) = ',a(4)
print *, 'a(5) = ',a(5)
end

subroutine alter_array(dum)
integer dum(1)
dum(1) = 0
```

```
        dum(2) = -1
        return
        end
```

The output of the main program is

```
        a(3) = 0
        a(4) = -1
        a(5) = 10
```

When a(3) is passed as the argument, what is actually passed is a pointer which points to the memory location where a(3) is stored. The subroutine "believes" it is getting an array dum where dum(1) is the first element. When the subroutine alter_array assigns 0 to dum(1), it is actually assigning this value to the third element of a. When it assigns −1 to dum(2), it is assigning this value to the fourth element of a.

Another trick makes use of the fact that, for multidimensional arrays, the leftmost index varies fastest. The following fragment,

```
        real a(20,30),t,c(20)
        integer i,n,k
        .
        .
        .
        do 2 j = 1,n
            do 1 i = 1,n
                c(j) = c(j) + t * a(i,k)
1           continue
2       continue
```

is equivalent to

```
        real a(20,30),t,c(20)
        integer i,n,k
        .
        .
        .
        do 2 j = 1,n
            call do_sum(a(1,k),c(j),t,n)
2       continue

        subroutine do_sum(x,sum,t,n)
```

```
      real x(1),sum,t
      integer n
      do 1 i = 1,n
          sum = sum + x(i) * t
1     continue
      return
      end
```

When calling the subroutine with the argument a(1,k), it passes to the subroutine a pointer that points to the 1,kth element of a. Then x(1) is the same as a(1,k), x(2) is the same as a(2,k), x(3) is the same as a(3,k), and so forth, while sum is equivalent to c(j), which is altered by the subroutine.

When calling a function, any arguments which are expressions are evaluated and passed as constants. The evaluation of arguments can be made in any order, and different compilers will do it differently. Thus, caution must be taken if the arguments contain other functions which can produce side effects.

CHAPTER 3

Hardware and Operating System Models

3.1 Introduction

The purpose of this chapter is to present a simple, abstract model of the hardware and software of a multiprocessor computer, a model which is sufficient to allow a programmer to create parallel programs. It is outside the scope of this text to present an introduction to the hardware of multiprocessors, nor is such knowledge needed to perform shared-memory parallel programming. This text is a programmer's manual, and it is normal to omit discussions of hardware in a programmer's manual. What is needed, rather, is an abstract model which is sufficient to allow sensible parallel programs to be written in a high-level language.

The abstract model for conventional programming on uniprocessors is called *the Von Neumann model*. In this model, the central processor performs the following actions over and over (until it gets to a "stop" instruction):

1. Read an instruction from memory;
2. Read any data required by the instructions from memory;
3. Perform the operation on the data;
4. Store results in memory;
5. Go to (1).

The hardware of modern computers acts in a much more complex manner than indicated by this model. Thus, instructions can be pipelined, the CPUs can perform in parallel, or in vector mode, there can be cache memory, there may be DMA, and so forth. Nevertheless, the simple model underlies all high-level programming. When the programmer writes

```
real x,y,f
.
.
.
x = x + 1.0
y = f(x)
.
.
.
```

he is implicitly thinking in terms of the Von Neumann model, so that x is first read, then incremented, and then stored back into the same location from which it was read. It is only then that the function f is called with the new value of x as the argument.

The model of parallel programming will be on a similar level of abstraction. Each CPU of a shared-memory multiprocessor computer behaves exactly as outlined above—that is, exactly as it does in a uniprocessor. All that is needed to make a multiprocessor model is to describe how CPUs act in concert, and this is the purpose of this chapter.

3.2   Hardware

An abstract model of the hardware is shown in Fig. 3-1. This is a model of a *shared-memory multiprocessor*, so called because the processors share a single pool of memory. In this model, there are many CPUs and I/O modules. The memory contains the instructions executed by each CPU, as well as the data on which the program operates. I/O will be neglected in this text.

The model of Fig. 3-1 is meant to imply that *any CPU can access any memory location at any time, with one exception: No single memory location can be accessed by two CPUs simultaneously.* If two processors try to access the same memory location at the same time, for read or write, one will always give way to the other. (All the processors can always read or write the same memory location, but two or more can't do so at exactly the same instant.) This precedence is an important practical and theoretical restriction, as without it no synchronization between processes would be possible. In the

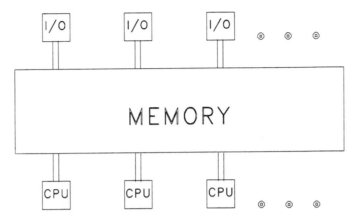

Figure 3-1.   Schematic model of a shared-memory multiprocessor computer.

model, different processes can access different memory locations simultaneously.

Although this schematic model is an idealization, fast overlapped access to the memory can be implemented, so memory access is almost simultaneous. The closer the implementation gets to the idealized model of Fig. 3-1, the more effective the parallel program will be in comparison with a comparable sequential one.

Two implementations of the model of Fig. 3-1 are shown in Fig. 3-2. Figure 3-2(a) shows a bus structure with "cards" plugged into a system bus. Any card that can be plugged into a uniprocessor bus can in principle be used in a multiprocessor. The most important cards are processor cards, each with one or more CPUs, memory cards, I/O modules, and a bus arbiter. In Fig. 3-2(b), the CPUs and I/O modules access memory through a switch. This is a mainframe-type model. Both these implementations can be modeled by Fig. 3-1. Hardware implementations will not be discussed further, and the programmer is urged to adopt the model of Fig. 3-1.

The strictly hardware model of Fig. 3-1 must be enhanced to encompass the pervasive influence of the operating system in the practice of shared-memory parallel programming. The next sections discuss those aspects of the operating system which are relevant for parallel programming.

3.3   Time-Sharing with a Single Processor

Before introducing the programming model of a multiprocessor computer, it will be useful to describe the comparable model of a uniprocessor. Figure 3-3 shows the familiar model of a time-sharing, uniprocessor computer.

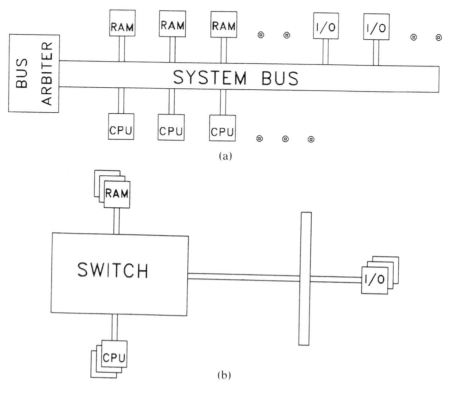

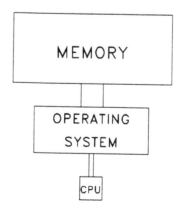

Figure 3-2.   Two implementations of a shared-memory multiprocessor.

Figure 3-3.   Illustration of the logical position of a multiprocessing operating system in a uniprocessor computer.

There is primary memory, a processor, and a number of peripherals, including secondary memory. The processor can be of any complexity. On the processor board, there may be cache memory, a memory-management unit, a floating point accelerator, and a pipelined CPU. The various components can be connected by a bus, switch, or some other arrangement. The hardware connecting the various modules is not shown in Figure 3-3.

Figure 3-3 is meant to imply that *the operating system controls the regions of memory which the CPU accesses.* In a multiprocessing, time-sharing operating system, many programs can be executing "simultaneously." That is, at any instant of time, one or more users could have started up one or more programs, and not all the programs have yet terminated. To the users, the programs are all running simultaneously even though there is only a single processor. The function of the operating system is to ensure that this situation proceeds smoothly and to give all programs equitable access to the processor. In addition, the operating system must make sure that the processor only accesses the memory of the executing program and not the memory of other programs. (This is actually a simplified view, but it is sufficient for our purposes.)

Consider, for example, two programs, a and b, both executing "at the same time." The situation is illustrated in Fig. 3-4. When the programs are loaded from disk, the data and instructions for program a go into the region of memory marked a in Fig. 3-4, while those for b go into the region marked b. These are different sections of physical memory. These two regions are called *processes*. The exact meaning of that term will be given in the next chapter. For now, we will continue to refer to these memory regions as programs.

Logically, time-sharing works as follows. The processor executes instructions in region a, say. All the program instructions and data required for program a are in this region. In particular, while running the program in region a, the processor never reads or writes a memory location in region b.

After program a has been running for a while, the operating system, on its own (as far as the user is concerned) causes a "switch," so the processor now runs the program in region b of memory. While b is executing, the operating system makes sure that no reference is made to region a of memory.

While one program is running, the other program is not running. We will say that the not-running program is *idle*. Actually, idled programs can be in many states. For example, in the Unix operating system, an idle program can be "asleep," "ready-to-run," "swapped" onto disk, and so forth. For pur-

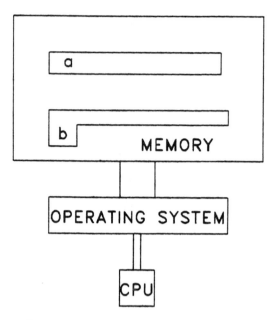

Figure 3-4.   Schematic illustration of a uniprocessor computer with a multiprocessing operating system and two programs a and b in memory which alternate use of the CPU.

poses of this book, it is not necessary to make these distinctions, and so the term *idle* will be used in all cases to describe a program that is not actually executing on a processor. Note that regions a and b of Fig. 3-4 can belong to the *same* user.

A diagram of the behavior of the programs a and b on the uniprocessor is shown in Fig. 3-5. Each line is a *timeline* for the program, and indicates whether the program is running or not. The solid line shows when the program is executing, and the spiral line shows when the program is idle. In the case of programs a and b, when one program is running, the other must be idle. (In fact, there is also *overhead*, where the operating system must use the processor, service interrupts, and so forth, but this is not shown.)

In summary, the operating system has two functions: *scheduling* (apportioning the single processor among all the users) and *memory management* (making sure that when a program is running, the correct region of memory is being accessed).

An operating system, of course, has many more functions than scheduling and memory management. For example, the operating system must manage I/O, provide an interface to the user, provide "services" to programs, communicate with other computers, offer utilities for program development, and

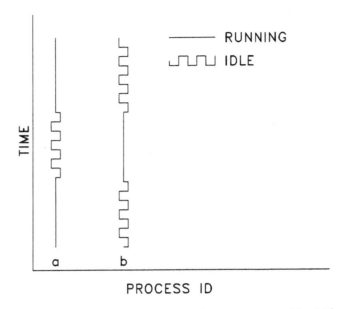

Figure 3-5. Timeline illustrating the execution of programs a and b of Fig. 3-4. The solid line means that the program is executing on the processor, while the curly line indicates that the program is idled (in memory, but not executing on the processor).

so forth. While all these are important in a real operating system, they are not relevant for our parallel programming model. All that is necessary to know is that *the operating system acts as an autonomous switch, allowing different programs to execute on the single processor at different times, and it protects the memory occupied by a given program from being accessed by any of the other programs.*

3-4   Time-sharing with Multiple Processors

The simplest use of a multiprocessor computer is to execute each program on a separate processor as much as possible. The model for this situation is shown in Fig. 3-6. This figure is meant to suggest that no processor is favored over any other. The operating system schedules a program to run on one of the available processors. The operating system treats all the processors as equal, and the operating system itself runs on any one of the processors (or on a number of processors simultaneously). Such a situation is referred to as *symmetric multiprocessing*. This is opposed to nonsymmetric multipro-

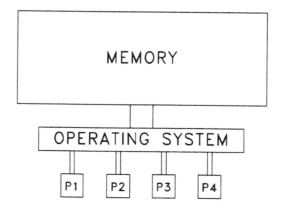

Figure 3-6.   Illustration of the logical position of a multiprocessing operating system in a multiprocessor computer. p1, p2, p3, and p4 are CPUs.

cessing, where one processor may be reserved for the operating system or other special functions.

Figure 3-7 shows how the operating system might distribute programs a, b, c, d, e, and f among the four processors p1, p2, p3, and p4. In Fig. 3-7(a), programs d, b, f, and a are running on processors 1, 2, 3, and 4 respectively, while programs c and e are idle. In 3-7(b) e, a, f, and c are running on processors 1, 2, 3, and 4 respectively, while b and d are idle. Note that program a has switched processors. Processor "jumping" occurs because, after a program has been idled, it can be restarted on any one of the available processors. A program does not "own" a processor merely because it has been executing on that processor for a while.

A possible "timeline" for this situation is shown in Fig. 3-8. At any instant, four programs are running, each referencing its own section of memory. The user never knows on which processor any particular program is running, and this information is not shown in the timeline diagram. In general, if a program has been idled, it will be started up again on a different processor than the one on which it ran previously. The program will migrate from one processor to another without the user ever being aware of it, unless he takes pains to examine the scheduling.

3.5   A Brief Description of Tightly Coupled Multiprocessing

A multiprocessor computer, if it is properly designed, can do more than apportion noninteracting programs among processors. It can also apportion a single program among many processors, so each processor only executes

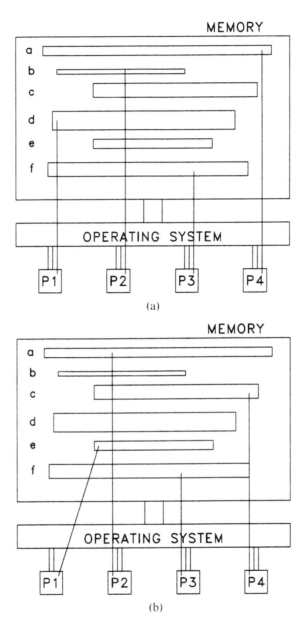

Figure 3-7.   Illustration of how programs a–f in memory may execute on the four processors p1–p4. (a) e and c are idle. (b) b and d are idle. Note that program a has switched processors.

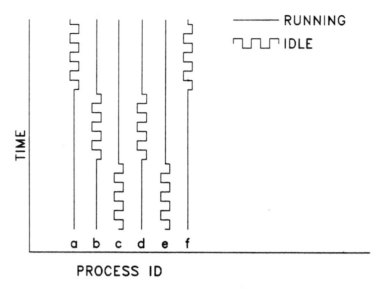

Figure 3-8.   Possible timeline for the execution of the programs a–f of Fig. 3-7. At any time, four programs are executing and two are idle.

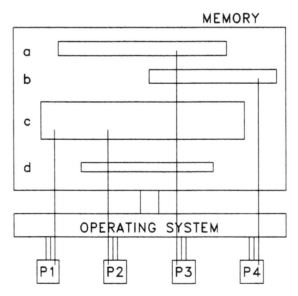

Figure 3-9.   Schematic illustration of the way in which a parallel program would execute on a multiprocessor computer. Program c is actually two programs, each one doing a portion of a calculation and each running on a different processor.

part of the calculation. This is done to get a *speedup*—the program may well run n times faster on n processors than it runs on a single processor. If it takes time t to run on a uniprocessor, it could take time t/n to run on a multiprocessor.

A schematic illustration of such a situation is shown in Fig. 3-9, where a single program "c" has been broken up into two programs, each running on its own processor. In this case, processors 1 and 2 are running program c, while processor 3 is running program a and processor 4 is running b. Program d is idle in Fig. 3-9.

The following program fragment, which multiplies two arrays, a and b, to produce a single number, is a typical job which could benefit from parallel processing.

```
real sum,a(1000),b(1000)
integer n,i
      .
      .
      .
sum = 0.
do 1 i = i,n
        sum = sum + a(i) * b(i)
  1     continue
```

Program 3-1

In this case, one would obtain a speedup in the computation if program 0 does the odd values of i, while program 1 does the even values. That is, each program does the slightly different program:

```
Program 0                            Program 1
     .                                    .
     .                                    .
     .                                    .
   sum1 = 0.                            sum2 = 0.
   do 1 = 1,n,2                         do 1 i = 2,n,2
      sum1 = sum1 + a(i) * b(i)            sum2 = sum2 + a(i) * b(i)
 1    continue                        1    continue
```

Program 3-2

When they are both finished, one of the programs (say program 0) can add the two partial sums,

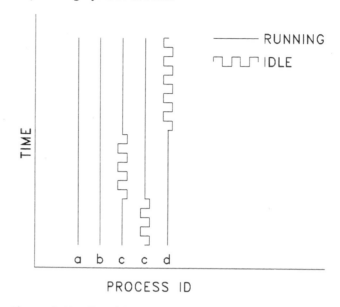

Figure 3-10.   Possible timeline for the situation of Fig. 3-9.

```
sum = sum1 + sum2
```

to complete the calculation. In this case, the calculation should run twice as fast as it did with a single processor, apart from the overhead of combining `sum1` and `sum2` at the end. It is this division of labor which characterizes parallel programming. In fact, one could split the sum up among even more programs and get even faster execution.

One possible timeline of this calculation is shown in Fig. 3-10. Two lines have been drawn for "program" c because it can be run by two processors at the same time. At any time, only four programs are running, and two of them may be, in some sense, the same program.

The two programs c (Fig. 3-10) running on two different processors are actually the same program, and some of the data they use is shared while other data must be private. When two or more programs share data, it means that they can all access the same physical memory location. When two programs share data, they are acting differently from the independent-program model, as illustrated, for example, in Fig. 3-4, where the memory regions of the two programs are disjoint. If a variable is declared as shared (see the next chapter), the operating system, in its function as memory manager, allows more than one program to access the same physical memory locations. A portion of the memory regions of different programs is the same. It is normal in a parallel program for some data to be shared and some to be private. In Program 3-2 above, programs 0 and 1 might share the variable sum2, and they may share the arrays a and b to save space, while each must have its own private value of i. The way in which memory can be shared is discussed in detail in Chapter 4.

Referring to the schematic hardware model of Fig. 3-1, it is seen that sharing memory is a natural way for two programs to communicate with each other. When one program changes the value of a variable, another program can read the new value from the same memory location. In the example above, when program 1 is finished with its partial sum, and stores its result in the shared variable sum2, then program 0 can read the new value and incorporate into the total sum.

3.6 Summary

In this chapter, an abstract model of a multiprocessor computer is developed. The basic features of the model are

1. Each CPU of the multiprocessor can be modeled by the Von Neumann model (Section 3.1).
2. Each CPU can access any memory location simultaneously, except that the same location can't be accessed by two CPUs simultaneously.
3. The operating system functions as a switcher (or scheduler) and memory manager. It switches programs among processors, and it ensures that a CPU accesses only one program at a time.
4. The scheduling of programs is random, so far as the user is concerned.

This model is sufficient for the development of parallel programs in a high-level language to run on a shared memory multiprocessor or on a uniprocessor.

CHAPTER 4

Processes, Shared Memory, and Simple Parallel Programs

4.1 Introduction

This chapter demonstrates how to create parallel programs. One way to distribute a single calculation among several different processors is to make each portion of the calculation appear to the operating system as if it were an independent program, even though the programs are related and may share some data. A framework for doing this is the concept of the *process*.

The *process* is a generalization of a program and is central to shared-memory multiprocessing. In this chapter, we discuss what a process is, how to create and destroy processes, and how processes share memory. Simple programs are presented which illustrate the ideas. It is assumed that, through its scheduling function, the operating system will distribute the processes among the available processors. Users need be concerned only with creating processes and not with the existence of multiple processors. The operating system will "put" the processes onto the processors. (Of course, if the user has the computer to himself, then for the best performance, and if the program allows it, the number of processes he creates should equal the number of processors.)

The process concept serves as the *logical* foundation of parallel programming. A refinement of this concept, called *threads*, is discussed in Chapter 10.

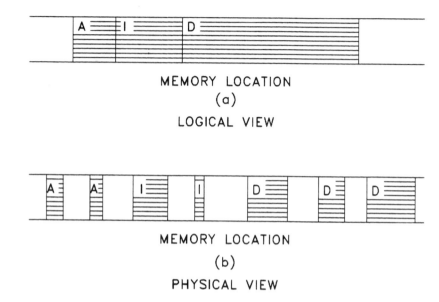

Figure 4-1.   Illustration of the occupation of memory by a process. (a) Logical view. (b) Physical view.

4.2   Processes and Processors

The description of the process given here is based on that of the Unix operating system. Whenever the user executes a program, the operating system creates a *process* in memory. The process contains the "program" itself (the machine instructions and space set aside for data) as well as other information required by the operating system, such as page tables, information about open files, the stack, and so forth. The process is a more general concept than a program and is useful in those cases where two different programs must share memory or communicate with each other in some way. The regions a and b of Figure 3-4, and the regions a, b . . . f of Fig. 3-7, are actually processes.

A schematic representation of a process is shown in Fig. 4-1(a). It is sufficient for our purposes to assume that each process has three parts—an administrative section, a section for program instructions, and a section for data (the variables that the program has allocated). These sections are labeled A, I, and D in Fig. 4-1(a).

The administration area has information that the operating system needs in order to execute the process and to time share with other processes and with itself. It contains, for example, pointers to the instruction and data sections and information about open files, page tables, the stack, and so forth. The instruction section contains the machine instructions which are executed, and the data section contains the values of the global variables. (Variables local to a subroutine are normally put on the stack, in the administration area of the process, unless they are "static" or "save" variables.)

The instruction and data sections need not be contiguous. If there are many processes executing, memory will in general be *fragmented*, so that the instruction and data sections of a process will occupy noncontiguous regions of physical memory (Fig. 4-1(b)). The sections are logically contiguous, however. The relation between the physical, possibly fragmented, memory and the logical view of the sections as contiguous is mapped by the *page tables*. The subject of page tables is beyond the scope of this text but is covered in most elementary treatments of operating systems.

For purposes of this text, the reader should always think of the three sections of the process as contiguous—that is, he should take the logical viewpoint, as illustrated in Fig. 4-1(a).

A process is a program along with its environment (its support structures). When the operating system does a switch—when it stops one process from executing (thereby idling it) and allows another process to use the processor—the registers and program counter of the original process are stored in the administration area of the process being idled. Then the analogous values for the new process are restored to the CPU and the second process commences running.

The operating system has a table of all existing processes. The table consists of pointers to the start of the administration area of each process. This table is the master list of executing or idled processes.

The only thing a process lacks is something to "run" on — the processor. (One function of the operating system is to schedule processes on processors.) A process has a life of its own, independent of the existence of processor(s) on which it may execute. The fact that, on a heavily loaded, time-sharing computer, many processes share a small number of physical processors is a detail over which the user has no control and which he is normally powerless to influence.

The important point is that *it is the process which has the independent existence, and it is the process with which the programmer must be concerned.* The existence of the processors, and the number of processors, is an insignificant detail, hidden from the user. (It is only important from the performance point of view and not from a logical point of view.) It is in this sense that the operating system was shown as standing between the CPU and the memory, as in Figs. 3-4 and 3-6.

From this point of view, the difference between the uniprocessor of Fig. 3-4 and the multiprocessor of Fig. 3-6 is merely the number of processors available to actually execute the processes. From the software point of view, there is no logical difference. However, there will be (or should be) a significant performance difference.

For the sake of completeness, we mention a relatively new concept called the *thread*. A thread is a small portion of a process, consisting of register contents, the program counter, private data, and a stack. The thread is the executing part of the process, and there may be many threads associated with the same process. The D, I, and A sections of the process are shared by all the threads, so that the thread concept is biased toward shared data, while the process concept is biased toward private data. The topic of threads is further discussed in Chapter 10. For purposes of the programmer's model, the logical nature of the thread and of the process is the same.

4.3   Shared Memory—1

To subdivide a calculation among two or more processes, one must create the desired number of processes, each able to carry out its own part of the calculation. Each process must have some portion of memory which is private, but there must be locations of physical memory which they can all access. Those memory locations which are accessed by all the processes are *shared*. Those memory locations which can be accessed by only a single process are *private*.

Figure 4-2 shows two different ways in which two processes might occupy memory such that some of the memory is shared and some of it private. The processes are the ones appropriate for the dot-product Program 3-2 of the previous chapter. In Program 3-2, the sum over i is partitioned among two processes (labeled programs 0 and 1), such that one process does the even values of i and the other does the odd values. In Fig. 4-2, the processes are labeled 0 and 1. Each process has its own instructions, and, in Fig. 4-2(a), both share the variables sum1 and sum2. Each process has a private copy of the variables i and sum, of arrays a(i) and b(i), and of a variable id (see below). Only process 0 accesses the variable sum, but both processes have a copy.

Later in this chapter, the functionality bestowed on the processes by memory arrangements such as Fig. 4-2 will be examined.

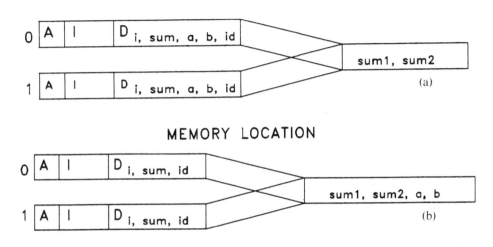

MEMORY LOCATION

MEMORY LOCATION

Figure 4-2.   Two ways in which the variables of Program 3-2 might occupy memory.

The arrays a and b may be shared, if just to save space. In this case, the memory layout would look like Fig. 4-2(b).

When one process alters the value of one of the shared variables sum1 or sum2 in Fig. 4-2(a), then the other process has immediate access to the new value, since the shared memory is part of his process as well. In the case of Program 3-2, when process 1 (called program 1 in 3-2) assigns sum2, process 0 can access the value when it assigns

```
sum = sum1 + sum2
```

The private variable id in Fig. 4-2 is used by each process to determine which part of the sum it should do—the even or odd part. It allows the process to identify itself either as process 0 or process 1. The variable id is discussed in the next section. It, too, is private, so each process has its own value (id is a user-defined name).

It does not affect either the scheduling or the memory management of the processes that a portion of the data area of two processes occupies the same region of physical memory. The operating system treats the two processes as completely separate, as if there were no physical memory in common. On a multiprocessor computer, the operating system can schedule process 0 (Fig. 4-2) to run on one processor, and process 1 to run on another. So far as scheduling is concerned, the operating system does not "care" that the two processes share memory, that they are two faces of the same die, so to speak. The two processes time-share with other processes, and *also with each other* in the normal manner.

If the two processes were executing on a uniprocessor, then the two processes would share the same processor. However, *the processes would still look like Fig. 4-2*. The nature of the processes is independent of the hardware available to execute them. This is why this book stresses the process and not the number of processors. It is also for this reason that parallel programming can be practiced on a uniprocessor. There is no performance advantage to running a parallel program on a uniprocessor, because both processes would have to share a single processor. In fact, execution time would be longer because of the overhead of creating new processes and because of the interprocess communication required. Even so, the principles of parallel programming are the same on multiprocessor and uniprocessor hardware, because the processes are the same.

4.4   Forking—Creating Processes

The first parallel programming examples involve creating processes. Processes are created by the operating system. The user can command the operating system to create a new process by calling the library function `process_fork`. It will be assumed that the user has access to a library which has a function similar to the function `process_fork` described below. There may be a library function which is equivalent to `process_fork`, but which has a different name. Appendix 3 shows how the function `process_fork` can be implemented based on the Unix `fork` system call.

The function `process_fork` is used in the following way:

```
integer id,nproc,process_fork
       .
       .
       .
id = process_fork(nproc)
```

The function `process_fork(nproc)`, when called from an executing process, creates nproc − 1 *additional* processes. *Each additional process is an exact copy of the caller.* After returning from the `process_fork` function, there are nproc − 1 additional and identical processes to time-share. The original process, which called `process_fork(nproc)` in the first place, is still running, so now there are nproc processes in all. Each of the nproc processes has a private copy of each of the variables of the parent, unless the variable is explicitly shared. The process which made the call is called the *parent*, and the nproc − 1 processes that are created are called the *children*. If nproc = 1, then no additional processes are created (that is, there are no children).

The process_fork function is rather unusual in that, while only one process invokes it, it returns nproc times to nproc identical processes of which nproc − 1 are new. After the return, each process continues executing at the next executable statement following the process_fork function.

The function process_fork returns an integer, called the *process-id*, which is unique to each process. It returns 0 to the parent and the integers 1, 2, . . . , nproc − 1 to the children, each child getting a different number. The fact that each process receives a different number allows the different processes to identify themselves and to do different parts of the same calculation (or to do entirely different calculations). Apart from the value of id, the processes are identical.

The use of the function process_fork is illustrated in the program below.

```
c       illustration of the use of process_fork. create
c       one child, and each process prints its own process-id.
        integer id,process_fork
        print *,'parent, before forking'
        id = process_fork(2)
        if (id .eq. 0) then
            print *, 'parent process, id = ',id
        else if (id .eq. 1) then
            print *, 'child process, id = ',id
        else
            print *, 'ERROR, fork did not work correctly'
            call exit()
        endif
        print *, 'both processes do this. id = ',id
        call process_join()
        end
```

Program 4-1

When Program 4-1 is run (either on a multiprocessor or uniprocessor computer), the output may be

```
parent,before forking
parent process,id = 0
child process,id = 1
both processes do this. id = 0
both processes do this. id = 1
```

We now explain how this comes about.

The statement

```
id = process_fork(2)
```

creates an additional process. This process is an exact copy of the original process in all respects, except for the value of id. Upon returning from the process_fork, the function returns to id an integer appropriate to the process being created. The parent always gets a value 0. The child gets 1. It is only by the value of id that the processes are distinguished. In all other respects, the processes are identical.

Program 4-1 starts out as a single process. After the call to process_fork, there are two processes, both identical except for the value of the variable id. When entering into the if-block, the process with id = 0 will do one of the branches, and the one with id = 1 will do the other. Each process executes the appropriate branch of the if-block, so the id values are printed only once. However, both processes will execute the final print statement, and so the message "both processes do this" is printed twice.

The call to process_join will be explained later. For now, view this statement in the same way as the "stop" statement—a signal that the program should be complete.

If Program 4-1 is run again, the output might look like this:

```
parent,before forking
child process,id = 1
parent process,id = 0
both processes do this. id = 1
both processes do this. id = 0
```

The output, the second time, is different from what it was the first time, in that the second and third lines of the output are reversed. (Several attempts may be required to reverse the output.) A possible reason for this behavior is shown in Fig. 4-3. In the first run, when the child is created, it immediately becomes idle. (Fig. 4-3 is a description of what could happen on a particular run. There are other possibilities, as will be seen below.) Therefore, the

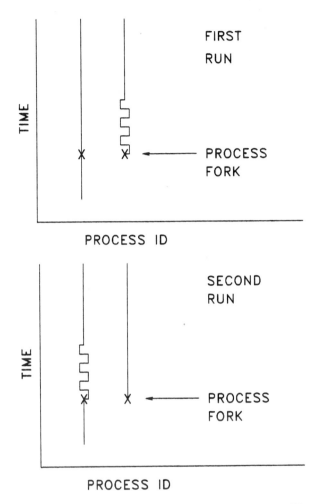

Figure 4-3.   Two possible timelines for the two processes of Program 4-1.

parent can race ahead of the child, and execute the if-block first. In the
second run, the parent becomes idle as soon as it creates the child. In this
case, the child races ahead and prints first. This is an example of the random
scheduling of processes, as discussed in the previous chapter.

It is also possible to obtain the following output:

```
parent,before forking
parent process,id = 0
both processes do this. id = 0
child process,id = 1
both processes do this. id = 1
```

In this case, the parent process executes both print statements before the child process executes one. The case where the child process goes first is also possible.

Problem: Is the following output possible? Explain why.

```
parent, before forking
both processes do this.  id = 1
parent process, id = 0
both processes do this.  id = 0
child process, id = 1
```

Partial answer: No.

Problem: What are the possible outputs of the following program:

```
c       program to create a single child.  Parent and child
c       each print 3 integers.
                integer id,k,process_fork
                id = process_fork(2)
                do 1 k = 1,3
                    print *,k * id
1               continue
                call process_join()
                end
```

Program 4-2

Answer: One possible result is

```
0
0
0
1
2
3
```

This will be written as (0 0 0 1 2 3) to save space. The following outputs are also possible: (1 2 3 0 0 0), (0 0 1 2 3 0), (1 0 2 0 3 0), (1 2 0 3 0 0), (0 1 0 2 0 3), and so forth. The different possible outputs are due to the random scheduling of processes. In practice, most of these outputs will be rare.

Problem: Sketch the memory occupation of the two processes of Program 4-2.

The `process_fork` function does not require the entire parent process to be copied in order to produce each child. Rather, the *logical* nature of the `process_fork` is to *start up* additional processes. It may do this by creating new processes or else by starting up already created but dormant processes. This latter approach is the one taken in the *thread* implementation. From the abstract (i.e., logical) point of view, both approaches do the same thing— yield one or more additional and identical processes following the appropriate function call, even though the implementations are quite different. A variable is private to each process, or to each thread, unless it has been explicitly shared, a feature that follows naturally from a process-copy implementation. Threads are discussed in Chapter 11.

4.5   Joining Processes

The join is the opposite of the fork—it destroys all the children, leaving only the parent running. The "join" is carried out by the statement

```
call process_join()
```

The subroutine `process_join` has no arguments, so the parentheses are optional. The user's library may have a program with a functionality similar to that of the `process_join` but with a different name. The user's function may also have arguments. An example of using `process_join` is given in the following program:

```
c       program to illustrate use of the process_join. Create
c       a child process, which prints its id, then destroy it.
c       The parent then prints its id.
        integer id,process_fork
        print *,'beginning'
        id = process_fork(2)
        print *,'id = ',id
        call process_join()
        print *,'only parent remains, id = ',id
        end
```

Program 4-3

Whenever a process makes the `process_join` call, if the process is a child, it is destroyed. If the process is the parent (id = 0), it *waits* until all the children are destroyed, and then it continues with the statement following the call to `process_join`. *For the parent, the join is a wait. For the children, the join is a kill.*

There are two possible outputs of Program 4-3. One is

```
beginning
id = 0
id = 1
only parent remains, id = 0
```

and the other is

```
beginning
id = 1
id = 0
only parent remains, id = 0
```

When Program 4-3 is run, the single process prints "beginning," then forks, creating a single child. Both the parent and the child print their respective ids, which can be printed in either order. Then the parent and child arrive at the join. The child is destroyed, and the parent waits until the child is destroyed and continues. Because of the built-in wait at the join, it would be impossible to have as output the following:

```
beginning
id = 0
only parent remains, id = 0
id = 1
```

The parent could never execute the "only parent remains" print statement until the child was destroyed, and the child could not be destroyed until it printed its id.

When a process is destroyed, the memory it occupied is freed for other uses. The operating system no longer has a record of the destroyed process. There is no way to access the data of the destroyed process, except by accident.

The join does not have to be in the same "place" in the program. Consider, for example, the following program:

```
c       program to illustrate use of joins called from different
c       positions in the program.

        integer id,process_fork
        print *,'beginning'
        id = process_fork(3)
        if (id .eq. 0) then
            print *,'parent,id = ',id
            call process_join()
        elseif (id .eq. 1) then
            print *,'child,id = ',id
            call process_join()
        elseif (id .eq. 2) then
            print *,'child,id = ',id
            call process_join()
        endif
        print *,'at end,id = ',id
        end
```

Program 4-4

The output of this program is

```
        beginning
        child,id = 2
        parent,id = 0
        child,id = 1
        at end,id = 0
```

The three intermediate statements could appear in any order. However, the first and last lines will always be output first and last respectively.

Program 4-4 works as follows. The subroutine process_join acts as if it has access to a counter in shared memory, which is initialized with the total number of processes (three in the case of Program 4-4 above). Each time a process calls process_join (it calls its private copy of process_join, which exists in the I area of the process), the counter is decremented. It does not matter "where" in the program the call comes from. In fact, this "place" really has no meaning. There is only a single counter which is shared and which is decremented in the subroutine process_join. The functioning of this subroutine does not depend on the "position" of the call in the calling routines. When the child makes the call, it is eliminated. When the parent makes the call, it waits until the counter is zero, and then it is allowed to continue.

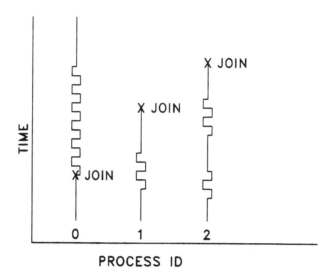

Figure 4-4. Possible time-line for Program 4-4.

A typical example of the time lines for the three processes of Program 4-4 is shown in Fig. 4-4.

Problem: How will the following program behave?

```
integer id,process_fork
id = process_fork(2)
if (id .eq. 0) then
    call process_join()
endif
end
```

Answer: Depending on the implementation, the program may never end. Only the parent calls process_join. The child does not. The parent could wait forever for the child, which never arrives. The child may actually be destroyed by the operating system when arriving at the "end" statement (as a default), but the parent, which is "in" the process_join subroutine, will never know it if process_join keeps its counter independently of the operating system.

One must be careful in writing parallel programs to make sure all processes call the process_join subroutine, or to determine the behavior of the particular parallel programming library.

Problem: Explain how the following program can have the outputs shown below it.

```
integer id,process_fork
id = process_fork(2)
if (id .eq. 0) then
     print *,'now is the time'
else
     print *,'THE BIG BROWN FOX'
endif
call process_join()
end
```

A possible output is:

```
now iTHE Bs the tIG BROWN FOX
ime
```

Another is:

```
Now THE BIG is the time
BROWN FOX
```

and another is

```
now is the time
THE BIG BROWN FOX.
```

Answer: Print statements are actually made up of many machine instructions. It is possible for both print statements to be executed at exactly the same time, with the instructions of one process interleaved with those of the other process, and so the outputs are interleaved.

4.6   Shared Memory—2

In this section, the shared subroutine is described. This subroutine would normally be recognized by the Fortran compiler, so it may not be in an external library. The syntax is

```
call shared(var_name,num_of_bytes)
```

Here, var_name is the name of the variable. It is actually a pointer to the variable. (In Fortran, all variables are passed to subroutines as pointers, as described in Section 2.12.) The term num_of_bytes is the number of bytes which the variable occupies in memory. The subroutine shared is called by the parent, before forking. This call arranges for var_name to be shared among all the children created by the calling process. That is, when the children are created, the shared variables occupy the same physical region of memory, as in Figure 4-2.

When the parent process calls process_fork and spawns a number of children, each child is an identical copy of the parent. All the variables and values are copied, and, unless memory is declared to be shared (as discussed in this section), changes in the data of one process do not appear in the data of another process.

Consider, for example, the following program:

```
c       program to illustrate that variables in children are
c       not shared with the parent in absence of the "shared"
c       function.
        integer id,k,process_fork
        print *, 'beginning'
        k = 985
        print *, 'k = ',k
        id = process_fork(2)
        if (id .eq. 1) then
            k = 1
            print *, 'Position A,id = ',id,'k = ',k
c       .......position A
        endif
c
        call process_join()
c       ......position B
        print *, 'Position B,id = ',id,'k = ',k
        end
```

Program 4-5

The output of this program is

```
beginning
k = 985
Position A,id = 1,k = 1
Position B,id = 0 k = 985
```

There is no other order for the output (unless the print statement becomes interleaved). The if-block is executed only by the child, id = 1. The child alters its copy of k to 1, and prints the value of k. At point B, only the parent is left (the child was destroyed), and the parent's value of k is still 985. It was not altered when the child altered its copy of k.

Problem: Sketch the arrangement of the two processes of Program 4-5 in memory. Where is k? What is changed when the child alters k? Show why the parent still prints k = 985 at the end. (Hint: Each process has its own value of k.)

Problem: What would happen if the variable id were shared?

Answer: Each process would have the same value of id, and different processes could not be distinguished from each other. The value of id would be determined by the last process to return from the process_fork function, and the program would act accordingly. In the previous example, if both processes end up with id = 1, the output would be

```
beginning
k = 985
Position A, id = 1, k = 1
Position A, id = 1, k = 1
Position B, id = 1, k = 1
```

In this case, both parent and child alter their private copies of k to 1, because each process has id = 1.

Problem: What would happen in the above case if both processes end up with id = 0.

As another example, suppose we break up a sum into two parts. (This example is purposely made very simple.)

```
c       simple program to sum four integers using two processes.
c       This program does not work correctly because
c       the variable sum1 is not shared among the two processes.
c       This illustrates how memory is private to each process
c       in absence of commands for it to be shared.

        integer id, sum0, sum1, sum, process_fork
        print *, 'sum 1 + 2 + 3 + 4 in two processes'
```

```
sum = 0
sum0 = 0
sum1 = 0
id = process_fork(2)
if (id .eq. 0) then
      sum0 = 1 + 2
elseif (id .eq. 1) then
      sum1 = 3 + 4
endif
call process_join()
sum = sum0 + sum1
print *,'Net sum = ',sum
print *,'process 0 subtotal, sum0 = ',sum0
print *,'process 1 subtotal, sum1 = ',sum1
end
```

Program 4-6

The output is

```
sum 1 + 2 + 3 + 4 in two processes
Net sum = 3
process 0 subtotal, sum0 = 3
process 1 subtotal, sum1 = 0
```

(There are no alternative orders for this output. Do you know why?) What has happened? Why isn't sum = 10, and sum1 = 7?

Before the fork, the variables sum, sum0, and sum1 are initialized to 0. After the fork, process 1 has its own, private copy of the variable sum1 (as does process 0). It dutifully sets sum1 to 7, and then process 1 and its value of sum1 are destroyed at the join. So far as process 0 is concerned, its copy of sum1 was never altered from its initial value of 0. Process 0 computes its own copy of sum0 as 3 and then creates the final result. Note that only process 0 creates and prints the final result.

The way in which memory is allocated to processes 0 and 1 in Program 4-6 is shown in Fig. 4-5. Figure 4-5(a) shows the values of the variables immediately after the fork. All the subtotals are 0. Figure 4-5(b) shows the subtotals just before the join. For process 1, sum1 has the correct value, while in process 0, sum1 is still 0. After the join, the value of sum1 held by process 1 is destroyed, along with process 1. All that remains is process 0's value of sum1.

What is needed for this program to work correctly is for sum1 to be shared by process 0 and process 1. Then when sum1 is assigned by process 1, process

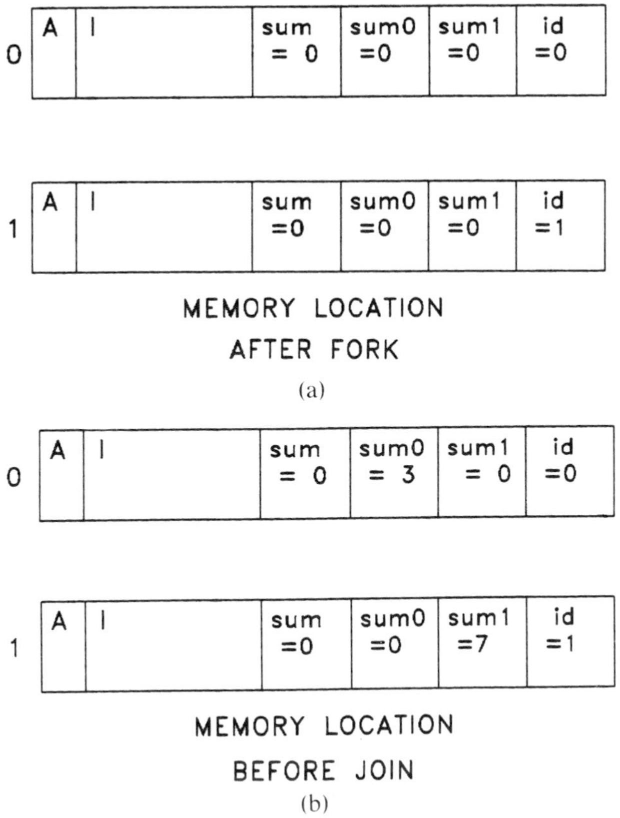

0	A	I		sum = 0	sum0 =0	sum1 =0	id =0

1	A	I		sum =0	sum0 =0	sum1 =0	id =1

MEMORY LOCATION

AFTER FORK

(a)

0	A	I		sum = 0	sum0 = 3	sum1 = 0	id =0

1	A	I		sum =0	sum0 =0	sum1 =7	id =1

MEMORY LOCATION

BEFORE JOIN

(b)

Figure 4-5. Memory occupation of Program 4-6.

0 will be able to access this updated value later on. One can modify this program by simply adding the statement

```
call shared(sum1,4)
```

immediately following the declaration section. The "4" in this call means that sum1 occupies four bytes.

With the addition of the shared call, Program 4-6 becomes

```
c       simple program to sum four integers using two processes.
c       This program works correctly because
c       the variable sum1 is shared among the two processes.
c       This illustrates how memory is private to each process
c       in absence of commands for it to be shared.
```

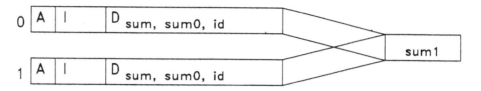

MEMORY LOCATION

Figure 4-6.   Memory occupation of Program 4-6(a).

```
          integer id,sum0,sum1,sum,process_fork

c         share sum1
          call shared(sum1,4)

          print *,'sum 1 + 2 + 3 + 4 in two processes'
          sum = 0
          sum0 = 0
          sum1 = 0
          id = process_fork(2)
          if (id .eq. 0) then
              sum0 = 1 + 2
          elseif (id .eq. 1) then
              sum1 = 3 + 4
          endif
          call process_join()
          sum = sum0 + sum1
          print *,'Net sum = ',sum
          print *,'process 0 subtotal,sum0 = ',sum0
          print *,'process 1 subtotal,sum1 = ',sum1
          end
```

Program 4-6(a)

When the shared call is added, the output becomes

```
          sum 1 + 2 + 3 + 4 in two processes
          Net sum = 10
          process 0 subtotal, sum0 = 3
          process 1 subtotal, sum1 = 7
```

which is correct. The memory allocation for this program, using the shared cell, is shown in Fig. 4-6. Note that sum1 is the same physical location for both process 0 and process 1, and so it is accessible to both. Figure 4-6 should be compared to Fig. 4-2.

The reader should note that programs 4-6 and 4-6(a) differ only in the inclusion of the shared call in the latter. The control flow is identical in the two programs. Yet, the outputs of the two programs are different. *The behavior of parallel programs can be extremely sensitive to shared memory.*

A general program for splitting a sum into two parts is

```
c       apportion sum of elements of a(i) over 2 processes.

        integer id, sum, sum0, sum1, i, a(1000)
        integer process_fork,n,nproc
        call shared(sum1,4)

        sum0 = 0
        sum1 = 0
c       initialize a(i)
        do 10 i = 1,1000
            a(i) = 1
  10    continue
        n = 1000
        nproc = 2
c       create a single child.
        id = process_fork(nproc)

c       do the partial sums.
c       process 0 does odd terms, process 1 does even terms.
        if (id .eq. 0) then
            do 1 i = 1,n,2
                sum0 = sum0 + a(i)
   1        continue
        elseif (id .eq. 1) then
            do 2 i = 2,n,2
                sum1 = sum1 + a(i)
   2        continue
        endif

        call process_join()
c       process 0 only does the final summation
        sum = sum0 + sum1
        print *,'at end,sum = ',sum
        print *,'sum0 = ',sum0
        print *,'sum1 = ',sum1
        end
```

Program 4-7

The output is

```
at end,sum = 1000
sum0 = 500
sum1 = 500
```

Problem: (a) How can Program 4-7 be written without using the variable sum0 (i.e., using only sum and sum1)?
(b) Why does it not matter that a(i) is not shared?

Answer: (a) One could write Program 4-7 without using sum0. In the if-branch for process 0, we could have set

```
sum = sum + a(i)
```

Then, in the final summation, carried out by process 0, we could have set

```
sum = sum + sum1
```

(b) It does not matter whether a(i) is shared or not because a(i) is not altered. Each process needs only to read the values of a(i), not to write new values. Thus, whether the processes get the values from their own copies of a(i), or from shared values, does not make any difference. However, if the array a(i) were very large, declaring it as shared would save space (since otherwise two copies of the entire array a(i) would be needed). Not sharing a(i) might result in very slow execution because each process might have to be swapped out of memory frequently. In this case, parallelization might result in a noticeable degradation in performance.

As a final example of sharing memory, consider a program that copies array a2 to array al using two processes. Initially, al(i) = 1, a2(i) = 2, for all i.

```
c       copy array a2(i) into al(i), using two processes.
        integer al(1000),a2(1000),i,id,process_fork,n,nproc
        call shared(al,4000)
        call shared(a2,4000)
        nproc = 2
        n = 1000
c       initialize al, a2
        do 11 i = 1,n
```

```
            al(i) = 1
            a2(i) = 2
11      continue
c    create a single child.
         id = process_fork(nproc)
c    do the copy in parallel, using 2 processes.
         if (id .eq. 0) then
            do 1 i = 1,n,2
               al(i) = a2(i)
1           continue
         elseif (id .eq. 1) then
            do 2 i = 2,n,2
               al(i) = a2(i)
2           continue
         endif
         call process_join()
c    print the first 10 values of al(i).
c    only process 0 executes the statements below.
         print *,'i      a(i)'
         do 3 i = 1,10
            print *, i,al(i)
3        continue
         end
```

Program 4-8

The output from this program is

```
i    al(i)
1    2
2    2
3    2
4    2
5    2
.
.
.
10   2
```

Problem: What would the output of Program 4-8 be if al(i) were not shared.

Answer: The output would be

```
i    al(i)
1    2
2    1
3    2
4    1
5    2
6    1
.
.
.
10   1
```

That is, for i = 2, 4, 6, . . . , the array a2(i) would not be copied into the copy of al(i) owned by process 0. While process 1's copy of al(i) would be altered, for i even, process 0 could not access the result.

Problem: (a) Does a2 need to be shared? Why?
(b) Draw the schematic memory layout for this program, in which al and a2 are shared. When only al is shared.

Partial answer: (a) No.

The behavior of a parallel program can be completely different depending on whether variables that are assigned new values by different processes are or are not shared. Several examples were presented in this section. Program behavior can be modified merely by modifying which variables are shared, without even altering the flow of control of the program. It will be seen later in the book that, sometimes, the behavior of shared variables can be quite complex. *Very common errors in parallel programming are not sharing variables which should be shared, sharing variables which should not be shared, or misusing shared variables.*

4.7 Processes Are Randomly Scheduled— Contention

Although this topic has already been covered in this and the previous chapters, it is so important that it has been given a separate heading. In analyzing shared-memory parallel programs, it is essential to assume that *all processes are randomly scheduled. That is, any process can be idled and restarted at any time.* It can be idle for any length of time. It is incorrect to assume that two processes will proceed at the same rate or that one process will go faster because it has less work to do than another process. The operating system can intervene at any time to idle a process.

The random scheduling of processes in this chapter has been invoked as causing the order of output of different processes to be different in each run. It is also possible for processes to incorrectly alter something in shared memory, so that *the final value of a shared variable will be different depending on the order in which the variable is altered.* As a simple example, consider the following "toy" program:

```
integer i,id,process_fork
call shared(i,4)
i = 0
id = process_fork(2)
i = i+1
print *,'id = ', id,'i = ',i
call process_join()
end
```

There can be several outputs of this program. One is

```
id = 0 , i = 1
id = 1 , i = 2
```

a second is

```
id = 0 , i = 2
id = 1 , i = 1
```

and a third is

```
id = 0 , i = 1
id = 1 , i = 1
```

An additional three outputs can reverse the order of the output.

The analysis of this program is based on the random scheduling of the processes when executing the machine instructions into which the source program is compiled. When the program is compiled, the source code statement

```
i = i + 1
```

becomes several machine language instructions. In general, one can expect each CPU to execute three separate instructions:

(a) The CPU loads the value of i from main memory into a CPU register.
(b) The contents of the register are incremented by 1.
(c) The value of i is stored back in main memory.

The important point is that *the CPU can be idled after any one of these steps*. Thus it can be idled after it loads i from memory, after it increments i, or after it stores i back into memory. Because i is shared, it is read and altered by each process. The differences in the output of the program depend upon the order in which each process executes the above steps.

To get the first output, the following series of steps occurs (assuming that each process gets ready to execute (a) at the same time). Note that each process may execute on a different CPU, or they may share the same CPU.

1. Process 1 is idled.
2. Process 0 executes steps (a), (b), and (c). The memory location referenced by i now contains 1. Process 0 prints the value of i.
3. Process 1 starts up and executes steps (a)–(c), which alters i to 2. It then prints the value of i.

To obtain the second output, the same series of events occurs, but with process 0 first being idled.

More interesting is the third output, which involves the following series of steps:

1. Process 0 performs step (a), then is idled. Its CPU register now contains 0.
2. Process 1 performs step (a)–(c) and then prints its value of i. It prints 1.
3. Process 0 now wakes up and increments the contents of its register, doing steps (b) and (c) and then printing i. In step (c) it stores 1 back into memory, and prints that value.

Problem: Can you think of other outputs? Assume that print statements are atomic.

The root of this problem is that two processes are trying to alter the value of a shared variable simultaneously. They are contending for the same variable, and such a situation is referred to as *contention*. It is clear that, if processes must alter shared variables, some way must be found to coordinate the processes, and this is discussed in the next two chapters.

Problem: In Program 4-7, what would happen if i were shared?

Answer: If i were shared, the loops would not work properly. Each process would increment the common value of i as it executed the loop. For example, the following chain of events may take place:

1. Process 0 sets i = 1, then becomes idle.
2. Process 1 sets i = 2 and computes the contribution of a(2) to sum1.
3. Process 0 starts up, computes the contribution of a(2) to sum0 (because i is now 2).

In this particular example, both process 0 and process 1 would calculate the contribution of a(2) to the sum. Then, a(2) would be counted twice, while a(1) would not contribute at all.

Problem: What would happen in Program 4-7 if the process_join statement came after the

```
sum = sum0 + sum1
```

statement? Draw the timeline illustrating your answer. (Hint: Consider a particular execution in which process 0 finishes ahead of process 1 (process 1 might have become idle). Then, when process 0 is ready to do the final summation, the value of sum1 would not be correct (process 1 still has work to do). With the proposed change, the program could in principle return a different answer for each run. The join serves a synchronization function. Because it forces the parent to wait until the child has completed its calculation, it causes the calculation to be carried out correctly.)

4.8 Summary

In this chapter, several parallel programming functions were introduced. These functions are summarized below:

process_fork:

integer id,process_fork,nproc

.

.

.

id = process_fork(nproc).

The process making this call causes the startup of nproc − 1 additional processes, whose logical nature is that they are exact copies of the original. However, the value of id is different in each process, being 0 in the parent (the one making the call) and having the values 1, 2, . . . , nproc − 1 in the children (the newly created processes). All variables are private to each process except for those explicitly shared. Note that process_fork can also be called from any child, thus creating a hierarchy of processes.

process_join:
call process_join()

When a child calls process_join, it is destroyed. When a parent calls process_join, it waits until all its children are destroyed, and then is allowed to continue.

shared:
integer num_of_bytes
any_declaration var_name

.

.

.

call shared(var_name, num_of_bytes)

This call is made in the parent, before process_fork is called. It arranges that the variable var_num, occupying num_of_bytes of memory, is shared among all the children.

CHAPTER 5

Basic Parallel Programming Techniques

5.1 Introduction

In this chapter, several elementary techniques for parallel programming are introduced. These include loop splitting and self-scheduling, two simple ways of apportioning the work done in a loop among several processes. In addition, a basic synchronization construct—the spin-lock—is presented. After reading this chapter, the reader should be able to create a variety of parallel programs.

The concept of *speedup* is also presented. The speedup is the increase in speed obtained by parallelizing a program and indicates how efficiently multiple processes are utilized. Techniques for computing the speedup are discussed.

5.2 Loop Splitting

Loop splitting is an efficient way to apportion the work done in a loop among processes. In the first example, the members of array a(i) are summed, from i = 1 to i = 300 inclusive.

```
c       Sum the elements of array a(i), using nproc processes.
```

```
c       The final sum is in variable "sum."
c       nproc is the total number of processes.
c       temsum(id) holds the partial sum done by process number id.
c       Assume <= 50 processes.

        integer id,i,a(1000),sum,temsum(0:49),nproc,
    s   process_fork,n

        call shared(temsum,200)

        n = 300
        nproc = 3
c       initialize a(i)
        do 10 i = 1,n
            a(i) = 1
 10     continue

c       create nproc - 1 additional processes
        id = process_fork(nproc)
c       now the loop splitting.
c       process id stores a partial sum in temsum(id).
        temsum(id) = 0
        do 1 i = 1 + id,n,nproc
            temsum(id) = temsum(id) + a(i)
  1     continue

c       destroy the children.
        call process_join()

c       parent only beyond this point.
c       Sum all the partial sums into the final sum and print.
c       Process 0 can't get here until all children finish their
c       work and are destroyed.
c       This part is overhead.
        sum = 0
        do 2 i = 0,nproc - 1
            sum = sum + temsum(i)
  2     continue

        print *,'final sum is ',sum
        end
```

Program 5-1

The loop

```
        do 1 i = 1 + id,n,nproc
```

1   2   3   4   5   6   7   8   9   10 11

○ PROCESS 0

✕ PROCESS 1

☐ PROCESS 2

Figure 5-1. Illustration of loop splitting. The filled circles represent the values taken by index variable i of Program 5-1 in successive iterations of a loop.

is the one demonstrating loop splitting. For the case of nproc = 3, process 0 does i = 1, 4, 7, 10, ... Process 1 does i = 2, 5, 8, 11, . . . , and process 3 does i = 3, 6, 9, 12, ...

The division of labor in loop splitting is illustrated in Fig. 5-1. There, the filled dots represent the successive values of i assigned in the loop. The circles, squares, and Xs indicate which process executes that particular iteration.

Because of loop splitting, each process computes a partial sum, which is stored in the shared array temsum(id). Process 0 stores the sum

```
temsum(0) = a(1) + a(4) + a(7) + ...
```

Process 1 stores the sum

```
temsum(1) = a(2) + a(5) + a(8) + ...
```

and so forth. After each process is finished computing its portion of the sum, it is destroyed at the call to process_join. After all the children are destroyed, process 0 accumulates all the partial sums into the final sum. Because process 0 must wait at the process_join statement for all the children to be destroyed, we are certain that all the partial sums will be complete before process 0 starts to calculate the final sum.

Problem: Why is temsum not lost when the children are destroyed?

Problem: Why does the array temsum have to be shared in Program 5-1? What are the values of temsum(id)? Can a(i) be shared? What would be the advantage of sharing a(i)? Can the variable sum be shared?

Answer: Each element of temsum(id) is accessed by two processes: the process with the appropriate id value and process 0. If it were not shared, each process would update its own copy of temsum(id). Each temsum(id) is 100. If temsum were not shared, the final sum would be 100 because process 0 would not have access to those elements of temsum updated by processes 1, 2, . . . , nproc − 1. The array a(i) need not be shared, because it is only read, not written. (Note that temsum is both written and read.) If a(i) were shared, then it would not be copied when the parent spawns the children, and all the processes would occupy less memory. It does not matter whether the variable sum is shared, since it is accessed only by process 0.

As a second example, the following program calculates the maximum value of the array a, using nproc processes.

```
c       Compute the maximum value of array a(i) using nproc
c       processes. Assume <= 50 processes.
c       amax = maximum value.
c       The loop is apportioned using loop splitting.
c       amax is private to each process.

        integer id,nproc,process_fork,i,n
        real a(1000),amax,local_max(0:49),float

        call shared(local_max,200)

        nproc = 10
        n = 1000
c       initialize a(i)
        do 10 i = 1,n
             a(i) = float(i)
  10    continue

c       create nproc - 1 children.
        id = process_fork(nproc)

c       loop splitting, each child calculates the maximum
c       value of a subset of the elements of a(i)
        amax = a(1)
        do 1 i = 1 + id,n,nproc
```

```
            if (a(i) .gt. amax) then
                  amax = a(i)
            endif
1       continue

c       Before the child id is destroyed, save its maximum value
c       in local_max(id).
            local_max(id) = amax

c       destroy children
            call process_join()

c       process 0, which is the only process remaining, finds
c       the maximum of all the partial maxima.
c       This part is overhead. At this point, amax is
c       the partial maximum found by process 0.
            do 2 i = 1,nproc - 1
                if (local_max(i) .gt. amax) then
                      amax = local_max(i)
                endif
2       continue

            print *,' max value of a(i) is ',amax
            end
```

Program 5-2

In this example, which utilizes ten processes, each process finds the maximum value of "its own" group of array elements. For example, process 0 finds the maximum value of the elements $a(1), a(11), a(21), \ldots$. Process 9 finds the maximum value of $a(10), a(20), a(30), \ldots$. The largest value of $a(i)$ for each set is stored in local_max(id). When all these partial maxima have been found, the children are all killed and the parent finds the maximum of all the maxima.

Note that one could replace the entire if-branch by any function, so the split loop could as well be written as

```
        do 1 i = 1 + id,n,nproc
            call check_for_max(a(i),amax)
1       continue
```

The fact that one can parallelize a loop which includes a subroutine call demonstrates the flexibility of parallel programming.

Problem: Write a parallel program using loop splitting which does a matrix vector multiply in parallel.

Answer:

```
c       matrix-vector multiply
c               c(i) = a(i,j) * b(j), summed over j

        integer a(100,100),b(100),c(100)
        integer nproc,i,j,id,sum,process_fork,n

        call shared(a,40000)
        call shared(b,400)
        call shared(c,400)

        nproc = 10
        n = 100
        (initialize a,b)

        id = process_fork(nproc)

        do 1 i = 1 + id,n,nproc
            sum = 0
            do 2 j = 1,n
                sum = sum + a(i,j) * b(j)
2           continue
            c(i) = sum
1       continue
        call process_join()

        (store results)
        end
```

Program 5-3

In this program, each of the 10 processes computes a subset of the c(i). Thus, process 0 computes c(1), c(11), c(21), . . . , process 1 computes c(2), c(12), c(22), . . . , and so forth.

Problem: Does c(i) have to be shared in the above program? Do a(i,j), b(j) have to be shared?

5.3   Ideal Speedup

The speedup of a parallel program is

$$\text{speedup} = \frac{\text{time required for the nonparallel program execution}}{\text{time required for parallel version execution}}$$

The maximum speedup possible is always the number of processes used. (But see Problem 1, Section 8.10.) However, in practice the speedup is often less than this.

The speedup describes how efficiently one is using multiple processes. For instance, if a parallel program has a speedup of 10 and is making use of ten processes, then the parallel version is as efficient as possible. On the other hand, if the speedup is 2 for 10 processes, then one is making rather ineffective use of the processes.

The discussion of speedup will be in terms of processes and not processors. It will be assumed throughout the text that *the number of processors available is greater than or equal to the number of processes*. In the case that, during a run, the number of processors is less than the number of processes, then the speedup may be smaller than the maximum possible. This is discussed at the end of this section.

In the case of parallelization of a single loop, the time required for parallel execution is

time for parallel execution =
     time to create processes
   + time to execute the loop
   + other overhead
   + time to destroy the children.

The time required to generate children from a single parent depends on the implementation of the `process_fork` function. In the case of Unix, where processes are created using the `fork` call, each process might require milliseconds to create on a 1 MIP processor. An implementation using threads can start up processes in tens of microseconds or less. Chapter 11 contains a discussion of this issue and how it affects writing parallel programs.

The "other overhead" involves *synchronization* and any *sequential parts* of the calculation. Synchronization will be introduced in the next section. The sequential part of Program 5-1, which sums the elements of an array, is the part of the calculation in which process 0 consolidates the partial sums into the final value. This part of the calculation has no analogue in the single-process version of the calculation, and so is *overhead*. For the case of finding the maximum value of an array, Program 5-2, the part of the calculation in which process 0 finds the maximum of all the partial maxima is overhead. Program 5-3 has none of this kind of overhead.

It is useful to consider the parallelized loop in isolation, ignoring the other overhead in the program. In this way, one can get an idea of how effectively one has parallelized the "core" of the program. The speedup so calculated will be termed the *ideal speedup*. *The ideal speedup is the maximum possible speedup that one can attain, assuming that there is no overhead.* The existence of overhead only causes the actual speedup, obtained in a real program, to be smaller than the ideal. The ideal speedup indicates how well one has utilized the processes in the "core" parallel part of the program. As will be seen, for large problems, the true speedup can approach the ideal but will never surpass it.

When a loop is parallelized using loop splitting, each process does not necessarily do the same number of iterations. For example, consider the simple split loop with nproc = 2:

```
        do 2 i = 1 + id,5,nproc
            (work)
2       continue
        call process_join()
```

Program 5-4

Process 0 does i = 1, 3, 5 while process 1 does i = 2, 4. If these processes are doing the same amount of work on each iteration, then when process 0 does its work for i = 5, process 1 will do nothing. (It will have been destroyed at the join). This is one example of a common inefficiency of parallel programming, in that it may be difficult, or even impossible, to apportion the work in a completely equitable manner.

In the case of the Program 5-4, the parallelized program will require a time of 3t to execute the loop, where t is the time required for a single pass through the loop. Even though one process only does two passes, the final result is not available until the other process completes the third pass. Thus, the execution time of process 0 is the *rate-determining step* of the calculation, and is 3t. The sequential program will execute the loops in time 5t, so that the speedup just for executing the loop, and neglecting any other overhead, is 5t/3t = 5/3, less than the number of processes.

In general, in computing the ideal speedup, it is necessary to find the process, or processes, which are the rate-determining step in the calculation.

Continuing with the example above, if the loop were

```
        do 2 i = 1 + id,6,nproc
            (work)
 2      continue
        call process_join()
```

Program 5-5

with nproc = 2, then the parallel execution time is still 3t, while the sequential execution time is 6t. The speedup is now 6t/3t = 2, equal to the number of processes.

The speedup is a measure of how effectively processes are utilized and not necessarily of the actual speed of execution. Note that both Programs 5-4 and 5-5 have the same execution time, while the speedups are 5/3 and 2 respectively.

The inefficiency due to inequitable distribution of work becomes less important as the size of the loop increases, as the following problem will demonstrate.

Problem: For the loop

```
        do 1 i = 1 + id,n,nproc
            (work)
 1      continue
```

Program 5-6

what is the ideal speedup if nproc = 10 and n = 10, 20, 100? What about n = 9, 19, 109? 11, 21, 101?

Answer:

n	ideal speedup
10	10
20	10
100	10
9	9
19	9.5
109	9.9
11	5.5
21	7
101	9.2

In the second triplet (9, 19, 109), the nonparallel execution time is 9t, 19t, 109t, where t is the time for each iteration of the loop, while the parallel time is t, 2t, and 11t. For the last three cases, the parallel execution time is 2t, 3t, and 11t. The reader should compare the speedups for the pairs n = 10, 11. For n = 20, 21.

The important point in the above example is that the larger is n the more the speedup approaches the number of processes (10 in all the cases above). The quantity n is the *characteristic size of the problem*. That is, it is a number characteristic of the amount of work which is distributed over the processes. Normally, as the problem size increases, the speedup will approach the number of processes.

In the case that nproc is greater than the number of physical processors, the speedup may be less than the ideal speedup of the program. Consider program 5-6 for the case that nproc = 15, n = 150 but the number of physical processors is only 10. That is, the loop

```
do 1 i=1 + id,150,15
```

with 10 processors.

The program must execute on the processors in two shifts. In the first shift, only 10 processes may execute, and in the second shift, 5 processes execute. If t is the time to complete 1 iteration of the loop, then in the first pass, each of the 10 processes require a time of 10t. After they are finished, the other 5 processes make the second pass, and the execution time of each of these is also $10t$. Since the single-stream execution time is $150t$, the ideal speedup is

$$\text{ideal speedup} = 150t/20t = 7.5$$

This is even smaller than the number of physical processors, and is half the number of processes.

On the other hand, if 15 physical processors were available, the parallel execution time is $10t$ and the ideal speedup is 15, equal to the number of processes.

Problem: Estimate the speedup of Programs 5-1 and 5-2, taking the sequential parts into account but neglecting the time for the `process_fork` and `process_join`. Assume that the time to execute each overhead statement (the "do 2" loops) is the same as that to execute each statement of the "do 1" loop.

5.4   Spin-Locks, Contention, and Self-Scheduling

One problem with loop splitting is that it could lead to an uneven distribution of work among the processes. The general form of loop splitting that we have encountered is

```
       do 1 i = 1 + id,n,nproc
           (work)
   1     continue
```

The "work" section can be long and involved for some values of i, short and sweet for others. A simple example is the case where several processes are exploring a maze. (The program is given in Section 13.5.) Some processes may reach a dead end in a short time; others may take longer. Some processes may explore many short paths while others may explore only a few long ones. Yet, in the loop splitting, each process must execute approximately the same number of iterations.

The alternative is self-scheduling—each processes "chooses" its next index value only when it is ready for one. Self-scheduling allows some processes to execute only a few iterations, while others may execute many iterations.

To illustrate self-scheduling, consider a simple program which adds a constant number to each element in an array. This is a very simple program, which in practice would not normally require self-scheduling. It is used here for illustrative purposes.

```
c       Add a constant to each element of an array.
c       Illustrate self-scheduling, but
c       the program below is incorrect and should not be run
c       as is.

        integer a(1000),next_index,i,process_fork,id,k

        call shared(next_index,4)
        call shared(a,4000)

        n = 1000
        next_index = n
        nproc = 3
        k = 4
        (initialize a(i))

        id = process_fork(nproc)

c       parallelized loop. This part is supposed to illustrate
c       self-scheduling, but it has a bug.
  10        continue
            i = next_index
            next_index = next_index - 1
            if (i .le. 0) goto 2
            a(i) = a(i) + k
            goto 10
   2        continue
c       end of the parallelized loop

        call process_join()

        (store result)
        end
```

Program 5-7

In the above program, next_index has the next available value of the index i that will be used by a process. As each process finishes its work (which consists only of the statement a(i) = a(i) + k), it jumps to statement label 10, and gets its next index value. After the process assigns the value of next_index to i, it decrements next_index, so that the next process can assign the next lower value of the index. If any process has

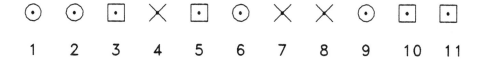

○ PROCESS 0

✕ PROCESS 1

☐ PROCESS 2

Figure 5-2.   Illustration of one way in which the values of i of Program 5-8 are allocated by self-scheduling.

i <= 0, it leaves the loop and is destroyed at the process_join statement.

The intention of the program is to allocate the values of i to processes on a first-come, first-served basis. The variable next_index is shared, the intention being that whenever a process decrements it, the new, decremented value is used by the next process.

The type of scheduling which is *intended* is illustrated in Figure 5-2. The filled dots represent the possible values of i. The Xs and open circles and squares show one possible way in which different processes may execute the loop with these values of i. For example, process 0 executes i = 1 and 2, process 2 does i = 3, process 1 does i = 4, and so forth.

Program 5-7 has one drawback, however. It will not work because of contention! The problem is similar to the one described in Section 4.7 and arises because processes are randomly scheduled. To see the problem, consider the following sequence of events:

1. Process 0 executes the instructions corresponding to the statement

```
i = next_index
```

2. Process 0 is idled.

3. Process 1 executes the two statements

```
i = next_index
next_index = next_index - 1
```

4. Process 0 starts up and executes the statement

```
next_index = next_index - 1
```

5. Process 2 executes the two statements

```
i = next_index
next_index = next_index - 1
```

The net result is that process 0 has i = 1000, process 1 has i = 1000 and process 2 has i = 998. This means, assuming no interference in assigning a(i), at the end of this sequence of events, a(1000) will be incremented by 8 and a(999) will remain unchanged.

In other words, the program acts incorrectly. The root of the problem is that three processes are trying to alter the value of the variable next_index all at the same time. As discussed in Section 4.7, the situation in which two or more processes try to alter a shared variable in parallel is called *contention*.

In order to eliminate contention for next_index, there must be a mechanism for ensuring that, if a process executes

```
i = next_index,
```

then no other processes can be allowed to execute that statement until the original process has decremented next_index. That is, the two source-code statements

```
i = next_index
next_index = next_index - 1
```

(which can be several assembly language statements) must be treated as a single indivisible unit by the processes. The terminology is that the section of code is *protected* or has *mutual exclusion*. While one process is executing a protected section of code, all other processes must be *locked out* or *excluded*.

In order to enforce protection, it is necessary that one process communicate to all other processes that it is in a protected portion of the program, and all other processes must behave in a responsible manner by staying away. Such communication is an example of *interprocess communication (IPC)* or *synchronization*. This communication normally involves the processes sharing one or more variables. When one process changes the value of the variable, in a mutually agreed upon manner, the other process can read the value and understand what the first process is doing. Note that mutual exclusion is not *enforced* by the operating system, or by hardware (it may be provided by these!), but it is a convention adhered to by all the processes.

In the case of self-scheduling, the required software structure for implementing such synchronization is the *spin-lock*. The spin-lock is normally provided either by the operating system or by the hardware itself. The implementation is not discussed here, but it is assumed that the appropriate function exists. Appendix 3 shows how the spin-lock may be implemented in Unix V. The functionality of the spin-lock will be described, starting with an illustrative program. Program 5-7, revised to make use of a spin-lock, is

```
c       Add a constant to each element of an array.
c       Illustrate self-scheduling.
c       This program uses spin-locks and works correctly.

        integer a(1000),next_index,i,process_fork,id,k
        integer lock_word,locked,unlocked,n,nproc

        call shared(next_index,4)
        call shared(a,4000)
        call shared(lock_word)

        locked = 1
        unlocked = 0
        n = 1000
        next_index = n
        nproc = 2
        k = 4
        (initialize a(i))

c       initialize the spin-lock
        call spin_lock_init(lock_word,unlocked)

        id = process_fork(nproc)

c       parallelized loop using self-scheduling.
   10       continue

        call spin_lock(lock_word)

c           start of protected region
            i = next_index
            next_index = next_index - 1
c           end of the protected region
```

```
              call spin_unlock(lock_word)

              if (i .le. 0) goto 2
              a(i) = a(i) + k
              goto 10
     2        continue
c          end of the parallelized loop

              call process_join()
              (store result)
              end
```

Program 5-8

The use of the spin-lock requires three function calls and a shared variable. The spin_lock_init statement

```
         integer lock_word,lock_condition
         call shared(lock_word,4)

         call spin_lock_init(lock_word,lock_condition)
```

initializes the spin-lock. A spin-lock has only two states—*locked* and *unlocked*. The integer variable lock_word is shared by all the processes and describes the state of the spin-lock. We can imagine that lock_word takes on two values, say 0 and 1. (The actual values depend on the implementation; 0 and 1 are used here for illustrative purposes only.) When the state of the spin-lock is "unlocked," then lock_word is 0. This means that there is no process executing the instructions in the protected region. When lock_word is 1, the spin-lock is in the locked state, indicating that there is a process in the protected region.

The shared variable lock_word serves as a signalling mechanism. Any process can read the value of lock_word and act accordingly. If a process finds that lock_word is 0 (i.e., "unlocked"), it can enter the protected region. Otherwise, it should stay out. Because lock_word is read and written by many processes, it must be shared.

When the spin-lock is initialized, the variable lock_condition describes the initial state of the lock. For purposes of this discussion, this variable is assumed to be an integer whose values can be 0 or 1. The value 0 initializes the lock to the unlocked state, while 1 initializes the lock in the locked state.

The user may have access to a library for which `lock_word` and `lock_condition` are different data types from those used here. In that case, he should follow the instructions in his documentation. The actual data types and values of `lock_word` and `lock_condition` depend upon the implementation, which is why one should use the function `spin_lock_init` for the initialization and not assign the variable `lock_word` directly.

When `lock_word` is 0, we say that the lock is *unlocked*, and when `lock_word` is 1 we say that the lock is *locked*. The appropriate terminology is to say that the lock is "unlocked" and "locked" rather than saying that `lock_word` is 0 or 1.

It is perhaps an unfortunate choice of terminology that we should say "process such-and-such locks the lock" or "the lock is unlocked," but this is how spin-locks are normally described. One way to overcome the confusion is, when something is described as "locked," to imagine that the variable `lock_word` is set to 1 (or is already 1), and if something is "unlocked," then the variable lock-word is set to 0 (or already is zero). Using the terminology "locked" and "unlocked" frees us from being committed to particular values of `lock_word`.

Besides the initialization, there are two functions which actually do the work of protecting a group of instructions. These are

```
call spin_lock(lock_word)
call spin_unlock(lock_word).
```

The `spin_lock` subroutine is called at the beginning of a protected region, and `spin_unlock` is called at the end. The variable `lock_word` is passed as a parameter to distinguish which particular lock is being invoked. There can be many different spin-locks in the same program. The program for an operating system may involve thousands of different spin-locks.

When the function `spin_lock` is called by a process, the logical action is that a check is made to see if the lock is unlocked. If it is, then the lock is locked and the process that called `spin_lock` is allowed to continue executing instructions (which would bring it into the protected region). Thus, when a process finds the lock unlocked, it locks it and then proceeds into the protected region.

However, if the lock was already locked when the process called the function `spin_lock`, then the calling process must wait until the lock becomes unlocked. That is, the process cannot proceed until the process, which is already in the protected region, finishes and then calls `spin_unlock`. When a process calls the function `spin_lock` and finds that the lock is locked, it must "spin its wheels" until the lock becomes unlocked. When a process which is in the protected region calls the function `spin_unlock`, it unlocks the lock so that the protected region is available to some other process.

When a process is blocked at a locked spin-lock, waiting for the lock to become unlocked, the process is actually in a loop of the form

```
90    continue
      if (lock_word .eq. 1) goto 90
```

(This loop would appear within the subroutine `spin_lock`.) That is, while the process is spinning, it is in a potentially infinite loop. It is also occupying a processor completely, executing a set of nonproductive instructions. Spin-locks should be used sparingly, and the protected regions should be as small as possible, so as to minimize the overhead of processes spinning unproductively at the locks. The function `spin_lock` takes care of the details of checking the state of the lock, allowing the process to continue or causing it to spin.

Many processes can be waiting at a locked lock at any particular time, because a single process is within the protected region. When the lock becomes unlocked, *only one* of the waiting processes can enter the protected region. The remaining processes keep spinning, awaiting their turns. The order in which waiting processes are selected to enter the protected region is undefined. The user should not assume that processes will be selected either in the order they arrive at the lock, in the order of `id` number, in the order of creation, or any other possibility.

Consider now how Program 5-8 above is executed. In the following illustration, suppose that only two processes are used (`nproc = 2`), the parent and a single child. The following description is illustrated in Figure 5-3.

Suppose, after the fork, that process 0 is first to call `spin_lock` (point A in Fig. 5-3). Since the lock was initialized as "unlocked," (`lock_word = 0` in our simple implementation), then the call to `spin_lock` locks the lock and process 0 begins executing the statements in the protected region.

Suppose, while it is there, process 1 makes the `spin_lock` call (point B in Fig. 5-3). The lock is locked so that process 1 must wait (spin its wheels). The spinning is illustrated in Fig. 5-3 by the dotted line. The program is not idle, but it is not doing any productive work. Meanwhile, process 0 executes both statements in the protected region, and then calls `spin_unlock` (point C in Fig. 5-3), which unlocks the lock. Now process 1 can acquire the lock" (point D, Fig. 5-3) and begin executing the code in the protected region.

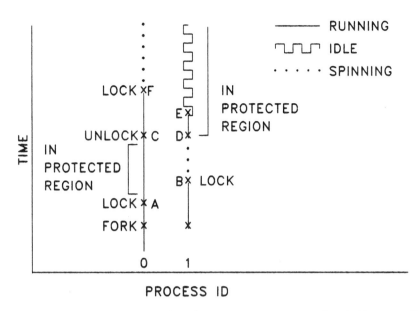

Figure 5-3.   One possible timeline for two processes executing in Program 5-8.

Let process 1 become idled at point E in Fig. 5-3. Process 0, after doing its work, branches back to the start of the protected region and calls spin_lock. The lock is locked and so process 0 starts to spin. The further action is left as a problem.

A spin-lock is used to eliminate contention and is used to enforce the following rule: *Only one process should ever be able to update a shared variable at a time.*

When more than two processes exist, there can be any number of processes "spinning" at a locked spin-lock. When the lock becomes unlocked, only one of the processes will be allowed to continue. The rest will be kept spinning.

However the spin-lock is implemented, there must be a guarantee that the call to spin_lock is indivisible, or *atomic*. That is, it must be guaranteed that, no matter how many processes are waiting at the lock, only one process at a time can possibly proceed past the lock into the protected region, and all other processes will be kept waiting until the lock is unlocked. This service is supplied either by the hardware or by software. Implementing it in hardware is essential if multiprocessing is to be efficient. The guarantee that the call to spin_lock be atomic can only be made if it is impossible that two processes can access the same memory location simultaneously. This was an assumption of the parallel-programming model discussed in Chapter 3.

The spin-lock is the most basic synchronization mechanism, and multi-tasking operating systems may have thousands of different locks. Practical parallel programming also requires liberal use of locks. An inefficient implementation can make a parallel program actually run slower than the sequential version.

It can be seen in Program 5-8 that, if there were a large number of processes (nproc large), then the processes could pile up at the lock, waiting to enter the protected region. This can cause the self-scheduling program to execute more slowly than the loop-splitting version.

On the other hand, if the calculation were long and involved (rather than merely incrementing an array element), then the self-scheduling technique will be more efficient than the loop-splitting version. It is up to the programmer to determine which technique is appropriate for the particular situation.

Problem: Explain what would happen in Program 5-8 if the variable lock_word were not shared.

Problem: Continue Fig. 5-3 for a few more iterations.

Problem: In Program 5-8, what would happen if the statement

```
if (i .le. 0) goto 2
```

were to come before the call to spin_unlock rather than after.

Answer: In this case, the first process for which i = 0 would branch out of the protected region without unlocking the lock. The remaining processes would wait at the lock but would never be able to enter the protected region because the lock would be forever locked. (That is, there would be no way for any other process to arrive at the call to spin_unlock.) The program would enter the limbo of the infinite loop. Each process would be "spinning" in an endless loop, waiting in vain for the lock to become unlocked. This is called *deadlock*. The lock is dead.

The spin-lock can be used for doing sums in parallel in a different manner than 5-1.

```
c       Sum the elements of array a(i), using nproc processes.
c       The final sum is in shared variable final_sum. This version
```

```
c      uses spin-locks when the partial sums are consolidated.
c      nproc is the total number of processes.
c      temsum holds the partial sums and is private to each
c      process.

       integer id,i,a(1000),final_sum,temsum,nproc
       integer process_fork,n,lock_word,unlocked,locked

       call shared(lock_word,4)
       call shared(final_sum,4)

       unlocked = 0
       locked = 1
       n = 1000
       nproc = 3
       final_sum = 0
c      initialize a(i)
       do 10 i = 1,n
            a(i) = 1
 10       continue

c      initialize the spin-lock
       call spin_lock_init(lock_word,unlocked)

c      create nproc-1 additional processes
       id = process_fork(nproc)

c      now the loop splitting.
c      process id stores a partial sum in temsum.
       do 1 i = 1 + id,n,nproc
            temsum = temsum + a(i)
  1       continue

c      accumulate partial sums in variable final_sum
       call spin_lock(lock_word)
            final_sum = final_sum + temsum
       call spin_unlock(lock_word)
c
       call process_join()
       print *,' final sum is ',final_sum
       end
```

Program 5-9

Each process calculates its portion of the sum, storing it in the private variable temsum. Each process has a private copy of temsum. Note that loop

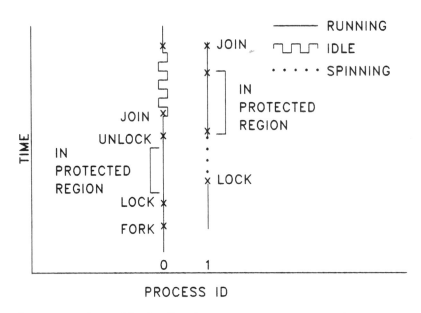

Figure 5-4.   A possible timeline for two processes executing Program 5-9.

splitting is used for calculating the partial sums. Self-scheduling would also work, but it would tend to be inefficient when many processes were involved.

In the protected region, each process adds its part of the sum to the shared variable `final_sum`. Because this is done in a protected region, the variable `final_sum` is accessed by only one process at a time, and the update is orderly. Note the difference between this version and Program 5-1. In the latter, process 0 consolidated all the partial sums into the final value. In 5-9, each process adds its own part of the sum to the final value.

The timeline for the case `nproc = 2` is given in Fig. 5-4.

Problem: What would happen if the statement in which `final_sum` were updated were not in a protected region? What would happen if `final_sum` were not shared?

Problem: Rewrite Program 5-9 using self-scheduling for the loop in which the partial sums are calculated. (Use a different variable for the spin-lock data structure that protects the assignment of i.)

Problem: In 5-9, what would happen if the statement

```
final_sum = 0
```

were located directly before the call to `spin_lock`?

Answer: This question will be answered by way of a particular situation that could arise. Suppose that process 1 has completed all its work and has been destroyed at the join. Suppose, now, that after process 1 is destroyed, process 0 finishes calculating its partial sum and arrives at the statement `final_sum = 0`. By zeroing `final_sum`, it also eliminates the partial sum which has already been stored in `final_sum` by process 1. Clearly, this state of affairs can continue, so that in the end `final_sum` may contain the partial sum of the very last process to finish the partial calculation.

Problem: Write a program to find the maximum value of an array. Use self-scheduling, and use spin-locks for the part that determines the maximum of all the maxima. (Hint: it is necessary to use two different spin-locks.)

Answer:

```
c       Compute the maximum value of array a(i) using nproc
c       processes and self-scheduling
c       and spin-locks for the calculation of the maximum of all the
c       partial maxima.
c       Assume <= 50 processes.
c       final_amax - the final maximum.
c       amax is private to each process.

        integer id,nproc,process_fork,i,locked,unlocked,n
        integer lock_word_1,lock_word_2,next_index
        real a(1000),amax,final_amax

        call shared(final_amax,4)
        call shared(lock_word_1,4)
        call shared(lock_word_2,4)
        call shared(next_index,4)

        unlocked = 0
        locked = 1
        nproc = 10
        n = 1000
        next_index = n
c       initialize a(i)
        do 10 i = i,n
            a(i) = float(i)
10      continue

        amax = a(1)
```

```
                    final_amax = a(1)

c       initialize spin-lock
                call spin_lock_init(lock_word_1,unlocked)
                call spin_lock_init(lock_word_2,unlocked)

c       create nproc - 1 children.
                id = process_fork(nproc)

c       loop splitting, each child calculates the maximum
c       value of a subset of the elements of a(i)

 20             continue

c       self-scheduling section
                call spin_lock(lock_word_1)
                    i = next_index
                    next_index = next_index - 1
                call spin_unlock(lock_word_1)
c       end of self-scheduling section

                if (i .le. 0)goto 1
                if (a(i) .gt. amax) then
                    amax = a(i)
                endif
                goto 20
 1              continue

c       Now each child updates the shared variable
c       final_amax by comparing its private amax with
c    .  the global one
                call spin_lock(lock_word_2)
                    if (amax .gt. final_amax) then
                        final_amax = amax
                    endif
                call spin_unlock(lock_word_2)

c       destroy children
                call process_join()

                print *,' max value of a(i) is ',final_amax
                end
```

Program 5-10

This program contains two different spin-locks, one of which accesses lock_word_1 and the other lock_word_2. A program which locks the lock governed by lock_word_1 will not affect the state of the lock governed by lock_word_2.

Problem: Why are two different spin-lock variables (lock_word_1 and lock_word_2) used in Program 5-10?

Answer: They are used for efficiency. The decrementing of next_index and updating of final_amax are independent operations and are protected separately. If only a single spin-lock variable were used, then while one process was updating final_amax, any process that wanted to get the next_index would have to wait.

5.5   Histogram

In this section, a program is presented which creates a histogram from the values stored in an array a(i). For purposes of illustration, self-scheduling is used, although it is likely to be less efficient than loop splitting.

```
c       Create histogram of values of a(i).
c       amin, amax are min and max values of a(i).
c       n is number of elements of a(i).
c       num_of_bins is number of bins of the histogram.

        integer id,i,histogram(50),int,n,nproc
        integer lok1,lok2,bin,process_fork
        integer unlocked,locked,num_of_bins,next_index
        real bin_size,float,a(1000),amin,amax

        call shared(a,4000)
        call shared(lok1,4)
        call shared(lok2,4)
        call shared(histogram,200)
        call shared(next_index,4)

c       initialize
        unlocked = 0
        locked = 1
        n = 1000
        nproc = 10
        num_of_bins = 20
        next_index = n
        (initialize a(i))
```

```
c       initialize spin-locks
        call spin_lock_init(lok1,unlocked)
        call spin_lock_init(lok2,unlocked)

c       find amin, amax - min and max values of array a(i)
        call find_min_max(a,n,amin,amax)

        bin_size = (amax - amin)/float(num_of_bins)

c       create nproc - 1 children
        id = process_fork(nproc)

c       iterate over all elements of a(i) using
c       self-scheduling.
  10       continue
        call spin_lock(lok1)
            i = next_index
            next_index = next_index - 1
        call spin_unlock(lok1)
        if (i .le. 0) goto 2
c       update histogram for element a(i)
c       function int converts real to integer
        bin = 1 + int(abs(a(i) - amin)/bin_size)
        if (bin .gt. num_of_bins)bin = num_of_bins
        call spin_lock(lok2)
            histogram(bin) = histogram(bin) + 1
        call spin_unlock(lok2)
        goto 10
   2       continue

        call process_join()
        (store result)
        end
```

Program 5-11

Program 5-11 works as follows. Following initialization, a call is made to subroutine find_min_max, which finds the minimum and maximum of array a(i) and returns these values in the private variables amin and amax respectively. Then the program forks nine additional processes. The elements of array a(i) are distributed to the processes through self-scheduling, using the region protected by lok1. Each process calculates the bin number in variable bin, which is not shared. It then updates the histogram in a region protected by lok2.

Problem: In Program 5-11, what would happen if variable `bin` were shared?

Partial answer: The program would give incorrect results.

The reason why updating `histogram` must take place in a protected region is that two or more processes may want to update the same element `histogram(bin)` simultaneously. When the program is compiled, the statement

```
histogram(bin) = histogram(bin) + 1
```

actually corresponds to a number of machine-language instructions, each of which does a small part of the work. In general, the steps that the CPU must go through to execute the statement are

(a) Load the value of `bin` into a CPU register from main memory (assume it is not already there).
(b) Using `bin` as an index, load `histogram(bin)` into a CPU register from main memory.
(c) Add 1 to the contents of the register used in (b).
(d) Store the result back into main memory.

As discussed in Section 4.6, *a process can be idled after any one of these steps*. That is, the process can be idled after loading `bin` into the register or before storing the incremented value of `histogram(bin)` back into main memory.

Neglecting `lok2`, the following chain of events can happen for two processes executing Program 5-11 in parallel. Suppose both processes find `bin = 8` and `histogram(8) = 17`, and then they set about incrementing `histogram(bin)`. Then

1. Process 0 does steps (a) and (b) and is then idled. (17 is now in a register of the CPU on which process 0 is executing.)
2. Process 1, on a different processor, also does steps (a) and (b), so its corresponding register also has contents 17.
3. Process 1 starts up and completes steps (c) and (d). It has then set `histogram(bin) = 18`.
4. Process 2 completes steps (c) and (d), so it also sets `histogram(bin) = 18`.

Thus, instead of histogram(bin) being 19, it is 18, which is the incorrect value. Updating histogram(bin) in the protected region prevents the incorrect assignment outlined above, and it obeys the general rule that a shared variable can be updated by only one process at a time.

Problem: Show that, by protecting the update of histogram(bin), the above scenario cannot occur.

In spite of using two locks, Program 5-11 is not nearly as efficient as it could be. The reason is that when a process wants to update a particular element of the array histogram, it locks the entire array, so no other process can update a different element at the same time. There is no reason, in principle, why different array elements of array histogram cannot be updated simultaneously. The way to do this is to protect each element of the histogram array with a different lock. This is done in the following program, which also uses loop splitting (which is more efficient than self-scheduling).

```
c       Create histogram of values of a(i).
c       amin, amax are min and max values of a(i).
c       n is number of elements of a(i).
c       num_of_bins is number of bins of the histogram.
c       Uses a different spin-lock lokl(i) to protect
c       each element of array histogram(i).

        integer id,i,n,histogram(50),int,nproc,next_index
        integer lokl(50),bin,process_fork
        integer unlocked,locked,num_of_bins
        real bin_size,float,a(1000),amin,amax

        call shared(a,4000)
        call shared(lokl,200)
        call shared(histogram,200)
        call shared(next_index,4)

        unlocked = 0
        locked = 1
        n = 1000
        nproc = 10
        num_of_bins = 20
        next_index = n
        (initialize a(i))
```

```
c      initialize spin-locks
           do 20 i = 1,num_of_bins
               call spin_lock_init(lokl(i),unlocked)
  20       continue

c      find min and max of array a(i)
           call find_min_max(a,n,amin,amax)

           bin_size = (amax - amin)/float(num_of_bins)

c      create nproc - 1 children
           id = process_fork(nproc)

c      iterate over all elements of a(i) using
c      loop splitting.
           do 1 i = 1 + id,n,nproc
c              update histogram for element a(i)
c              function int converts real to integer
               bin = 1 + int(abs(a(i) - amin)/bin_size)
               if (bin .gt. num_of_bins)bin = num_of_bins

c              each element of histogram(bin) is protected
c              by a separate lock.
               call spin_lock(lokl(bin))
                   histogram(bin) = histogram(bin) + 1
               call spin_unlock(lokl(bin))

   1       continue

           call process_join()
           (store result)
           end
```

Program 5-12

Program 5-12 is similar to 5-11, except that there is a spin-lock for each element of the array histogram. Each lock is initialized as unlocked in the do 20 loop. When any process updates the element histogram(bin), it first calls the appropriate lock lokl(bin). This locks the update section only against other processes that want to update the exact same element of histogram. A different bin of the histogram can be updated simultaneously.

The subroutine find_min_max can be implemented either in single-stream or in parallel. Doing it single-stream would defeat the subsequent parallelization of the histogram formation, in the sense that it would require a relatively long time to execute. Efficient implementation requires barriers, which are described in the next chapter. At the end of that chapter, 5-12 will be enhanced so that `find_min_max` is done in parallel.

Program 5-12 for the histogram may be somewhat inefficient, because of the `spin_lock` and `spin_unlock` call on each iteration of the do 1 loop. This means that there is process synchronization on each iteration of the "core" loop, so that the overhead is proportional to n, which can become large.

Another way to create a histogram is to have each process update a private `histogram`, which is a histogram of a subset of array elements a(i), and then the partial histograms are accumulated into the final version. The advantage of this approach is that the "core" loop do 1, in which most of the work is done, is the same for both the single-stream and parallel versions, and the overhead is not proportional to n. The disadvantage is that there is considerable initialization and consolidation overhead. The following program carries out this approach.

```
c        Create histogram of values of a(i).
c        Each process first creates a partial histogram
c        temhist(i), from a subset of array elements,
c        and then these partial histograms
c        are merged into the final one, histogram(i).
c        amin, amax are min and max values of a(i).
c        n is number of elements of a(i).
c        num_of_bins is number of bins of the histogram.
c        uses a different spin-lock lokl(i) to protect
c        each element of array histogram(i).

         integer id,i,histogram(50),int,n,nproc
         integer lokl(50),bin,process_fork
         integer unlocked,locked,num_of_bins
         integer temhist(50)
         real bin_size,float,a(1000),amin,amax

         call shared(a,4000)
         call shared(lokl,200)
         call shared(histogram,200)

         unlocked = 0
         locked = 1
         n = 1000
         nproc = 10
```

```
            num_of_bins = 20
            (initialize a(i))

c       initialize spin-locks
            do 20 i = 1,num_of_bins
                call spin_lock_init(lokl(i),unlocked)
 20         continue

c       find min and max of array a(i).
            call find_min_max(a,n,amin,amax)

            bin_size = (amax - amin)/float(num_of_bins)

c       initialize histogram(i)
            do 30 i = 1,num_of_bins
                histogram(i) = 0
 30         continue

c       create nproc - 1 children.
            id = process_fork(nproc)

c       each process initializes temhist
            do 25 i = 1,num_of_bins
                temhist(i) = 0
 25         continue
c       Each process creates partial histogram temhist(i)
            do 1 i = 1 + id,n,nproc
c               function int converts real to integer
                bin = 1 + int(abs(a(i) - amin)/bin_size)
                if (bin .gt. num_of_bins)bin = num_of_bins
                temhist(bin) = temhist(bin) + 1
  1         continue

c       each process updates histogram(i) with its private
c       partial histogram. Lock each element of histogram(i)
c       separately.
            do 40 i = 1,num_of_bins
                call spin_lock(lokl(i))
                    histogram(i) = histogram(i) + temhist(i)
                call spin_unlock(lokl(i))
 40         continue

            call process_join()
            (store result)
            end
```

Program 5-13

In Program 5-13, the array `temhist(i)` is private to each process. In the do 1 loop, each process makes a partial histogram of those elements of `a(i)` which the process can access. For example, process 0 makes its partial histogram, in its copy of `temhist`, from the array elements `a(1)`, `a(11)`, `a(21)`, ... In the protected region, each process adds its partial histogram to the shared array `histogram`. Program 5-13 will execute faster than 5-12 for large n, because the do 1 loop has fewer statements to execute, but it uses more memory and has more overhead. For small n, 5-13 may well run slower than 5-12.

Problem: Estimate the speedup of 5-12 and 5-13 for various values of n and `nproc`.

Problem: Could `histogram(i)` be initialized in parallel, after forking?

Partial answer: No.

5.6   Summary

This chapter introduced two basic mechanisms for apportioning loops among several processes. These are loop splitting and self-scheduling.

In order to implement self-scheduling correctly, the spin-lock was required. The spin-lock is used to protect a region of the program, so that only one process at a time can execute the code therein. The spin-lock has two states—locked and unlocked. The spin-lock is first initialized, then it can be locked and unlocked. The initialization is

```
integer lock_word,condition
call shared(lock_word,4)

call spin_lock_init(lock_word,condition)
```

where condition is an integer which sets the state of the lock to be locked or unlocked.

A process accesses the spin-lock with the subroutines

```
call spin_lock(lock_word)

call spin_unlock(lock_word)
```

Spin-locks are used to enforce the following rules: *Only one process at a time should update the value of a shared variable.*

5.7 Additional Problems

1. Write a parallel program to evaluate a polynomial of any order.
2. Write a parallel program to do numerical integration, using your favorite integration algorithm.
3. Write a parallel program to count the number of characters in one or more character strings.
4. Write a parallel program to compute $n!$, using two processes.
5. Write a parallel program to compute the derivative

$$g(x) = \frac{d}{dx} f(x)$$

where $f(x)$ is given numerically at points $x(i)$ in some interval, and $g(x)$ is returned as an array at equally spaced points of the interval.

CHAPTER 6

Barriers and Race Conditions

6.1 Introduction

A barrier causes processes to wait and allows them to proceed only after a predetermined number of processes are waiting at the barrier. It is used to ensure that one stage of a calculation has been completed before the processes proceed to a next stage which requires the results of the previous stage. Barriers are used to eliminate *race conditions*, in which the result of a calculation depends on the relative speed at which processes execute. Along with spin-locks, barriers are the most important synchronization mechanism for fine-grained parallel programming. In Chapter 14, and in Appendix 3, it is shown how to create the barrier function from a spin-lock.

6.2 The Barrier Calls

Barriers will be introduced in a program to find the absolute deviation from the average of a set of numbers. If a(i) contains the numbers, the average is

$$\langle a \rangle = (1/n) \, sum(i) \, a(i)$$

and the absolute deviation is

$$deviation = (1/n) sum(i) \mid a(i) - \langle a \rangle \mid$$

where the vertical bars denote the absolute value. The sums in the two expressions above run from 1 to n inclusive. The average deviation gives an average of the difference between each array element and the average value.

The calculation requires two steps. First, the average is calculated; second, the deviation is found. The calculation is done (incorrectly!) in the following program:

```
c       Calculate absolute deviation of array a(i).
c       deviation = (1/n) sum(i) | a(i) - <a>|
c       where <a> is the average of a.
c       The sum over j goes from 1 to n inclusive.
c       This program is incorrect because it suffers from
c       a race condition.

        real  a(1000),average,deviation,sum
        integer lok,n
        integer i,nproc,id,unlocked,locked
        integer process_fork

        call shared(lok,4)
        call shared(average,4)
        call shared(deviation,4)

        unlocked = 0
        locked = 1
        nproc = 10
        n = 1000
        (initialize a(i))
        call spin_lock_init(lok,unlocked)

        average = 0
        deviation = 0
        id = process_fork(nproc)

c       average value
        sum = 0.
        do 1 i = 1 + id,n,nproc
            sum = sum + a(i)
```

```
1       continue

        call spin_lock(lok)
            average = average + sum/float(n)
        call spin_unlock(lok)

c       ---------------------------------------------------
c       The calculation of the average is now complete.
c       Calculate the deviation.
c       ---------------------------------------------------

        sum = 0.
        do 2 i = 1 + id,n,nproc
            sum = sum + abs(a(i) - average)
2       continue

        call spin_lock(lok)
            deviation = deviation + sum/float(n)
        call spin_unlock(lok)

        call process_join()
        (output result)
        end
```

Program 6-1

Program 6-1 has two parts. First the average is calculated, and then the deviation. The problem is this: The calculation of the deviation should not be started until the calculation of the average is complete. Program 6-1 does not have this property.

Consider the following chain of events, assuming two processes (nproc = 2):

1. Processes 0 forks, then becomes idle.
2. Process 1 executes the entire program, then is terminated at the process_join.
3. Process 0 starts up and executes the entire program.

When process 1 is computing its contribution to deviation, process 0 has not computed its contribution to average. Therefore, process 1's contribution to deviation will be incorrect.

This situation is known as a race condition, because the result depends on the relative speed at which the processes execute the program. If both processes keep abreast with each other, so that the calculation of `deviation` is not begun until the calculation of `average` is complete, the answer would be correct. However, there are other, incorrect possibilities.

A race condition is different from contention. There is no contention in Program 6-1, because the shared variables `average` and `deviation` are both updated in protected regions.

What is needed is a mechanism to force all processes to wait at the end of the calculation of the average, and before the start of the calculation of the deviation, until all processes have finished the calculation of the average. This mechanism is the *barrier*, which is used in Program 6-1(a), the correct version of the calculation.

```
c       Calculate absolute deviation of array a(i).
c       deviation = (1/n) sum(i) | a(i) - <a>|
c       where <a> is the average of a.
c       The sum over j goes from 1 to n inclusive.
c       Illustrates use of barriers

        real  a(1000),average,deviation,sum
        integer bar_array(4),lok,n
        integer i,nproc,id,unlocked,locked
        integer process_fork

        call shared(bar_array,16)
        call shared(lok,4)
        call shared(average,4)
        call shared(deviation,4)

        unlocked = 0
        locked = 1
        nproc = 10
        n = 1000
        (initialize a(i))
        call spin_lock_init(lok,unlocked)

c       initialize the barrier
        call barrier_init(bar_array,nproc)

        average = 0
        deviation = 0
        id = process_fork(nproc)

c       average value
        sum = 0.
```

```
          do 1 i = 1 + id,n,nproc
              sum = sum + a(i)

  1       continue

          call spin_lock(lok)
              average = average + sum/float(n)
          call spin_unlock(lok)

c         ------------------------------------------------
c         The calculation of the average is now complete.
c         Calculate the deviation.

c         no process can continue past the barrier until
c         all the processes are there
c         ------------------------------------------------

          call barier(bar_array)

          sum = 0.
          do 2 i = 1 + id,n,nproc
              sum = sum + abs(a(i) - average)
  2       continue

          call spin_lock(lok)
              deviation = deviation + sum/float(n)
          call spin_unlock(lok)

          call process_join()
          (output result)
          end
```

Program 6-1(a)

The initialization of the barrier is performed using the subroutine call

```
          call barrier_init(bar_array,blocking_number)
```

where blocking_number is the number of processes that will halt at the barrier. This is the number of processes that the barrier can block. The array bar_array is used to keep track of the information required by the barrier, which includes the blocking number, the actual number of processes waiting at the barrier, and other things. If the barrier is implemented in software, using a spin-lock, as is described in Section 14.2.4 or Appendix 3, then a dimension of 4 is needed, and this is the value used in this text. The user's library may require a different dimension and different arguments as well.

The barrier is invoked in the program by using the subroutine `barrier`,

```
call barrier(bar_array)
```

where `bar_array` is the same array that appeared as an argument in the call to `barrier_init`. The `barrier` subroutine call works as follows. When a process "arrives" at the barrier (i.e., makes the `barrier` call), the subroutine checks to see how many processes have already made this call. If the number of processes, including the newly arrived one, is less than the blocking number, the newly arrived process must wait (along with all the processes that have already arrived at the barrier). On the other hand, if the number of processes which have made the call, inclusive of the new one, equals the blocking number, then all the processes that are waiting are allowed to proceed, including the last one to make the call. That is, the `barrier` subroutine returns, and the processes continue by executing the statement following the call to `barrier`.

Problem: Why must the array `bar_array` be shared?

Answer: One integer of `bar_array` serves as a counter for the number of processes that are waiting at the barrier. When the barrier is initialized, the counter is set to the blocking number. Each time a process calls the subroutine `barrier`, the counter is decremented. The decrementing is carried out in the subroutine `barrier`. If the counter is not zero, the calling processes "wait" at the barrier, either by spinning or by being idled, depending on the implementation. The waiting is carried out within the subroutine `barrier`. When the counter is zero, the processes are permitted to continue, meaning that each process returns from the subroutine `barrier`. If `bar_array` were private, then when one process decremented the counter, the new value of the counter could not be made known to the other processes. The value of each private counter would be equal to `blocking_number − 1` for each process that called the barrier. The counter would never become zero and the processes could never proceed past the barrier.

Program 6-1(a) works as follows. First, variables are initialized, including the spin-lock and the barrier. Then the average value is calculated, the value being held by the variable `average`. In the `do 1` loop, using loop splitting, each process makes a partial sum. In the following protected region, each process adds its partial sum to average, which is a shared variable.

The barrier call follows the first protected region. No process can execute any instruction following the call to barrier until all the processes have made the barrier call. This ensures that the calculation of the average value is complete before the calculation of the absolute deviation can begin.

Problem: In Program 6-1(a), can the statement "deviation = 0" come directly after the barrier call?

Partial answer: No. To see why, imagine that a process is idled just after it passes the barrier and wakes up after several processes have reached the process_join.

Problem: How would the Program 6-1(a) have to be revised if the variables average and deviation were set to 0 after the process_fork?

Partial answer: There would have to be a barrier following the initialization and before the start of the protected region. To see why, consider the following possible sequence of events:

1. A process becomes idle immediately after being created and before assigning 0 to average and deviation.
2. The other processes update the variable average with their partial sums and then are blocked at the barrier following the protected region.
3. The idled process starts up, sets average = 0 and deviation = 0, and continues.

Barriers need not be in the same "place" in the program. The following fragment, while it would never be used in a real program, performs the exact same function as the single barrier call in 6-1(a).

```
if (id .eq. 0) then
    call barrier(bar_array)
else if (id .eq. 1) then
    call barrier(bar_array)
else if (id .eq. 2) then
    call barrier(bar_array)
    .
    .
```

```
      .
   else
         call barrier(bar_array)
```

This fragment will act as a single barrier to the processes. The call to the barrier involves a shared array which keeps track of how many processes have arrived at the barrier. The same shared array is manipulated on each call, no matter "where" the call comes from.

The barrier has two phases: a *trapping* phase and a *release* phase. The trapping phase was discussed above. A *release* means that the function returns from the barrier subroutine call. In the release phase, all the processes that are trapped at the barrier must be released, and *this release must occur before any other process can be trapped*.

Normally, the release is sequential, so that first one process is released, then the second, then the third, and so forth. (This is not necessary. A nearly simultaneous release can be implemented in hardware, but such an implementation is rare.) The fact that the release is sequential means that a process which was released can call the same barrier again, before all the other processes are released. To see how this comes about, consider the following fragment, where bar_array is a barrier for nproc processes:

```
      .
      .
      .
   call barrier(bar_array)
   (work)
   call barrier(bar_array)
      .
      .
      .
```

Suppose the following happens:

1. nproc processes become trapped at the first barrier.
2. One process (say process A) is released. The other processes are idled in the barrier function.
3. The released process rushes through the work area, then makes the second barrier call.

There are now nproc processes at the barrier, nproc − 1 waiting "at" the first barrier to be released, the other (process A) waiting at the second call. If the barrier were not implemented correctly, then *all* nproc processes would be released. This is an error, because process A should wait at the second barrier for all the other processes to be released from the first barrier, execute the work area, and then become trapped at the second barrier. What must happens is that process A spins at the second barrier, not decrementing the internal counter of the barrier, waiting for the other processes to be released. After the other nproc − 1 processes are released, the counter is reset to the blocking_number, and *only then* can process A be trapped at the barrier, the trapping involving a decrementing of the internal counter of the barrier.

Barriers can be used to fully parallelize the histogram calculation, including the determination of the minimum and maximum values of the array a. This example is instructive because it also invokes a subroutine call. The complete code is

```
c       Create histogram of values of a(i).
c       shr_amin, shr_amax are min and max values of a(i).
c       n is number of elements of a(i).
c       num_of_bins is number of bins of the histogram.
c       A different spin-lock array lokl(i) protects
c       each element of array histogram(i).

        integer id,nproc,i,n,histogram(50),int,process_fork
        integer lokl(50),bin,lok,bar_array(4)
        integer unlocked,locked,num_of_bins
        real bin_size,float,a(1000),shr_amin,shr_amax,abs

c       shared variables
        call shared(a,4000)
        call shared(lokl,200)
        call shared(histogram,200)
        call shared(bar_array,16)

c       additional shared variables used in subroutine
c       find_min_max.
        call shared(lok,4)
        call shared(shr_amax,4)
        call shared(shr_amin,4)

c       (initialize a(i))
        unlocked = 0
        locked = 1
        nproc = 10
        n = 1000
```

```
                num_of_bins = 20

                call spin_lock_init(lok,unlocked)
c         initialize num_of_bins spin-locks
                do 20 i = 1,num_of_bins
                    call spin_lock_init(lokl(i),unlocked)
  20        continue

c         initialize barrier
                call barrier_init(bar_array,nproc)
                id = process_fork(nproc)

c         each process calls find_min_max. min and max returned
c         in shared variables shr_amin, shr_amax.
                call find_min_max(a,n,id,nproc,shr_amin,shr_amax,
     s                  lok,bar_array)

                bin_size = (shr_amax-shr_amin)/float(num_of_bins)

c         initialize histogram array
                do 10 i = 1 + id,num_of_bins,nproc
                    histogram(i) = 0
  10        continue

                call barrier(bar_array)

c         compute histogram
                do 1 i = 1 + id,n,nproc
                    bin = 1 + int(abs(a(i) - shr_amin)/bin_size)
                    if (bin .gt. num_of_bins)bin = num_of_bins
                    call spin_lock(lokl(bin))
                        histogram(bin) = histogram(bin) + 1
                    call spin_unlock(lokl(bin))
  1         continue

                call process_join()
                (output result)
                end


c         **********************************************find_min_max


                subroutine find_min_max(a,n,id,nproc,shr_amin,
     s      shr_amax,lok,bar_array)

c     Find minimum amin and maximum amax
c     of an array a(i), 1 <= i <= n.
```

```
c       Each process calls this routine separately and
c       returns results in shared variables shr_amin, shr_amax.
c       lok is shared, and spin-lock must be initialized
c       before entry.

        integer lok,id,nproc,i,bar_array(1),n
        real a(1),amin,amax,shr_amin,shr_amax

c       only process 0 does initialization
        if (id .eq. 0) then
            shr_amax = a(1)
            shr_amin = a(1)
        endif

c       initialization must be complete before continuing
        call barrier(bar_array)

        amax = a(1)
        amin = a(1)

c       each process finds the max and min values.
        do 1 i = 1 + id,n,nproc
            if (amax .lt. a(i)) then
                amax = a(i)
            endif
            if (amin .gt. a(i)) then
                amin = a(i)
            endif
  1     continue
c       each process updates shr_amin and shr_amax
        call spin_lock(lok)
            if (shr_amax .lt. amax) then
                shr_amax = amax
            endif
            if (shr_amin .gt. amin) then
                shr_amin = amin
            endif
        call spin_unlock(lok)

c       all processes must wait for calculation to be complete before
c       returning.
        call barrier(bar_array)

        return
        end
```

Program 6-2

After the fork, each process calls subroutine `find_min_max`. The shared variables `shr_amin` and `shr_amax` hold the minimum and maximum values of `a(i)`.

Problem: In Program 6-2, why is a barrier call needed before any process can begin executing the `do 1` loop?

Answer: The initialization of `bin_size` and of the `histogram` array must be complete before the processes can begin to use these variables in the `do 1` loop. Even if this initialization were carried out by a single process, the barrier would be necessary.

Program 6-2 has the unfortunate feature that the shared variables used by the subroutine `find_min_max` are declared in the main program and passed as arguments to the subroutine. This is a result of the limitations of tiny Fortran (it has, for example, no global variables). It is probable that such machinations will not be required for the user's implementation.

6.3   Expression Splitting

It is not necessary that a barrier block all processes which exist. Rather, the barrier will block up to the blocking-number of processes and then let them proceed. The blocking number can be any number between 1 and the total number of processes. In a single program, there can be many barriers, all with different blocking numbers. The different barriers are distinguished by different arrays as arguments in the call to subroutine `barrier`, or by different portions of the same array. An example of using different barriers for different processes arises in expression splitting.

If one has a loop with relatively few iterations, then loop splitting may lead to an inequitable distribution of the work, as discussed in Section 5.3. If the expression being executed within the loop is large enough, it can be split among two or more processes, leading to a more equitable distribution of the workload.

Consider the following example, which is a slight alteration of one of the Livermore Loops and is used in Navier Stokes (hydrodynamic) simulations:

```
c       Hydrodynamic simulation fragment
        real x(1000),u(1006),y(1000),z(1000),r,t
        integer k,n
```

```
        (initialize u,y,z,r,t)
        n = 1000
        do 7 k = 1,n
        x(k) = u(k) + r * (z(k) + r * y (k) ) +
   s            t * (u(k + 3) + r * ( u(k + 2) + r * u(k + 1))) +
   s            t * t * (u(k + 6) + r * (u(k + 5) + r * u(k + 4)))
   7    continue
```

Program 6-3

This typical loop assigns x(k) as a sum with nine elements. This can be parallelized as follows:

```
c       Hydrodynamic simulation fragment, parallelized
c       Use expression splitting.
c       Assume <= 20 processes.

        real x(1000),u(1006),y(1000),z(1000),r,t,sum(0:19)
        integer bar_array(4,0:19),id,nproc,k,n
        integer process_fork,mod,i

        call shared(sum,40)
        call shared(bar_array,320)
        call shared(x,4000)

        n = 1000
        nproc = 10
        (initialize u,y,z,r,t)

c       initialize nproc/2 barriers
c       nproc must be even
        do 10 i = 0,(nproc-1)/2
            call barrier_init(bar_array(1,i),2)
  10    continue

c       fork nproc-1 additional processes
        id = process_fork(nproc)

c       Pairs of processes execute the
c       same value of k. The process for which id is even
c       does half the sum for given k, the process for which id is
c       odd does the other half.
        do 7 k = 1 + id/2,n,nproc/2
            if (mod(id,2) .eq. 0) then
                sum(id) = u(k) + r * (z(k) + r * y(k)) +
   s                t * (u(k + 3) + r * u(k + 2))
```

```
                         else
                             sum(id) = t * r * r * u(k + 1) +
       s                         t * t * (u(k + 6) + r * (u(k + 5) + r * u(k + 4))))
                         endif

c                        Make sure both processes have completed their work
c                        before the "even" process accumulates the final sum.
c                                                   ********* Point A
                         call barrier(bar_array(1,id/2))

c                        accumulate the final sum.
                         if (mod(id,2) .eq. 0) then
                             x(k) = sum(id) + sum(id + 1)
                         endif

c                        This barrier call eliminates a race condition.
                         call barrier(bar_array(1,id/2))

   7             continue
                 call process_join()
                 (output results)
                 end
```

Program 6-4

In Program 6-4, a total of five barriers are defined, each with blocking number 2. The initialization is

```
        call barrier_init(bar_array(1,i),2)
```

for i = 0, 1, 2, 3, 4. This initializes five barriers, and each barrier uses a different part of the same two-dimensional array bar_array. The first barrier (i = 0) uses the first four elements of the array. The next barrier (i = 1) uses the next four elements, and so forth. (Recall from Section 2.6 that arrays in Fortran are stored in column order, so that the left-most index varies most rapidly.)

Following the initialization, two processes each execute the same value of k. For example, if nproc = 10, processes 0 and 1 both execute k = 1, 6, 11, 16,.... Processes 2 and 3 each execute k = 2, 7, 12, 17,..., and so forth. The expression within the do-loop is split (thus leading to the term *expression splitting*) among the two processes. Processes with an odd id number do one part of the expression; those with an even id number do the other part.

The barrier call

```
call barrier(bar_array(1,id/2))
```

will block only two processes. It will block the pairs (0,1), (2,3), (4,5), (6,7), and so forth. For example, for both processes 0 and 1, id/2 = 0, so these two processes make the call

```
call barrier(bar_array(1,0))
```

passing to the subroutine the first four elements of bar_array. For processes 2 and 3, we have id/2 = 1, and these two processes then make the call

```
call barrier(bar_array(1,1))
```

passing to the subroutine the next four elements of bar_array, and so forth.

In other words, in Program 6-4, processes are synchronized in pairs, and different pairs can execute the loop at different rates.

Note that a barrier does not "belong" to a process. Rather, the process must call the appropriate barrier, passing the relevant array to it as the argument to identify which barrier it is calling.

Problem: What is the purpose of the second barrier call in Program 6-4, the one directly above the 7 continue statement.

Answer: If this barrier call were absent, the loop would not work correctly. While the process with the even id number assigns x(k) to the sum of the partial sums, the "odd" process can proceed to the next value of k and alter the value of sum(id) before it is accessed by the "even" process. This in turn could lead to an incorrect value of x(k). This is another example of a *race condition.*

Problem: Is it necessary to share x(i) in 6-4?

Problem: In Program 6-4, why couldn't one have a call to a single barrier, for nproc processes? Then, instead of the processes proceeding in pairs, they would all be synchronized. (Hint: Will all the processes always make the barrier call? Consider the loop

```
      do 7 k = 1 + id/2,10,4
```

for eight processes.)

Problem: In Program 6-4, executing two barrier calls for each value of k is expected to introduce extra loop overhead. Rewrite the program so that there is only a single barrier call, no matter what the value of k.

Answer:

```
c        Hydrodynamic simulation fragment, parallelized
c        use expression splitting.
c        This version is more efficient than 6-4
c        but uses more memory (in temporary arrays sum1,sum2).
c        Assume <= 20 processes.

         real x(1000),u(1006),y(1000),z(1000),r,t
         real sum1(1000),sum2(1000)
         integer bar_array(4),id,nproc,mod,process_fork,k,n

         call shared(bar_array,16)
         call shared(x,4000)
         call shared(sum1,4000)
         call shared(sum2,4000)

         nproc = 10
         n = 1000
         (initialize u,y,z,r,t)

c        initialize the barrier
         call barrier_init(bar_array,nproc)

c        fork nproc-1 additional processes
         id = process_fork(nproc)

c        Pairs of processes execute the
c        same value of k. The process for which id is even
c        does half the sum for given k, the process for which id is odd
c        does the other half.
         do 7 k = 1 + id/2,n,nproc/2
         if (mod(id,2) .eq. 0) then
             sum1(k) = u(k) + r * (z(k) + r * y(k)) +
     s               t * (u(k + 3) + r * u(k + 2))
         else
             sum2(k) = t * r * r * u(k + 1) +
```

```
      s              t * t * (u(k + 6) + r * (u(k + 5) + r * u(k + 4)))
             endif
  7          continue

  c    Make sure all processes have completed before
  c    accumulating the partial sums
             call barrier(bar_array)

  c    accumulate the partial sums
             do 8 k = 1 + id,n,nproc
                       x(k) = sum1(k) + sum2(k)
  8          continue

             call process_join()
             (output results)
             end
```

Program 6-5

While Program 6-5 will execute much more rapidly than 6-4, it does require more memory.

Problem: Could you dispense with the barrier and move the assignment

```
      x(k) = sum1(k) + sum2(k)
```

to just before the statement 7   continue? Explain your answer. Make sure you take into account the possibility that processes with odd id all become idle immediately upon being created.

6.4   Summary

Barriers are initialized using the call

```
          integer barrier_array(4),blocking_number
          call shared(barrier_array,16)
          call barrier_init(barrier_array,blocking_number)
```

where blocking_number is the number of processes that will wait at the barrier. A barrier is "erected" using the subroutine call

```
          call barrier(barrier_array)
```

6.5   Additional Problems—Elementary Statistics

1. Write a single parallel program to compute the variance, skewness, and kurtosis of a set of data in array a(i). The variance is

    $$variance = (1/n)sum(i)(a(i) - \langle a \rangle)**2$$

    where <a> is the average of a(i), and the sum goes from 1 through n. The skewness is

    $$skewness = (1/n)sum(i)((a(i) - \langle a \rangle)/std)**3$$

    where std is the standard deviation

    $$std = sqrt(variance)$$

    The kurtosis is

    $$kurtosis = ((1/n)sum(i)((a(i) - \langle a \rangle)/std)**4) - 3$$

2. Write a parallel program to find the median of a set of data in array a(i). The median is the value j such that

    $$sum(i = i{:}j)a(i) = sum(i = j + 1{:}n)a(i)$$

    or a value of j such that this relation holds as closely as possible.

3. Write a parallel program to evaluate the chi-squared value of a distribution. If a histogram h(i) has been made of a set of points, where i is the bin number, and if p(i) is a theoretical probability distribution function (or another binned data set), then the chi-squared estimate of how well p(i) approximates h(i) is

    $$chi\text{-}squared = sum(i)((h(i) - p(i))/p(i))**2$$

4. Write a parallel program to evaluate the correlation coefficient of two sets of data, a(i) and b(i). The correlation coefficient is defined as

    $$correlation = \frac{sum(i)(a(i) - \langle a \rangle)(b(i) - \langle b \rangle)}{sqrt(std(a)std(b))}$$

    where std(a) is the standard deviation of a.

5. Write a parallel program to smooth a data set, using your favorite smoothing algorithm.

CHAPTER 7

Introduction to Scheduling— Nested Loops

7.1 Introduction

Making efficient use of processes is a problem in *scheduling. Scheduling is concerned with apportioning the workload among processes in the most equitable manner.* Note that, as programmers, we are concerned about using processes rather than processors. It is at run time that the decision as to exactly how many processes to create must be made, based on the number of available processors.

According to this definition, loop splitting, self-scheduling, and expression splitting are examples of scheduling.

Writing parallel programs is complicated by the desirability of balancing the workload among processes (and, by implication, the available processors). For example, suppose that one has sixteen processors available, so that one wants to use sixteen processes, but a loop being executed in parallel only has ten iterations. It is inefficient to have sixteen processors available but to be able to use only ten of them in a particular program section. If there is only a single loop, then only expression splitting can improve the situation. However, for nested loops, there is hope.

In this chapter, the problem of scheduling will be discussed with reference to two nested small loops. The problem of small loops arises when the number of iterations of each of the loops is comparable to or smaller than the number of processes. The small-loop problem, and several possible resolutions, will be illustrated using the example of the multiplication of a vector by an array.

In all the examples of this chapter, the following program is parallelized:

```
c        Multiply vector v(j) by array a(i,j).
c                result(i) = a(i,j) * v(j),summed over j
c        Single-stream program
         integer v(10),a(10,10),result(10),i,j,temsum,n

c        ----------initialization
         n = 10
         (initialize a,v)

c        ----------calculation
         do 1 i = 1,n
             temsum = 0
             do 2 j = i,n
                 temsum = temsum + a(i,j) * v(j)
2            continue
             result(i) = temsum
1        continue
         (output results)
         end
```

Program 7-1

This routine is written as a main program, but it could also be a subroutine.

There are more efficient ways to code this loop, but since the program is for illustrative purposes, we shall let it stand.

It will be useful to illustrate the scheduling graphically. The notation to be used is shown in Fig. 7-1, where the scheduling of Program 7-1 is illustrated. There is only one process, represented by the vertical line with squares. Starting at the bottom of the figure, the single process first sets i = 1 (the vertical, solid line). Then it iterates over j, doing all values of j from 1 through 10, as illustrated in the square. Next it sets i = 2, as expressed by the vertical line, and then iterates over all values of j again (the square), and so forth. The numbers in any square are the values of j over which the process iterates, for the value of i given on the line below the square.

The simplest way to parallelize Program 7-1 is to parallelize the outer

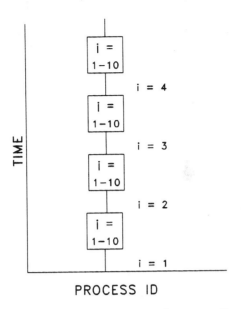

PROCESS ID

Figure 7-1.   Illustration of the scheduling of the single-stream Program 7-1. The solid line represents the assignment of i in the outer loop, and the square represents the assignment of j in the inner loop. In this simple case, first the process assigns i = 1, then it iterates through all values of j, then it assigns i = 2, then iterates through all value of j, and so forth.

loop (over i) using loop splitting. This results in the version 1, Program 7-2:

```
c       Parallel matrix — vector multiplication
c       Version 1. Simple loop splitting.
c               result(i) = a(i,j) * v(j), summed over j

        integer v(10),a(10,10),result(10),i,temsum,n,j
        integer process_fork,id,nproc

        call shared(result,40)

c       ----------- intialization
        n = 10
        nproc = 16
        (initialize a, v)

        id = process_fork(nproc)
```

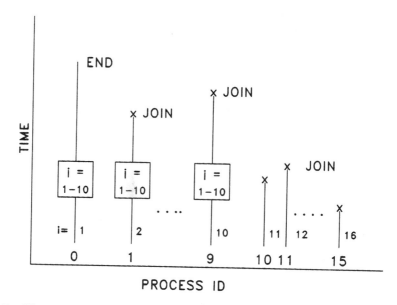

Figure 7-2. Illustration of the scheduling of Program 7-2, in which the outer loop split among 16 processes. Processes 0-9 can perform the calculation, while processes 10-15 have no work.

```
c          ---------- calculation
           do 1 i = 1 + id,n,nproc
               temsum = 0
               do 2 j = 1,n
                   temsum = temsum + a(i,j) * v(j)
2              continue
               result(i) = temsum
1          continue

           call process_join()
           (store results)
           end
```

Program 7-2

The scheduling used in Program 7-2 is illustrated in Fig. 7-2. Although sixteen processes are created, the parallelized loop only utilizes ten processes. Six processes have no work to do and are straightaway destroyed at the process_join. In Fig. 7-2, processes 10-15 have no assignments of i and no squares, because they don't do anything.

While the parallelized version will run approximately 10 times faster than the sequential version (ignoring overhead), 30% of the processing power is

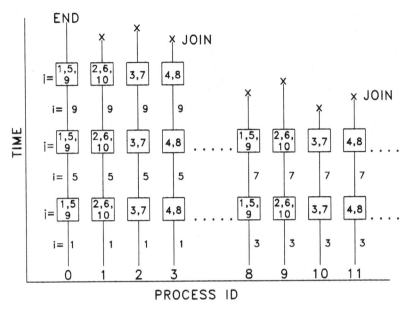

Figure 7-3. The scheduling in Program 7-3. Four processes always have the same value of i, but they execute the inner loop for different values of j.

unused. The speedup of Program 7-2, compared to the sequential version 7-1, and ignoring overhead, is 10. (The maximum speedup of Program 7-2 is 10, for any number of processes greater than 10.) One would like an ideal speedup of 16.

7.2 Variations on Loop Splitting

To increase process utilization in the parallel version of Program 7-1, one must parallelize both loops simultaneously. This approach is taken next. As an introduction to the approach, the outer loop is parallelized in such a way that four processes do the same values of i (see Fig. 7-3). That is, assuming that sixteen processes are created, processes 0, 1, 2, and 3 will execute the iterations i = 1, 5, 9. Processes 4, 5, 6, and 7 will do i = 2, 6, 10. Processes 8, 9, 10, and 11 will do i = 3, 7, and processes 12, 13, 14, and 15 will do i = 4, 8.

The inner loop (over j) is also parallelized. For a given i, four processes are available to work on the inner loop. Consider i = 1, so that processes 0, 1, 2, and 3 are available. Process 0 can do j = 1, 5, 9. Process 2 can

do j = 2, 6, 10. Process 3 can do j = 3, 7 and process 4 can do
j = 4, 8. This division of labor is illustrated in Fig. 7-3.

The following is version 2-a. It uses the mod function mod(a,b), which
returns the remainder of the division a/b. For example, mod(4,4) = 0,
mod(3,4) = 3, mod(5,4) = 1, and mod(9,4) = 1.

```
c       Parallel matrix - vector multiplication
c       Version 2 - a.
c               result(i) = a(i,j) * v(j), summed over j

        integer v(10),a(10,10),result(10),temsum(0:19)
        integer process_fork,id,nproc,i,j,k
        integer barrier_array(4,0:3),n

        call shared(barrier_array,64)
        call shared(result,40)
        call shared(temsum,80)

c       ---------- initialization
        n = 10
        nproc = 16
        (initialize a,v)
c       initialize 4 barriers, for 4 processes each
        do 10 k = 0,3
        call barrier_init(barrier_array(1,k),4)
10      continue

        id = process_fork(nproc)

c       ---------- calculation
c       four processes do the same value of i
c       split the inner loop up among the 4 available processes

        do 1 i = 1 + (id/4),n,nproc/4
        temsum(id) = 0
        result(i) = 0
        do 2 j = 1 + mod(id,4),n,4
            temsum(id) = temsum(id) + a(i,j) * v(j)
2       continue

c       Consolidate the partial sums into the result.
c       Processes 0,4,8,12 do the consolidation.
c       first barrier
        call barrier(barrier_array(1,id/4))
        if (mod(id,4) .eq. 0) then
            result(i) = result(i) + temsum(id)
```

```
      s               + temsum(id + 1) + temsum(id + 2)
      s               + temsum(id + 3)
              endif
      c       processes must wait for the process doing consolidation
      c       second barrier
              call barrier(barrier_array(1,id/4))

      1       continue

              call process_join()
              (store results)
              end
```

Program 7-3

Four separate barriers are created in Program 7-3, one for each group of four processes. Four processes are used for the calculation of each value of i, and before result(i) can be determined, the individual inner-loop (j) calculations of the four processes must be completed.

Problem: Why couldn't one use a single barrier instead of four separate ones?

Answer: In Program 7-3, processes 8, 9, . . . , 15 each do only two iterations of the loop over i, while the other processes do three iterations. Thus processes 8, 9, . . . , 15 will only make two calls at the first barrier, while the other processes will make three. If the first barrier had a barrier number of 16, then at the third iteration, only eight processes could make the barrier call and the program would hang.

Problem: In Program 7-3, why are two barrier calls necessary for each group of four processes rather than one?

Answer: The process doing the consolidation may become idle during the consolidation phase. If the other processes in the same group did not wait at the second barrier, they could alter the value of temsum(id). When the process doing the consolidation begins to run again, it would have the incorrect value(s) of temsum(id). The second barrier circumvents this race condition and is analogous to the second barrier in Program 6-4.

Problem: What is the ideal speedup of Program 7-3? How does this compare to that of version 1, Program 7-2?

Answer: The ideal speedup of the double loop is calculated, ignoring such overhead as the consolidation phase, the barrier calls, the extra arithmetic of computing the mod function, the divisions id/nproc, and so forth. The ideal speedup is determined by recognizing that the outer loop must be iterated three times, and the inner loop calculation must also be done three times. If t is the time to execute the statement

```
sum = sum + a(i,j) * v(j),
```

then the maximum possible speedup is

```
100t/9t = 10.1
```

where 100t is the single-stream ideal execution time. This speedup is not a significant savings over the speedup of 10 obtained by version 1 (Program 7-2). In fact, the extra overhead of version 2 will probably make it run slower than version 1. To try and enhance the speedup, consider the next problem.

Problem: Rewrite Program 7-3 so that the inner loop is split up among idiv processes. (Then nproc/idiv processes each do the same value of i.) idiv must be a factor of nproc. In the case of sixteen processes, the possible values of idiv are 1, 2, 4, 8, and 16. Figure 7-4 illustrates the scheduling when idiv = 2. Assume a maximum of twenty processors are available.

Answer:

```
c       Parallel matrix - vector multiplication
c       Version 2 - b.
c       Split the inner loop among idiv processes.
c               result(i) = a(i,j) * v(j), summed over j
c       idiv must divide nproc evenly

        integer v(10),a(10,10),result(10),temsum(0:19)
        integer process_fork,id,nproc,idiv,i,j,k
        integer barrier_array(4,0:19),n,mod

        call shared(barrier_array,320)
        call shared(result,40)
        call shared(temsum,80)

c       --------- initialization
        n = 10
```

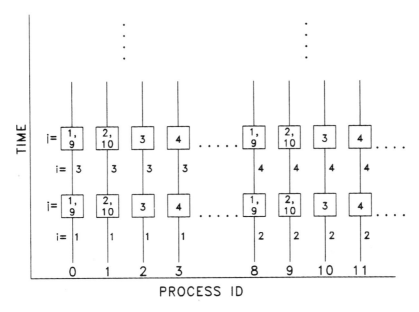

Figure 7-4. The scheduling in Program 7-4, for the case idiv = 2.

```
          nproc = 16
          if (mod(nproc,idiv) .ne. 0) then
              print *,'idiv must divide nproc evenly'
              call exit(-1)
          endif
          (initialize a,v,idiv)
c     initialize nproc/idiv barriers,
c     for barrier-number of idiv each.
          do 10 k = 0,nproc/idiv - 1
              call barrier_init(barrier_array(1,k),idiv)
  10      continue

          id = process_fork(nproc)

c         ---------- calculation
c     idiv processes do the same value of i
c     split the inner loop up among idiv processes
          do 1 i = 1 + (id/idiv),n,nproc/idiv
              temsum(id) = 0
              result(i) = 0
              do 2 j = 1 + mod(id,idiv),n,idiv
                  temsum(id) = temsum(id) + a(i,j) * v(j)
  2           continue
```

```
c               Consolidate the partial sums into the result.
c               first barrier
                call barrier(barrier_array(1,id/idiv))
                if(mod(id,idiv) .eq. 0) then
                    do 3 k = 0,idiv - 1
                        result(i) = result(i) + temsum(id + k)
    3               continue
                endif

c               processes must wait for the process doing
c               consolidation
c               second barrier
                call barrier(barrier_array(1,id/idiv))
    1       continue

        call process_join()
        (store results)
        end
```

Program 7-4

The program above can be made more efficient by setting up the arrays

```
        idmodn(id) = mod(id,idiv)
        idn(id) = id/nproc
```

before forking.

Problem: Calculate the ideal speedup of Program 7-4 for each appropriate value of *idiv*, for *nproc* = *16* and *20*.

Answer: The speedup is calculated by noting that the outer loop must be done at least *[10/(nproc/idiv)]* times, where *[i/j]* is *i/j* if *j* divides *i* evenly, and otherwise is *(i/j)* + *1*, where integer arithmetic is assumed. For each of these iterations, the number of times that the inner loop is done is at *[10/idiv]*. Thus the speedup is

$$ideal\ speedup = \frac{100}{[(10/(nproc/idiv)]\,[10/idiv]}.$$

Assuming *16 processes*, the speedup is

idiv	speedup
1	10
2	10
4	10.1
8	10
16	10

For *20 processes*, we have

idiv	speedup
1	10
2	20
4	16.7
5	16.7
10	20
20	10

It is seen that the possible speedup depends on the number of processes, and that considerably greater speedup can be obtained for twenty processes than for sixteen. This means that this particular algorithm can make better use of the processes when twenty processes are created than when sixteen are created. The reason why a large speedup is obtainable with twenty processes is that the work is divided in an equitable manner among all the processes. No processes are idle while others are still executing (assuming equal rate of execution for all processes).

Problem: Estimate the speedup when the consolidation phase is included. Assume that additions and multiplications require about the same amount of time.

Problem: The first barrier call in 7-4 can be eliminated by having each process update result(i) in a protected region. The protected region will replace the if(mod(i,idiv) .eq. 0) . . . endif group of statements. Rewrite 7-4 using this technique. The second barrier call must be retained.

The third version is similar to the second, except that it is done without the first barrier call and uses only a single barrier right before the consolidation phase. This version requires a large array temsum(10,0:19) to hold the intermediate results.

```
c       Parallel matrix - vector multiplication
c       Version 3.
c       Split the inner loop among idiv processes.
c               result(i) = a(i,j) * v(j), summed over j
c       Assume <= 20 processes.

        integer v(10),a(10,10),result(10),temsum(10,0:19)
        integer process_fork,id,nproc,idiv,i,j,k,sum
        integer barrier_array(4),n,mod

        call shared(barrier_array,16)
        call shared(result,40)
        call shared(temsum,800)

c       --------- initialization

        n = 10
        nproc = 16
        idiv = ...
        (initialize a,v)
        call barrier_init(barrier_array,nproc)

        id = process_fork(nproc)

c       --------- calculation
        do 1 i = 1 + (id/idiv),n,nproc/idiv
            sum = 0
            result(i) = 0
            do 2 j = 1 + mod(id,idiv),n,idiv
                sum = sum + a(i,j) * v(j)
2           continue
            temsum(i,id) = sum
1       continue

        call barrier(barrier_array)

c       consolidation
        if (mod(id,idiv) .eq. 0) then
            do 4 i = 1 + (id/idiv),n,nproc/idiv
                do 3 k = 0,idiv - 1
                    result(i) = result(i) + temsum(i,id + k)
```

```
3                     continue
4                 continue
        endif

        call process_join()
        (store results)
        end
```

Program 7-5

Program 7-5 suffers from the same defects as version 2, Program 7-4, namely, that for some values of nproc (for example, 16) there will not be much speedup. However, version 3 has considerably less overhead than version 2, and is expected to run faster. In version 2, there is a barrier call for each value of i. In version 3, there is only a single barrier call. Because all partial sums in 7-5 are stored in separate array elements, synchronization is kept to a minimum. A significant drawback of the technique in Program 7-5 is that it uses considerably more memory than Program 7-4.

7.3   Variation on Self-Scheduling

The fourth version uses self-scheduling and is based on the fact that there are n**2 calculations to do. Each process does one of these calculations. A process obtains both a single value of i and a single value of j from self-scheduling. It then executes the single statement

```
        result(i) = result(i) + a(i,j) * v(j)
```

for this pair of indices and then goes back for another pair of indices i and j. This type of scheduling is illustrated in Fig. 7-5. Each square in Fig. 7-5 has only a single number, standing for the particular value of j. The program is

```
c       Parallel matrix - vector multiplication
c       Version 4 - self-scheduling.
c               result(i) = a(i,j) * v(j), summed over j

        integer v(10),a(10,10),result(10),i,temsum,n,m,j
        integer process_fork,id,nproc,lok,next_index
        integer lok_result(10),unlocked,locked,n,mod
```

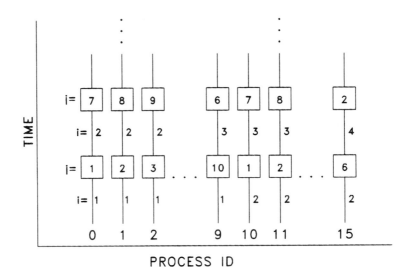

Figure 7-5.   The scheduling of Program 7-6.

```
            call shared(result,40)
            call shared(lok,4)
            call shared(lok_result,40)
            call shared(next_index,4)

c          ---------- initialization
            unlocked = 0
            locked = 1
            n = 10
            nproc = 16
            (initialize a,v)
            next_index = n**2
            call spin_lock_init(lok,unlocked)
c          initialize spin locks
            do 20 i = 1,n
                call spin_lock_init(lok_result(i),unlocked)
 20         continue
c          initialize result(i)
            do 5 i = 1,n
                result(i) = 0
  5         continue

            id = process_fork(nproc)

c          ---------- calculation
c          start parallelized loop
```

```
10        continue
          call spin_lock(lok)
                m = next_index
                next_index = next_index - 1
          call spin_unlock(lok)
          if (m .le. 0) goto 1
c      calculate i and j from m
          i = mod(m - 1,10) + 1
          j = (m - 1)/10 + 1
          call spin_lock(lok_result(i))
                result(i) = result(i) + a(i,j) * v(j)
          call spin_unlock(lok_result(i))
          goto 10
1        continue

          call process_join()
          (store results)
          end
```

Program 7-6

This version makes the best use of multiple processes. That is, it distributes the work over the available processes in the most equitable manner possible.

The ideal speedup is calculated as follows. For equitable scheduling, the maximum number of iterations done by a single process is

$$[100/nproc]$$

(Recall that $[i/j] = i/j$ is j divides i evenly and $(i/j) + 1$ otherwise.) The ideal speedup is

$$\text{ideal speedup} = 100/[100/nproc]$$

This is

nproc	speedup
10	10
12	11.1
14	12.5
16	14.3
18	16.7
20	20

The speedup increases with the number of processes, even though it is smaller than the number of processes. It is not possible to get a speedup greater than this.

However, there are several drawbacks to Program 7-6. One is that i and j must be calculated for each value of m. Another is that the self-scheduling spin-lock becomes a bottleneck when the number of processes is large. That is, when the time required to calculate each new addition to result(i) is comparable to or shorter than the time to execute the self-scheduling protected region (including executing the synchronization functions), then the processes will pile up at the spin-lock lok. Therefore, the processes can become blocked as they wait to trickle through the protected region.

The efficiency of Program 7-6 can be considerably enhanced by using loop splitting for the variable m. However, an even more efficient version uses indirect scheduling, as discussed in the next section.

The region in Program 7-6 protected by lok_result(i) protects each component of result(i) separately, so that different array elements can be updated simultaneously.

7.4   Indirect Scheduling

Another approach, which is similar to that of Program 7-6, but which eliminates self-scheduling, is *indirect scheduling*. In indirect scheduling, one determines the scheduling before the parallelization begins and sets up subsidiary arrays which are used to split up the work among the processes. The setup is overhead and in general would not be worth the effort if the parallelized loop is to be executed only once. Rather, it is useful if the algorithm is to be repeated many times (in a subroutine, for example). The setup would be done once, before the subroutine is called the first time.

The calculation of the matrix-vector multiply using indirect scheduling is illustrated in version 5 below. The manner in which the work is distributed among the processes is essentially the same as in Fig. 7-5.

```
c       Parallel matrix - vector multiplication
c       Version 5. Indirect scheduling
c             result(i) = a(i,j) * v(j), summed over j

        integer v(10),a(10,10),result(10),i,j
        integer process_fork,id,nproc,m,ival(100),jval(100)
```

```
            integer mmax,unlocked,locked
            integer lok_result(10),n

            call shared(result,40)
            call shared(lok_result,40)

c       --------- initialization
            unlocked = 0
            locked = 1
            n = 10
            do 25 i = 1,n
                call spin_lock_init(lok_result(i),unlocked)
 25         continue

            nproc = 16
            (set up a,v)

c       set up arrays needed for indirect scheduling
            m = 1
            do 20 i = 1,n
                do 21 j = 1,n
                    ival(m) = i
                    jval(m) = j
                    m = m + 1
 21             continue
 20         continue
            mmax = m - 1
c       end set-up section
c       initialize result(i)
            do 2 i = 1,n
                result(i) = 0
  2         continue

            id = process_fork(nproc)

c       --------- calculate
c       now do matrix-vector multiply using
c       indirect scheduling.
            do 1 m = 1 + id,mmax,nproc
                i = ival(m)
                j = jval(m)
                call spin_lock(lok_result(i))
                    result(i) = result(i) + a(i,j) * v(j)
                call spin_unlock(lok_result(i))
  1         continue
```

```
call process_join()
(store results)
end
```

Program 7-7

The term "indirect scheduling" comes from the fact that i and j are calculated from the "scheduling arrays"

```
i = ival(m)
j = jval(m)
```

This is indirect addressing, meaning that the "address" (values of i and j give the address of the appropriate elements of a(i,j), v(j)) is calculated from the contents of another variable. In indirect scheduling, the actual loop indices i and j are not directly scheduled, but rather they are computed based on a different index (in this case, m), which is itself directly scheduled.

Problem: Rewrite Program 7-7 so that each process updates result(i) by

$$a(i,j) * v(j) + a(i,j + 1)v(j + 1)$$

on each iteration (n must be even). Is this more efficient?

The speedup attainable from Program 7-7 will, in practice, depend upon how frequently two or more processes attempt to update the same array element result(i) simultaneously. If such simultaneous update is frequent, then the protected region will impose a relatively large overhead, as processes spin while waiting for other processes to leave the protected region.

Problem: Rewrite Program 7-7 so that each process updates a variable tem_result(i, id), and a protected region is not used. Then result(i) can be updated at the end. Is this more efficient? (tem_result is similar to the variable temsum in Program 7-5.)

7.5   Summary

In this chapter, a double loop performing matrix-vector multiplication was parallelized using a number of different scheduling techniques. It was shown that, for small loops, parallelizing only a single loop can result in an inequitable distribution of work among the processors, leading to a speedup that can be less than the number of processes. A number of techniques were then employed to try to level the load. These include self-scheduling and indirect scheduling. However, these scheduling techniques introduced additional overhead, which can serve to limit the speedup.

7.6   Additional Problems

In the problems below, choose the most efficient scheduling mechanism.

1. Use the technique of Program 7-4 for three-dimensional loops.
2. Write a routine to do matrix-matrix multiplication in parallel.
3. Write a routine to do the two-dimensional integral

$$\int_0^1 dx \int_0^x dy\, f(x)g(x - y)$$

   in parallel.
4. The following is a fragment which is similar to one used to integrate the Navier Stokes equations for fluid flow. Assume that

```
jav(1,m)  <= jav(2,m)
```

and that `jav(2,m)` varies between 1 and 20 in a random manner as a function of m. Also, assume that, if m .ne. m', then

```
jav(3,m) .ne. jav(3,m').
```

```
      do 144 k = 1,2
      do 145 m = 1,20
           imin = jav(1,m)
           imax = jav(2,m)
           j = jav(3,m)
           do 65 i = imin,imax
            dbar = db(i,j,k) + db(i,j - 1,k)

           vn(i,j,k) = vb(i,j,k)
   s          - (fldt * (uv(i,j) + uv(i + 1,j)) * d(i,j)
   s          + f2dt * (uv(i,j - 1) +
   s          uv(i + 1,j - 1)) * d(i,j - 1))
```

```
s                - gdtdy * (d(i,j) + d(i,j - 1)) *
s                (pr(i,j) - pr(i,j - 1))
s                - dtdx2 * (((uc(i + 1,j,k) +
s                uc(i + 1,j - 1,k)) * (vv(i,j) + vv(i + 1,j)))
s                - ((uc(i,j,k) + uc(i,j - 1,k)) *
s                (vv(i - 1,j) + vv(i,j))))
s                - dtdy2 * (((vc(i,j + 1,k) + vc(i,j,k)) *
s                (vv(i,j) + vv(i,j + 1)))
s                - ((vc(i,j - 1,k) + vc(i,j,k)) *
s                (vv(i,j - 1) + vv(i,j))))
s                + dbar * (akdtdy * (vd(i,j + 1,k) +
s                vd(i,j - 1,k) - 2. * vd(i,j,k))
s                + akdtdx * (vs(i + 1,j) +
s                vs(i - 1,j) - 2. * vs(i,j)))
s                - cdt(k) * ty(i,j) * vv(i,j)
s                + cidt * vi(i,j) * (vl(i,j,1) - vl(i,j,2)) -
s                cdt(k) * ty(i,j) * vv(i,j)

65       .       continue
145      continue
144      continue
```

5. Parallelize the following loop in the most efficient manner.

```
         integer i,a(1000),n
         do 1 i = 1,n
              if (a(i) .eq. 0) then
                   (work)
              endif
1        continue
```

Assume that the work section does not alter a(j) for j .ne. i.

6. Suppose subroutine matvec(a,v,c,n) is the matrix-vector multiply

```
c(i) = sum(j)a(i,j)v(j)
```

Parallelize this subroutine so that it can be called with the arguments

```
call matvec(a,c,c,n)
```

CHAPTER 8

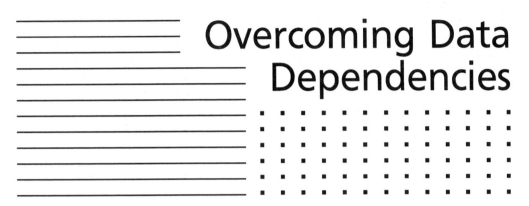

Overcoming Data Dependencies

8.1 Introduction

A common example of a *data dependency* is a situation in which a variable (scalar or array element) which is assigned in one iteration of a loop is read in another iteration. For example, a loop which sums the elements of an array, and which has the statement

```
        do 1 i = 1,n
            sum = sum + a(i)
  1     continue
```

has a data dependency for the variable sum, since it is assigned in an iteration (say i = 1) and read in a different iteration (i = 2). In the same way, the program for finding a maximum value (Program 5-2) contains a data dependency, because the variable amax is assigned in an iteration and read in a different iteration.

There can be other kinds of data dependencies as well, such as a situation in which the value of a variable causes a branch out of a loop.

The existence of data dependencies complicates the creation of parallel programs. Data dependencies normally require that the statements of the loop be executed in a particular sequential order. On the other hand, in parallelizing a loop, one attempts to allow different iterations to occur simultaneously, so that in practice the iterations can occur in arbitrary order (because processes are randomly scheduled). As a result, there is a conflict between the serial requirement for the dependencies and the random-order requirement of the parallel programming model.

Parallelizing loops with data dependencies, so that the parallelized version is executed efficiently and provides a useful speedup, can be difficult. The technique used depends on the situation. Fortunately, many loops fall into one of several categories. In this chapter, a number of typical data dependencies are described, and in most cases the ways to circumvent the dependencies are given.

It is frequently found that, when a calculation involving data dependencies is formulated in a way that allows it to be carried out in parallel, more arithmetic is done in the parallel version than is done in the sequential version. This leads to an ideal speedup which is less than the number of processes. The inefficiency resulting from overcoming data dependencies is different from that resulting from poor scheduling (as discussed in the previous chapter). In poor scheduling, the calculation is not apportioned evenly among the available processes. In the case of reformulating a problem with data dependencies, the work may be apportioned evenly, but there is *more work* than is done in a sequential calculation.

8.2   Induction Variable

One of the simplest cases of data dependency involves the use of an *induction variable*. The variable m in the following program is an induction variable.

```
c       Assign x(4 * i) = a(i). m is an induction variable
        integer m,k,i
        real x(1000),a(1000)
        .
        .
        .
        k = 4
        m = 0
        do 1 i = 1,1000
            m = m + k
            x(m) = a(i)
```

```
1    continue
     .
     .
     .
```

Program 8-1

For Program 8-1 to work correctly, it is essential that i = 1 be done first,
then i = 2, and so forth. For example, on the first iteration (i = 1), 4 is
assigned to m. On the second iteration, 4 is added to the exiting value of m,
giving 8, and so forth. This program has a data dependency because the
variable m, which is assigned in one iteration, is read in the next iteration.

If we blindly parallelize this loop, using loop splitting, we would have the
following fragment:

```
c        Incorrect parallelization of loop with induction variable.
c        Data dependencies are not treated correctly.

         integer m,k,i,lok,locked,unlocked,process_fork,id,nproc
         real x(1000),a(1000)

         call shared(lok,4)
         call shared(x,4000)
         call shared(m,4)
         .
         .
         .
         call spin_lock_init(lok,unlocked)
         .
         .
         .
         k = 4
         m = 0
         id = process_fork(nproc)
         do 1 i = 1 + id,1000,nproc
              call spin_lock(lok)
                   m = m + k
                   x(m) = a(i)
              call spin_unlock(lok)
1        continue
         .
         .
         .
```

Program 8-2

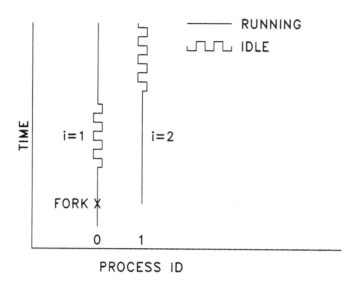

Figure 8-1.   One possible timeline for Program 8-2.

The most important aspect of the single-stream Program 8-1 is that there is a strict one-to-one relation between m and i, which is

```
m = 4 * i
```

However, in the parallel Program 8-2, the iterations will in general be done out of order, so that it is virtually certain that m will not be equal to i * 4.

To see how this comes about, suppose nproc = 2. One possible time line (for the initial iterations) is shown in Fig. 8-1. The parent forks and then becomes idle. The child executes its first iteration, assigning i = 2, m = 4, and x(4) = a(2). This, of course, is incorrect. Next, process 0 wakes up and executes its first iteration, assigning i = 1. Since m has already been assigned to 4, process 0 assigns m to 8 and assigns x(8) = a(1), also incorrect.

This incorrect execution occurs even though the spin-lock essentially serializes the loop in Program 8-2. The problem is not due to contention, since any updating of shared variables is done in a protected region. Rather, the problem is a race condition.

The simplest way to circumvent the data dependency is to rewrite the loop so that the induction variable is computed directly from the loop index, as in Program 8-3 (the bookkeeping has been left out of Program 8-3).

```
c       Rewrite program 8-2 with no data dependencies
        .
        .
        .
        k = 4
        id = process_fork(nproc)
        do 1 i = 1 + id,1000,nproc
            m = i * k
            x(m) = a(i)
1       continue
        call barrier(...)
        m = 1000 * k
        .
        .
        .
```

Program 8-3

The last statement assigns m its final value.

Note that the parallelized version 8-3 is lexically different than the sequential version. The statement

```
m = m + k
```

of the sequential version have been transformed to the statement

```
m = i * k
```

In general, loops with data dependencies will have to be transformed into a form in which the dependencies do not exist. In the above case, the transformed version substitutes a multiplication for an addition.

Problem: Explain the data dependencies of the sequential versions of Programs 5-1 and 5-2 and 5-11 (you will have to create the sequential versions yourself), and explain how they were overcome in the parallel versions.

8.3 Forward Dependency

Another example of a data dependency is a *forward dependency*.

```
c       Forward data dependency fragment
        integer i
```

```
            real x(1001)
                  .

                  .

                  .

            do 1 i = 1,1000
                  x(i) = x(i + 1)
    1         continue
                  .

                  .

                  .
```

Program 8-4

In Program 8-4, x(i) is assigned its value *after it is read*. This is a data dependency according to the definition in the introduction, because a value assigned in one iteration of a serial loop is used in another iteration, but in this case the iteration that reads the value comes *before* the iteration that assigns the value.

This sounds like a declaration that time travels backwards, but in fact the problem arises because processes are randomly scheduled, so that the iterations can be executed in any order.

To illustrate the problem, note that, when the loop is executed sequentially, the elements of x(i) are assigned in the following order:

```
        x(1) = x(2)
        x(2) = x(3)
        x(3) = x(4)
        etc.
```

so each x(i) is assigned the "old" value of x(i+1).

Suppose Program 8-4 were blindly parallelized using loop splitting, to give Program 8-5.

```
    c       Incorrect parallelization of program 8-4 with
    c       forward dependency.

            integer i,id,nproc,process_fork
            real x(1001)
            call shared(x,4004)
                  .

                  .

                  .

            id = process_fork(nproc)
```

```
        do 1 i = 1 + id,1000,nproc
            x(i) = x(i + 1)
1       continue
        call barrier(...)
        .
        .
        .
```

Program 8-5

Because of random scheduling, the assignments in Program 8-5 might occur in the following order:

```
    x(2) = x(3)  (process 1)
    x(1) = x(2)  (process 0)
    etc.
```

The result of the parallelization is that x(1) gets the incorrect value, receiving the old x(3) as its value rather than the old x(2). (In fact, the situation is even worse because of contention, but this can be overcome by using a lock.) The fundamental problem with Program 8-5 is the race condition.

One way to parallelize the forward-dependency Program 8-4 is to define a new array xold(i) = x(i), containing the old values, and then set x(i) = xold(i), as in the following program:

```
c       Correct parallelization of loop with forward dependency.

        integer i,id,nproc,process_fork,bar_array(4)
        real x(1001),xold(1001)
        call shared(x,4004)
        call shared(xold,4004)
        .
        .
        .
        call barrier_init(bar_array,nproc)
        id = process_fork(nproc)

        do 2 i = 1 + id,1000,nproc
            xold(i) = x(i + 1)
2       continue

        call barrier(bar_array)
```

```
        do 1 i = 1 + id,1000,nproc
            x(i) = xold(i)
1       continue
            .
            .
            .
            .
```

Program 8-6

In Program 8-6, xold is assigned but not read in the first loop, while x(i) is assigned but not read in the second loop, and therefore there is no data dependency in either loop.

The problem with the above solution is that the ideal speedup is nproc/2, half the number of processes. Twice as much work is done in the parallel Program 8-6 that in the original sequential version 8-4. That is, in the sequential program, there were 1000 assignments of x(i), while in the parallel version there are 2000 assignments (first xold is assigned, then x is assigned). While all the processes may be utilized in the calculation (in the sense that some processes are not idle while other processes are executing), *too much work* has been assigned to the processes.

Problem: In the above example, does xold have to be shared? What would happen if it were not shared?

8.4 Block Scheduling and Forward Dependency

There is a more efficient way to parallelize Program 8-4 with the forward dependency than was done in Program 8-6. This technique involves *block scheduling*. In block scheduling, each processor executes the loop for a sequential set (or block) of loop indices. Thus for a loop

```
        do 1 i = 1,n
            (work)
1       continue
```

divide the "points" i = 1, 2, ..., n into *blocks*, as illustrated in Fig. 8-2. In that figure, the dots correspond to the different values that i takes in successive iterations of the loop. (The case for n = 13 is illustrated in the figure.) Assuming two processes, the circled points of Fig. 8-2 correspond to iterations executed by process 0. In Fig. 8-2(a), loop splitting is illustrated,

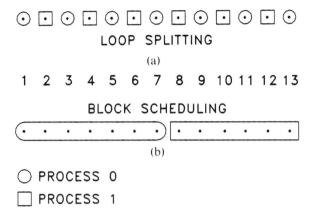

LOOP SPLITTING

(a)

1 2 3 4 5 6 7 8 9 10 11 12 13

BLOCK SCHEDULING

(b)

○ PROCESS 0

□ PROCESS 1

Figure 8-2. Illustration of (a) loop splitting and (b) block scheduling.

while 8-2(b) illustrates block scheduling. In 8-2(b), two blocks are used. The first block is executed by process 0, the second by process 1.

The crudest way to create the blocks is such that each block except two executes npts = n/nproc points. In this method of creating the blocks (which is revised below), process 0 does points i = 1, 2, ..., npts − 1, process 1 does points i = npts, ..., 2 * npts − 1, and so forth. The final process, nproc − 1, must then execute points i = (nproc − 1) * npts, (nproc − 1) * npts + 1, ..., n. Defining

$$\text{imin(id)} = \begin{cases} \text{id * npts} & \text{if id .ne. 0} \\ 1 & \text{if id = 0} \end{cases}$$

$$\text{imax(id)} = \begin{cases} \text{(id + 1) * npts − 1} & \text{if id < nproc − 1} \\ \text{n} & \text{if id = nproc − 1} \end{cases}$$

then process id executes the assignments

```
x(i) = x(i + 1)
```

for i = imin(id), ..., imax(id).

The only hitch now is to resolve the data dependencies at the boundaries of the regions. Note that, for id < nproc − 1, the assignment

```
x(imax(id)) = x(imax(id) + 1)
```

must be executed. But the right side of the above assignment must involve the "old" value of x(imax(id) + 1), whereas it is likely that process id + 1 will have assigned to x(imax(id) + 1) its new value before process id can assign the old value of x(imax(id) + 1) to x(imax(id)).

The resolution of this problem is to save the old value of x(imax(id) + 1) in the array xsav(id) before executing the blocks in parallel, and then assign it at the end. This approach leads to the following program:

```
c       Parallel execution of forward dependencies, using
c       block scheduling.
c       Uses inefficient version of block scheduling.
c       Assume <= 50 processes.

        real x(1001),xsav(0:49)
        integer imin(0:49),imax(0:49)
        integer bar_array(4),n,nproc,i,id,process_fork,npts

        call shared(x,4004)
        call shared(xsav,200)
        call shared(imin,200)
        call shared(imax,200)
        call shared(bar_array,16)

        (initialize n, nproc, x(i))

        call barrier_init(bar_array,nproc)
        id = process_fork(nproc)

c       ------------------subdivide the n points into blocks.
        npts = n/nproc
c       set up arrays imin,imax in parallel
        if (id .ne. 0) then
              imin(id) = id * npts
        else
              imin(id) = 1
        endif
        if (id .ne. nproc - 1) then
              imax(id) = (id + 1) * npts - 1
        else
              imax(id) = n
        endif
c       --------------end of creation of the blocks

c       save boundary point
        xsav(id) = x(imax(id) + 1)

        call barrier(bar_array)
```

```
c       now the assignments, using block scheduling
        do 1 i = imin(id),imax(id) - 1
            x(i) = x(i + 1)
 1      continue
c       now assign the "boundary"
        x(imax(id)) = xsav(id)

        call proc_join()
        (store results)
        end
```

Program 8-7

In Program 8-7, each process executes only four overhead statements. The overhead involves assigning `npts`, `imin`, `imax`, and `xsav`.

Problem: In Program 8-7, why is the barrier needed before executing the do 1 loop? Why is no barrier needed before assigning the boundary, following 1 continue?

There is an inequity in the scheduling of Program 8-7. If n is not an exact multiple of nproc, then process number nproc − 1 will execute more statements in the do 1 loop than any of the other processes. In the worst case, the number of extra statements will be nproc − 1, so that, for small n or large nproc, process number nproc − 1 will do significantly more work than the other processes.

This inequity in scheduling can be quite significant, as can be seen by calculating the ideal speedup of the do 1 loop of Program 8-7. Assuming the worst case, where process number nproc − 1 executes an extra nproc − 1 iterations of the loop, the parallel execution time is

```
((n/nproc) + (nproc - 1))t
```

where t is the time to execute a single assignment. Since the single-stream execution time is nt, the ideal speedup is approximately

$$\text{ideal speedup} = \frac{nproc}{1 + (nproc**2)/n}$$

Note that nproc enters squared in the denominator. If n = 999, which is a reasonably sized problem, and nproc = 25, the ideal speedup is approximately

```
ideal speedup = (2/3) nproc
```

which is a considerable loss of efficiency.

Problem: Rewrite Program 8-7 using more efficient scheduling, so that some processes do n/nproc + 1 points and some do n/nproc points (integer arithmetic assumed in the division).

Answer: The program fragment below calculates imin and imax in such a way as to provide the most equitable distribution of work among the nproc processes. It assigns the overflow (the excess of points beyond npts) to the processes with the lowest id numbers, one extra point per process.

```
c       Parallel execution of forward dependencies, using
c       block scheduling.
c       Uses very efficient version of block scheduling.
c       Assume <= 50 processes.

        real x(1001),xsav(0:49)
        integer imin(0:49),imax(0:49),iexcess
        integer bar_array(4),n,nproc,i,id,process_fork,npts

        call shared(x,4004)
        call shared (xsav,200)
        call shared(imin,200)
        call shared(imax,200)
        call shared(bar_array,16)

        (initialize n,nproc,x(i))

        call barrier_init(bar_array,nproc)
        call process_fork(nproc)

c       ---------------------- create the blocks
c       calculate imin and imax, using most
c       equitable distribution of work.
c       n is number of "points" to be distributed among nproc
c       processes.
           npts = n/nproc
c       iexcess is the number of extra points at the end
```

```
        iexcess = n - nproc * npts
        if (iexcess .eq. 0) then
c           no excess of points
            imin(id) = id * npts + 1
            imax(id) = id * npts + npts
        else
            if (id .lt. iexcess) then
c               processes 0,1,..,iexcess - 1
c               do npts + 1 points
c               the remaining processes do npts points
                imin(id) = id * (npts + 1) + 1
                imax(id) = imin(id) + npts
            else
                imin(id) = id * npts + 1 + iexcess
                imax(id) = imin(id) + npts - 1
            endif
        endif
c       --------------------------end creation of the blocks

c       save x(imin(id))
        xsav(id) = x(imax(id) + 1)
        call barrier(bar_array)

c       now the assignments, using block scheduling
        do 1 i = imin(id),imax(id) - 1
            x(i) = x(i + 1)
1       continue
c       assign the "boundary"
        x(imax(id)) = xsav(id)

        call process_join()
        (store results)
        end
```

Program 8-8

Problem: Show that, for Program 8-8, process nproc − 1 always does n/nproc points, no matter what the value of n and nproc. (It is seen that this is just the opposite of the case of 8-7, where process n always did the extra points.)

Problem: Determine the speedup of Program 8-8.

8.5   Backward Dependency

A less tractable kind of data dependency is the *backward dependency*. The following is an example:

```
c       Example of backward dependency
        integer i
        real a,b,x(1000)
        .
        .

        .
        do 1 i = 2,100
        x(i) = a * x(i) + b * x(i - 1)
1       continue
        .

        .

        .
```

Program 8-9

The array element x(i) is assigned before it is read, which is the opposite of the forward dependency discussed above. In this case, it does no good to assign x(i) to a holding array. In the sequential loop, the values of x are assigned as follows:

```
x(2) = a * x(2) + b * x(1)
x(3) = a * x(3) + b * x(2)
x(4) = a * x(4) + b * x(3)
etc.
```

Note that x(2) is assigned its new value, and then x(3) is assigned its value from the *new* value of x(2). Then x(4) is assigned its value from the *new* value of x(3), and so forth. The new value of x(i) must be available before the assignment of x(i + 1) is made.

If one were to blindly parallelize this loop, using loop splitting, the assignments would in general not occur in the proper order. For example, the assignments could occur in the following order:

```
x(3) = a * x(3) + b * x(2)  process 1
x(2) = a * x(2) + b * x(1)  process 0
```

In this case, x(3) obtains its value from the *old* value of x(2), and so receives the incorrect result.

There is no simple way to parallelize the above loop. Rather, one must reformulate the problem. Parallelizing loops such as 8-9 is described in detail in Chapter 10.

Problem: Show why the recurrence relation, Program 8-9, cannot be parallelized using block scheduling.

There are many cases of backward dependencies where it appears that no effective parallelization can be performed. An example is the loop below.

```
c       This program does not appear parallelizable in
c       a way that the speedup is proportional to the
c       number of processes, if p is not 0 or 1.

        integer i,n
        real x(1000),p
        (initialize)
        do 1 i = 1,n
            x(i) = x(i - 1)**p
1       continue
        (store results)
        end
```

8.6 Break Out of Loop

Some programs manipulate the elements of an array one-by-one so long as some condition holds, then terminate the manipulation when the condition is no longer true. This is done, for example, in a linear search and in the following program fragment:

```
c       Sequential program to illustrate break-out-of-loop
c       data dependency.
        integer a(1000),n,predicate,i
        .
        .
        .
        do 1 i = 1,n
        if (predicate(a(i)) .eq. 1) then
            call transform(a(i))
        else
            goto 2
        endif
```

```
1        continue
2        continue
         .
         .
         .
```

Program 8-10

In Program 8-10, predicate is an integer function returning an integer, the value of the integer depending on the value of the argument to the function, while transform is a subroutine that assigns a new value to a(i). It is assumed that neither of these functions involves any data dependencies.

Program 8-10 modifies the value of a(i) for all values of i such that predicate(a(i)) is 1. As soon as a value of i is found such that predicate(a(i)) is not 1, the alterations cease.

The problem in parallelizing Program 8-10 is to make sure that a(i) is not altered for values of i larger than the smallest one for which predicate(a(i)) is not equal to 1. Since the iterations can be done in any order, it is important to preserve the old values of a(i). Suppose i0 is the smallest value of i for which predicate(a(i)) is not 1. If any processes called transform(a(i)) for i > i0, then when the loop is terminated, those a(i) must be reassigned their old values.

One algorithm for parallelizing Program 8-10 is to use loop splitting. The first process that finds that predicate(a(i)) is not equal to 1 then assigns a predetermined value to a shared variable. The other processes continuously check the value of this variable and terminate when the predetermined value is found. Then, the appropriate old values of a(i) are restored. This idea is implemented in Program 8-11.

```
c        Initial parallelized version of break-out-of-loop.
c        This version is incorrect if predicate(a(i)) can be .ne. 1
c        for more than one value of i between 1 and n inclusive.
c        lasti(id) - initialized to -1. If positive, contains the
c        largest value of i for which process id called
c        transform(a(i)). i0 - predicate(a(i0)) is not equal to 1.
c        Other processes exit if i0 is not 0.

         integer predicate,lokl,process_fork,nproc,id,n,i
         integer a(1000),aold(1000),locked,unlocked
         integer lasti(0:49),i0,bar_array(4)

         call shared(lokl,4)
```

```
          call shared(lasti,200)
          call shared(i0,4)
          call shared(a,4000)
          call shared(aold,4000)
          call shared(bar_array,16)
c
          (initialize n,nproc,a(i))

          call barrier_init(bar_array,nproc)
          locked = 1
          unlocked = 0
          call spin_lock_init(lokl,unlocked)
          i0 = 0
          id = process_fork(nproc)

          lasti(id) = -1
          do 1 i = 1 + id,n,nproc
               call spin_lock(lokl)
                    if ((i0 .ne. 0) .and. (i .gt. i0)) then
                         call spin_unlock(lokl)
                         goto 2
                    endif
               call spin_unlock(lokl)
               aold(i) = a(i)
               if (predicate(a(i)) .eq. 1) then
                    call transform(a(i))
               else
c                    only one process ever executes this statement
                    call spin_lock(lokl)
                    i0 = i
                    call spin_unlock(lokl)
                    goto 2
               endif
               lasti(id) = i
1         continue
2         continue

          call barrier(bar_array)

c    restore old values of a(i)
          if (i0 .eq. 0)goto 4
          do 3 i = (i0/nproc) * nproc + 1 + id,lasti(id),nproc
                if (i .gt. i0) then
                     a(i) = aold(i)
                endif
3         continue
```

```
4         continue
          call process_join()
          (store results)
          end
```

Program 8-11

Program 8-11 works in the following way. Before attempting the transformation of a(i), each process checks the variable i0. If i0 is nonzero, then some other process (say j) has already found a value of i for which predicate(a(i)) is not 1. That value of i has been assigned to i0 by process j. For a process other than j, if i > i0 when i0 is nonzero, the process terminates its loop. If i < i0, the process must continue until i becomes greater than i0. In the do 3 loop, the old values of a(i) are restored, for i > i0.

Problem: In Program 8-11, do a and aold have to be shared?

Problem: In Program 8-11, what might happen if there were no barrier after the statement 2 continue?

Problem: In Program 8-11, show that the values of i executed by process id for loop do 3 are exactly the same values of i as are done in the do 1 loop, except that i > i0 and i <= lasti(id) in the do 3 loop. This is necessary if lasti(id) is to be used as the upper limit of this loop. Why?

Problem: What is the purpose of the spin-lock lokl in 8-11? (Hint: The two logical expressions in the if-statement may be evaluated in arbitrary order.)

Program 8-11 must be revised to handle the possibility that predicate(a(i)) is not equal to 1 for more than one value of i. Let i0 be the *smallest* value of i between 1 and n for which predicate(a(i)) is not 1. Suppose that process j determines that predicate(a(ix)) is not 1. The problem with Program 8-11 is that ix may not be equal to i0. The value of predicate(a(i)) may be not equal to 1 for many values of i, and since, in a parallel program, the iterations can be done in any order, the first process to determine that predicate(a(ix)) is not equal to 1 may not have ix = i0.

Problem: Modify Program 8-11 to eliminate the problem discussed above.

Answer:

```
c       Parallelized version of break-out-of-loop.
c       This may be incorrect if there are data dependencies
c       in subroutines "transform" and "predicate."
c       lasti(id) - initialized to -1. If positive, contains the
c       largest value of i for which process id called
c       transform(a(i)). i0 - initialized to 0. This is set
c       to 1 whenever predicate(i) is not equal to 1.
c       Other processes exit if i0 is not 0.

        integer predicate,process_fork,nproc,id,n,i
        integer a(1000),aold(1000),locked,unlocked
        integer lasti(0:49),i0,bar_array(4),lok

        call shared(lok,4)
        call shared(lasti,200)
        call shared(i0,4)
        call shared(a,4000)
        call shared(aold,4000)
        call shared(bar_array,16)
c
        (initialize n,nproc,a(i))

        locked = 1
        unlocked = 0
        call spin_lock_init(lok,unlocked)
        call barrier_init(bar_array,nproc)
        i0 = 0

        id = process_fork(nproc)

        lasti(id) = -1
        do 1 i = 1 + id,n,nproc
            call spin_lock(lok)
                if ((i0 .ne. 0) .and. (i .gt. i0)) then
                    call spin_unlock(lok)
                    goto 2
                endif
            call spin_unlock(lok)
            aold(i) = a(i)
            if (predicate(a(i)) .eq. 1) then
                call transform(a(i))
```

```
                    else
                        call spin_lock(lok)
                            if (i0 .eq. 0) then
                                    i0 = i
                            elseif (i0 .gt. i) then
                                    i0 = i
                            endif
                        call spin_unlock(lok)
                        goto 2
                    endif
                    lasti(id) = i
    1           continue
    2           continue
    c       restore old values of a(i)

            call barrier(bar_array)

            if (i0 .eq. 0)goto 4
            do 3 i = (i0/nproc) * nproc + 1 + id,lasti(id),nproc
                    if (i .gt. i0) then
                            a(i) = aold(i)
                    endif
    3           continue
    4           continue

            call process_join()

            (store results)
            end
```

Program 8-12

Program 8-12 is valid so long as the functions predicate and transform do not have side effects. If these functions alter some other variable, then the sequential program prevents these alterations from occurring when i is greater than i0. On the other hand, the parallel version 8-12 only restores the old values of a(i) for i > i0, but it does not undo the side effects. In addition, it is assumed that these functions do not have any data dependencies which would prevent parallelization by loop splitting.

8.7   Splittable Loops

Certain kinds of data dependencies can be removed by creating two or more loops from a single loop. This kind of data dependency is illustrated by the simple example below:

```
c       Illustrate splittable loop
        integer i,n,k
        real a(0:1000),b(1000),c(1000),f(2000),d
        .
        .
        .
        do 1 i = 1,n
            a(i) = b(i) + c(i) * d + f(i + k)
            c(i) = a(i - 1)
1       continue
        .
        .
        .
```

Program 8-13

Problem: Describe the data dependency in 8-13.

Answer: c(i) is assigned its new value based on the "new" value of a(i - 1). After a(i) is assigned a new value in one iteration, it is read in a later iteration (in order to assign a new value to c(i)).

Problem: If the statement c(i) = a(i - 1) in Program 8-13 were replaced with the statement

```
c(i) = b(i)
```

would there be a data dependency? Explain your answer.

Partial answer: No.

Problem: Does the loop below have a data dependency? Explain your answer.

```
        integer i,n,k
        real a(1000)
        do 1 i = i,n
            a(i) = a(i) + k
1       continue
```

Program 8-13 can be rewritten by splitting the loop into two loops:

```
c       Program 8-13 split into two loops
        integer i,n,k
```

```
            real a(0:1000),b(1000),c(1000),f(2000),d
            .
            .

            .
            do 1 i = 1,n
                 a(i) = b(i) + c(i) * d + f(i + k)
     1      continue
            do 2 i = 1,n
                 c(i) = a(i - 1)
     2      continue
            .

            .

            .
```

Program 8-14

Neither of the loops in Program 8-14 has a data dependency, and parallelization can proceed using any of the scheduling algorithms already discussed that is appropriate.

Problem: Parallelize Program 8-14.

Determining when a loop can be split into two or more loops, and then rewriting it in the correct manner, requires careful analysis on the part of the programmer. For example, consider 8-15 below, which is almost the same as 8-13:

```
     c      Illustrate splittable loop
            integer i,n,k
            real a(0:1000),b(1000),c(1000),f(2000),d
            .

            .

            .
            do 1 i = 1,n
                 a(i) = b(i) + c(i) * d + f(i + k)
                 c(i) = a(i + 1)
     1      continue
            .

            .

            .
```

Program 8-15

The difference between 8-15 and 8-13 is that, in 8-15, $c(i)$ is assigned the old value $a(i + 1)$, while in 8-13 it is assigned the new value $a(i - 1)$.

Problem: Split the loops of 8-15.

Answer: In this case, the loop to assign c(i) must be written before the loop to assign a(i).

```
c       Program 8-15 split up into two loops
        integer i,n,k
        real a(0:1000),b(1000),c(1000),f(2000),d,x(1000)
        .
        .
        .
        do 2 i = 1,n
            x(i) = c(i)
            c(i) = a(i + 1)
2       continue
        do 1 i = 1,n
            a(i) = b(i) + x(i) * d + f(i + k)
1       continue
        .
        .
        .
```

Program 8-16

The old value of c(i) is stored in x(i) so it can be used in the second loop, so that Program 8-16 does more work than the original version 8-15.

Problem: Parallelize 8-16. What is the speedup of the parallel version, compared with Program 8-15?

Problem: Can you parallelize 8-15 so that the ideal speedup equals the number of processes, for large n?

Splitting loops can be useful for certain algorithms which find iterative solutions to problems, such as eigenvalue problems or simultaneous equations. The following double loop arises in the Gauss-Seidel algorithm for iterative solution of n simultaneous equations. (The explanation of this algorithm is outside the scope of this text. It is not necessary to understand the algorithm in order to appreciate how loop splitting is implemented in the program.)

```
c       Program to illustrate forward and backward data
c       dependencies
```

```
            real x(1000),b(1000),c(1000),a(1000,1000),sum
            integer i,j
            (initialize n,x,b,c,a)
            do 1 i = 1,n
                  sum = 0.
                  do 2 j = 1,n
                        sum = sum + a(i,j) * x(j)
      2           continue
                  x(i) = b(i) + c(i) * sum - c(i) * a(i,i) * x(i)
      1     continue
            (store results)
            end
```

Program 8-17

The new value of x(i) involves a sum over both new and old x(j). The calculation proceeds as follows. First, x(1) is calculated, using only the "old" values of x(i), i = 2, 3, . . . , n. Then x(2) is calculated from the new x(1) and the old x(3), . . . , x(n). Then x(3) is obtained from the new x(1), x(2), and the old x(4), . . . , x(n), and so forth.

It is possible to rewrite 8-17 in a form which explicitly reveals the dependencies.

```
      c       8-17 with inner loop split to compute forward
      c       and backward dependencies separately.

            real x(1000),b(1000),c(1000),a(1000,1000),sum
            integer i,j

            (initialize n,x,b,c,a)

      c       forward dependency - partial sum involves the
      c       old values of x(j)
            do 4 i = 1,n
                  sum = 0.
                  do 3 j = i + 1,n
                        sum = sum + a(i,j) * x(j)
      3           continue
                  x(i) = b(i) + sum * c(i)
      4     continue

      c       backward dependency. Partial sum involves the
      c       new values of x(j).
            do 1 i = 1,n
                  sum = 0.
```

```
          do 2 j = 1,i - 1
                sum = sum + a(i,j) * x(j)
2         continue
          x(i) = x(i) + c(i) * sum
1     continue

      (store results)
      end
```

Program 8-18

One can parallelize 8-18 in a straightforward manner. The part with forward dependencies can be reasonably efficiently parallelized using self-scheduling. The parallelization of the backward dependency part is less efficient.

```
c       Parallelization of 8-18
        real x(1000),b(1000),c(1000),a(1000,1000),tem(1000),sum
        integer lok,bar_array(4),process_fork
        integer i,j,locked,unlocked,next_index

        call shared(next_index,4)
        call shared(lok,4)
        call shared(bar_ array,16)
        call shared(x,4000)
        call shared(tem,4000)

        (initialize n,x,b,c,a)
        unlocked = 0
        locked = 1
        call spin_lock_init(lok,unlocked)
        call barrier_init(bar_array,nproc)
        next_index = n

        id = process_fork(nproc)

c       forward dependencies - self-scheduling
4       continue
          call spin_lock(lok)
              i = next_index
              next_index = next_index - 1
          call spin_unlock(lok)
          if (i .le. 0)goto 10
          sum = 0.
          do 5 j = i + 1,n
                sum = sum + a(i,j) * x(j)
5         continue
```

```
                      tem(i) = b(i) + c(i) * sum
                      goto 4
   10         continue

              call barrier(bar_array)

              do 11 i = 1 + id,n,nproc
                      x(i) = tem(i)
   11         continue

              call barrier(bar_array)

   c      backward dependencies - loop splitting
              do 1 i = 1,n
                      sum = 0.
                      do 2 j = 1 + id,i - 1,nproc
                              sum = sum + a(i,j) * x(j)
   2              continue
                      call spin_lock(lok)
                              x(i) = x(i) + c(i) * sum
                      call spin_unlock(lok)
                      call barrier(bar_array)
   1          continue
              call process_join()
              (store results)
              end
```
Program 8-19

Problem: Explain the use of the temporary array `tem(i)` in the forward-dependency section of Program 8-19.

Problem: In Program 8-19, why is the barrier necessary in the do 1 loop?

Problem: In Program 8-19, why can't the do 1 loop be parallelized using the method of self-scheduling? (Consider what happens when i = 2 is done before i = 1.)

There are several inefficiencies in Program 8-19. One is that there is a barrier call for each value of i. The second is discussed in the following problem.

Problem: Program 8-19 makes inefficient use of the processes for the do 2 loop, because the sums over j are only over part of the range of n points. Calculate the ideal speedup of the backward-dependency part of 8-19 as compared to the backward-dependency part of the single-stream Program 8-18.

Answer: Consider the speedup of the following parallel fragment

```
      do 1 i = 2,n
          do 2 j = 1 + id, i - 1, nproc
              (work)
2         continue
          call barrier(...)
1     continue
```

Program 8-20

compared with the single-stream fragment

```
      do 1 i = 2,n
          do 2 j = 1, i - 1
              (work)
2         continue
1     continue
```

Program 8-21

Let t = time to do a single iteration of the do 2 loop. Then the time required for 8-21 is

$$single\text{-}stream\ time = t + 2t + 3t + ... + (n - 1)t$$

t is the execution time for the do 2 loop if $i = 1$, $2t$ is the execution time if $i = 3$ and so forth. Adding up all these times,

$$single\text{-}stream\ time = n(n - 1)t/2$$

For the parallelized version 8-20, the execution time depends on both n and nproc. Take the simple case when nproc = 2. For $i = 2$, the do 2 loop requires one iteration, which involves only process 0, and so requires time t. For $i = 3$, the do 2 loop again requires only 1 iteration, where both processes 0 and 1 do the iteration simultaneously. For $i = 4$, the do 2 loop requires 2 iterations, one in which both processes 0 and 1 are active, and a second executed only by process 0.

Then, for n even, say, the total time is

$$parallel\ time\ =\ 2(t\ +\ 2t\ +\ 3t\ ...\ +\ (n/2)t)\ (\text{nproc}\ =\ 2)$$

This is

$$parallel\ time\ =\ n(n\ +\ 2)t/4 \qquad (nproc\ =\ 2)$$

The ideal speedup is the single-stream time divided by the parallel time, which is

$$speedup\ =\ 2(n\ -\ 1)/(n\ +\ 2) \qquad (n\ even,\ nproc\ =\ 2)$$

The speedup is

n	speedup (nproc = 2)
4	1
8	1.4
12	1.6
16	1.7
20	1.7
50	1.9

The reason for the relatively small speedup for small values of n is that, for even values of i, one iteration of the do 2 loop is carried out with one process idle. The actual speedup will be smaller than that calculated above because of the barriers.

For the case of an arbitrary number of processes, the calculation is simple if nproc evenly divides n. We assume that this is the case. Then for the first nproc values of i, the do 2 loop requires a single iteration, and hence requires time t. For the next nproc values of i, the do 2 loop requires 2 iterations, and so forth. Thus the parallel time is

$$parallel\ time\ =\ nproc(t\ +\ 2t\ +\ 3t\ +\ ...\ +\ (n/proc)t)$$

This is

$$parallel\ time\ =\ n(n\ +\ nproc)t/2nproc$$

and the speedup is

$$speedup = (n - 1)nproc/(n + nproc)$$

For nproc = 2, this reduces to the previous result. In the case of 10 processes, we have the following speedup. (The assumption is that nproc evenly divides n):

n	speedup (nproc = 10)
10	4.5
20	6.3
30	7.3
40	7.8
50	8.2
100	9.0

The maximum possible speedup for 10 processes is 10, and the actual speedup does not attain 90% of that value until n = 100. Comparing the speedups for 2 and 10 processes, it is seen that, the larger the number of processes, the larger must n be in order to approach within 90% of the ideal speedup. As n becomes very large, the speedup approaches nproc.

The true speedup is less than the ideal speedup, because of the process synchronization.

In the next section we discuss another technique, called loop reordering, which will allow more efficient parallelization of the do 1 and do 2 loops and will give greater ideal speedup for smaller values of n.

8.8 Reordering Loops

Sometimes a double loop with a backward dependency can be reordered to increase the efficiency of parallelization. This reordering is illustrated by parallelizing the backward-dependency part of Program 8-18 of the previous section. The appropriate fragment of 8-18 is

```
c       fragment of 8-18
c       THIS IS THE PROGRAM THAT WILL BE PARALLELIZED
```

```
c     IN THIS SECTION.
      .
      .
      .
c     x(i) are assumed initialized
c     backward dependency.
      do 1 i = 1,n
          sum = 0.
          do 2 j = 1,i - 1
              sum = sum + a(i,j) * x(j)
2         continue
          x(i) = x(i) + c(i) * sum
1     continue
      .
      .
      .
```

Program 8-22

The following is the sequence of calculations in 8-22:

1. x(2) is calculated from new x(1);
2. x(3) is calculated from new x(1), x(2);
3. x(4) is calculated from new x(1),x(2),x(3); etc.

Once the new value of x(1) is found, each x(i) may be incremented as follows:

$$x(i) = x(i) + a(i,1) * c(i) * x(1)$$

for i = 2, 3, ..., n. At this point, x(2) is now known, and each x(i) may be updated as follows:

$$x(i) = x(i) + a(i,2) * c(i) * x(2)$$

for i = 3, 4, 5, ..., n, and so forth.

What is being described is a reversal of the loops over i and j (the do 1 and do 2 loops of Program 8-22). For each new x(j) that is calculated, all the x(i), i > j are updated. Thus 8-22 can be rewritten as

```
        .
        .
        .
c       8-22 rewritten by reordering of do 1 and do 2 loops.
c       This program is equivalent to 8-22.
        do 1 j = 1,n
            do 2 i = j + 1,n
                x(i) = x(i) + a(i,j) * c(i) * x(j)
2           continue
1       continue
        .
        .
        .
        .
        .
```

Program 8-23

Note that Program 8-23 is not as efficient as it could be. The multiplication by c(i) could be carried out after the do 1 loop is completed. The reader can streamline the programs if desired.

Problem: Parallelize 8-23. Calculate the ideal speedup relative to 8-22. Compare to the speedup of the backward-dependency part of the parallel Program 8-19.

Answer:

```
c       Parallelization of 8-23.
        .
        .
        .
        (fork nproc processes, initialize barrier)
        .
        .
        .
        do 1 j = 1,n
            do 2 i = j + 1 + id,n,nproc
                x(i) = x(i) + a(i,j) * c(i) * x(j)
2           continue
            call barrier(bar_array)
```

```
1       continue
          .
          .
          .
          .
          .
          .
```

Program 8-24

The ideal speedup of 8-24 is about the same as the backward-dependency part of Program 8-19. Program 8-24 should be faster, because x(i) is not updated in a locked region.

If n is much larger than nproc, then either 8-19 (or 8-19 using 8-24 for the backward-dependency part) provides an adequate parallelization of 8-16. However, in the case that n is not much larger than nproc, the speedup is much less than optimal. The reason is that, for many iterations of the inner loop, one or more processes may be idle.

It is possible to enhance 8-23 in a way that is not possible for 8-22. The basic observation is as follows: If x(1) is known, a single process (say process 0) can compute the contribution of a(i,1) * x(1) to x(2), x(3), ..., x(n). As soon as the contribution to x(2) is finished, then x(2) is also known, and process 1, say, can compute the contribution of a(i,2) * x(2) to x(3), x(4), ..., x(n). As soon as the contribution to x(3) is complete, then the next process (process 2) can compute the contribution of a(i,3) * x(3) to x(4), x(5), ..., x(n), and so forth.

In order to allow processes to communicate the information about what they have completed, the shared variable done(i) is introduced; done(i) is initialized to 1 for all i. When a process computes the contribution of x(j) to x(i) (j = 1, 2, ..., i − 1), the process increments done(i) by 1. After i − 1 of these manipulations, done(i) = i, and x(i) has attained its final value. At this point, the contribution of a(m,i) * x(i) to x(m), m = i + 1, i + 2, ..., n may be computed.

The parallelized version of 8-22, then, is as follows:

```
c       Parallelized version of 8-22
        real x(1000),b(1000),c(1000),a(1000,1000),sum
        integer lok,bar_array(4),process_fork
        integer i,j,locked,unlocked,next_index
        integer lok_x(1000),done(1000)

        call shared(next_index,4)
```

```
              call shared(lok,4)
              call shared(lok_x,4000)
              call shared(done,4000)
              call shared(bar_array,16)
              call shared(x,4000)

              (initialize n,x,b,c,a)
              unlocked = 0
              locked = 1
              call spin_lock_init(lok,unlocked)
              call barrier_init(bar_array,nproc)
              do 50 i = 1,n
                   call spin_lock_init(lok_x(i),unlocked)
    50        continue
              next_index = 1

              id = process_fork(nproc)

c     initialize done(i) in parallel
              do 5 j = 1 + id,n,nproc
                   done(j) = 1
     5        continue

              call barrier(bar_array)
    10        continue
                   call spin_lock(lok)
                        j = next_index
                        next_index = next_index + 1
                   call spin_unlock(lok)
                   if (j .gt. n) goto 20
c                  now compute the contribution of a(i,j) * x(j) to
c                  x(j + 1), ..., x(n). Wait until x(j) has attained
c                  its new value
    90             continue
                   if (done(j) .ne. j) goto 90
c                  update x(i) with x(j)
                   do 2 i = j + 1,n
                        call spin_lock(lok_x(i))
                             x(i) = x(i) + a(i,j) * c(i) * x(j)
                             done(i) = done(i) + 1
                        call spin_unlock(lok_x(i))
     2             continue
                   goto 10
    20        continue
              call process_join()
              (output results)
              end
```

Program 8-25

The updates of x(i) and done(i) are done in a protected region, where each array element is protected by a different lock. The barrier call is eliminated. The array done(i) provides synchronization.

Problem: Could 8-25 give incorrect results if done(i) were not updated in a protected region? Give an example.

The algorithm of 8-25 imposes some sequential behavior on the processes. A process which, for some j, computes the update to x(i), cannot begin unless x(j) is known (done(j) = j). Thus the process responsible for j = 5 cannot begin until the process responsible for j = 4 has completed the update of x(5). This sequentiality is a reflection of the data dependencies of the original problem 8-22.

Whether or not 8-25 executes more rapidly than 8-24 or 8-19 will depend on the size of the problem, the number of processes and the efficiency of the spin-lock implementation. If n is very large compared with nproc, then 8-25 will almost certainly be less efficient than the simpler 8-19 or 8-24. It is when n/nproc < 4, i.e. n not much larger than nproc, that 8-25 has a chance of being more efficient.

Problem: Estimate the speedup of 8-25.

In Section 14.3, 8-25 will be rewritten using events for the synchronization. However, it is anticipated that 8-25 will be more efficient than the version of Chapter 14.

8.9   Special Scheduling—Assign Based on Condition

The examples of this chapter have shown, among other things, that there is no single technique that can be applied to all data dependencies, but rather the method must be developed to suit the occasion. The method may involve scheduling, as in previous examples, or the problem may have to be reformulated.

In this section, another scheduling example will be introduced. Consider the following loop:

```
c       Assignment, involving backward dependency, which is
c       based on a condition.

        integer a(0:1000),i,mod,k,n

        (initialize a,n,k)

        do 1 i = 1,n
            if (a(i) .eq. 0) then
                a(i) = mod(a(i - 1),k)
            else
                call transform(a(i))
            endif
1       continue
        (output results)
        end
```

Program 8-26

Similar loops are encountered in calculations involving fractals.

The loop in 8-26 has a partial backward dependency, whereby only some-time does a(i) require the new value of a(i - 1) for its own assignment.

There are several ways to parallelize 8-26. A modified form of block scheduling will be used here (see Section 8.4).

The algorithm is as follows. Divide the n points into nproc sets of contiguous points, where the left-hand and right-hand point of the set number id is imin(id) and imax(id), id = 0, 1, ..., nproc - 1. Then, for id > 0, if a(imin(id)) = 0, decrement imin(id) by 1, decrement imax(id - 1) by 1. Repeat this until a(imin(id)) is not 0.

So long as a(imin(id)) is not 0, the calculation of a(i) for points in the region id can be computed independently of the values of the region id - 1. That is, the data dependency has been removed.

The parallelized version of 8-26 is

```
c       Assignment, involving backward dependency, which is
c       based on a condition.
c       Parallelized version of 8-26, using special scheduling.
c       Assume number of process <= 50.

        integer a(0:1000),i,mod,k,n,process_fork
        integer id,nproc,npts,iexcess,bar_array(4)
        integer imin(0:49),imax(0:49),lok_block(0:49)
        integer unlocked,locked,iexit
```

```
                call shared(bar_array,16)
                call shared(lok_block,200)
                call shared(a,4000)
                call shared(imin,200)
                call shared(imax,200)
                call shared(iexit,4)

                iexit = 0
                unlocked = 1
                locked = 0
                (initialize a,n,k,nproc)
                call barrier_init(bar_array,nproc)
                do 50 i = 0,nproc - 1
                    call spin_lock_init(lok_block(i),unlocked)
     50         continue

                id = process_fork(nproc)

c       divide points 1... n into nproc blocks.
c       (see 8-8)
                npts = n/nproc
c       iexcess is the number of extra points at the end
                iexcess = n - nproc * npts
                if (iexcess .eq. 0) then
c                   no excess of points
                    imin(id) = id * npts + 1
                    imax(id) = imin(id) + npts - 1
                else
                    if (id.lt.iexcess) then
c                       processes 0, 1, ..., iexcess - 1 do npts + 1
c                       points. The remaining processes do npts points
                        imin(id) = id * (npts + 1) + 1
                        imax(id) = imin(id) + npts
                    else
                        imin(id) = id * npts + 1 + iexcess
                        imax(id) = imin(id) + npts - 1
                    endif
                endif

                call barrier(bar_array)
c       now correct imin(id), and imax(id - 1) in the case that
c       a(imin(id)) is 0.
                if (id .ne. 0) then
      5             continue
                    if (a(imin(id)) .eq. 0) then
                        call spin_lock(lok_block(id))
                            imin(id) = imin(id) - 1
```

```
          call spin_unlock(lok_block(id))
          call spin_lock(lok_block(id - 1))
                imax(id - 1) = imax(id - 1) - 1
c               check boundary

                if (imax(id - 1) .gt. imin(id - 1)) then
                     call spin_unlock(lok_block(id - 1))
                     goto 5
                else
                     call spin_unlock(lok_block(id -1))
                     print *,'bad blocks'
                     iexit = 1
                     goto 50
                endif

                call spin_unlock(lok_block(id - 1))
          endif
       endif
50     continue

       call barrier(bar_array)
       if (iexit .eq. 1)call exit()
c      now compute the new a(i)
       do 1 i = imin(id),imax(id)
          if (a(i) .eq. 0) then
                a(i) = mod(a(i - 1),k)
          else
                call transform(a(i))
          endif
1      continue
       call process_join()
       (output results)
       end
```

Program 8-27

This algorithm is a form of *special scheduling*. It provides a work-around the data dependency, because it is specially designed for the particular situation. It is not likely that this exact technique could be used for many problems.

Note that 8-27 is not robust, because the program will exit in the case that $a(i)$ is 0 for all points in a region.

Problem: Explain the logic of the spin-locks following the 5 continue statement. Can you think of cases (pathological or otherwise) where it would not work as intended? (Suppose one process becomes idled immediately after executing the 5 continue statement.)

Problem: If the number of zeros of a(i) is large, then one could use a different form of block scheduling to parallelize 8-26. One could define the block such that the left boundary had a(imin(id)).ne. 0, rather than using the method of 8-8. Then there could be many more blocks than processes, and one could use self-scheduling to assign the processing of the blocks to processes. Write this version of the parallelization of 8-26. Can one create the blocks in parallel? How does the time spent creating the blocks affect the speedup?

8.10   Additional Problems

1 . Write a routine to do a linear search in parallel. This is similar to the break-out-of-loop program of Section 8.6. Find the ideal speedup. Can one get super-linear speedup (speedup greater than the number of processes) in certain cases?

2. Write a parallel program to do an indexed search. Does this make sense?

3. Parallelize 8-13 and 8-15 using block scheduling rather than loop splitting.

4. Parallelize the following program:

```
integer m,n,k,i,a(1000)
(initialize a(i),n)
m = n
do 1 k = 1,n/2
      a(k) = a(k - 1) + a(k)
      m = m - 1
      do 2 i = k + 1,m - 1
           if (a(i) .eq. 0) then
                 a(i) = a(i - 1) + a(i)
           else
                 a(i) = 0
           endif
2          continue
1     continue
end
```

5. Write a parallel program to find all the values of x at which an arbitrary function f(x) is 0, for x1 <= x <= x2. For f(x) a polynomial, find the ideal speedup as a function of the degree of the polynomial and the number of processes. Try to make the program as efficient as possible.

6. Do as in problem 5 for a two-dimensional function f(x,y).

7. Write a parallel program to find the local minima of any function f(x). Find the absolute minimum in any range of x.

8. Do as in problem 7 for a two-dimensional function f(x,y).

9. Parallelize the evaluation of the integral

$$I(x) = \int_0^x g(x - y) \, f(y) \, dy$$

for a range of values of x.

10. Write a parallel program to sort a sequence of character strings, using your favorite sorting algorithm.

11. Parallelize the nested loop

```
        integer i,j,n,m
        real u(100,100),v(100,100),f,g
        do 1 j = 1,n
            do 2 i = 1,m
                u(i + 1,j) = f(v(i,j),v(i,j + 1),
    s                          v(i + 1,j),v(i + 1,j + 1),
    s                          u(i + 1,j))

                v(i,j + 1) = g(u(i,j),u(i,j + 1),
    s                          u(i + 1,j),u(i + 1, j + 1),
    s                          v(i,j + 1))
    2           continue
    1   continue
```

where f, g are functions which do not alter their arguments and which cause no hidden changes. How would it change things if u(i − 1,j) were added as an argument to f?

CHAPTER 9

Scheduling Summary

9.1 Introduction

In this chapter, a brief summary is presented of the scheduling techniques which were introduced in previous chapters. Recall that scheduling is the way in which work is apportioned among processes, and the goal of scheduling is to apportion the work in the most equitable manner possible, with the least amount of overhead. The scheduling techniques discussed here involve parallelizing loops. In all cases, nproc is the number of processes, id is the process-id returned by the process_fork function, and i, j, k, l, m, and n are integers.

9.2 Loop Splitting

The loop to parallelize is

```
        do 1 i = a,b,c
             (work)
    1    continue
```

where a, b, and c are integers or integer-valued expressions. The parallel version is

```
      do 1 i = a + c * id,b,c * nproc
            (work)
1     continue
```

In the case of two nested loops

```
      do 1 i = a1,b1,c1
            do 2 j = a2,b2,c2
                  (work)
2           continue
1     continue
```

If the inner loop is split among idiv processes, the parallel version is

```
      do 1 i = a1 + c1 * (id/idiv),b1,c1 * (nproc/idiv)
            do 2 j = a2 + c2 * mod(id,idiv),b2,c2 * idiv
                  (work)
2           continue
1     continue
```

where integer division is assumed for all expressions in parentheses.

9.3   Expression Splitting

The loop to parallelize is

```
      do 1 i = a,b,c
            (work)
1     continue
```

where a, b, and c are integers or integer-valued expressions. The "work" can be a single statement or many statements.

In this case, idiv processes will execute each value of i, and the expressions within the loop will be partitioned among idiv processes. Thus,

```
      do 1 i = a + c * int(id/idiv),b,c * int(nproc/idiv)
      if (mod(id,idiv) .eq. 0) then
            (part of the work)
      elseif (mod(id,idiv) .eq. 1) then
            (part of the work)
```

```
        .
        .
        .
      elseif (mod(id,idiv) .eq. idiv - 1) then
            (part of the work)
      endif
1     continue
```

In this example, expression splitting is shown in combination with loop splitting. In fact, it could be used with self-scheduling or other scheduling techniques as well.

Problem: Rewrite the loop so the value of idiv can be set at run time.

9.4   Self-Scheduling

The loop to parallelize is, again

```
      do 1 i = a,b,c
            (work)
1     continue
```

In this case, the shared integer variable next_index is required.

```
      integer next_index, lok
      call shared(next_index,4)
      call shared(lok,4)
        .
        .
        .
      next_index = a
1     continue
      call spin_lock(lok)
            i = next_index
            next_index = next_index + c
      call spin_unlock(lok)
      if (i .gt. b) goto 10
      (work)
      goto 1
10    continue
```

This technique can be adapted for multiple loops as follows. In the case of the double loop,

```
        do 1 i = a1,b1,c1
            do 2 j = a2,b2,c2
                (work)
2           continue
1       continue
```

The loop is parallelized as

```
            integer lok,i,j,i0,j0

            call shared(lok,4)
            call shared(i0,4)
            call shared(j0,4)
```

```
c       fork here
            .
            .
            .
            i0 = a1
            j0 = a2 - c2
            call barrier (....)
10          continue
            call spin_lock(lok)
                j0 = j0 + c2
                if (j0 .gt. b2) then
                    j0 = a2
                    i0 = i0 + c1
                endif
                i = i0
                j = j0
            call spin_unlock(lok)
            if (i .gt. b1) goto 1

            (work)

            goto 10
1           continue
```

9.5   Indirect Scheduling

In indirect scheduling, the loop indexes are stored in preset index arrays. This technique is useful if indexing can be established once, while the parallel calculation is executed many times using the same indices. As an example, the loop to be parallelized is

```
        do 1 i = a1,b1,c1
            do 2 j = a2,b2,c2
                do 3 k = a3,b3,c3
                    (work)
3                continue
2            continue
1    continue
```

Define arrays index_i, index_j, and index_k to hold the indices, as follows.

```
            integer index_i(1),index_j(1),index_k(1)
            integer mmax

c       Initialize index arrays.
c       This should be done once only
            m = 0
            do 1 i = a1,b1,c1
                do 2 j = a2,b2,c2
                    do 3 k = a3,b3,c3
                        m = m + 1
                        index_i(m) = i
                        index_j(m) = j
                        index_k(j) = k
3                    continue
2                continue
1            continue
            mmax = m

c       Now the calculation, which is repeated many times.

            do 4 m = 1 + id,mmax,nproc
                i = index_i(m)
                j = index_j(m)
                k = index_k(m)
                (work)
4            continue
```

Self-scheduling could also be used in the work loop, rather than loop splitting.

This technique could also be useful if the loop is over a predefined subset of points of some domain.

9.6   Block Scheduling

In the case of block scheduling, each process number id executes successive values of i, between imin(id) and imax(id). The values of i differ by the amount c.

The loop to parallelize is, as usual,

```
      do 1 i = a,b,c
            (work)
1     continue
```

The parallel version is

```
            integer npts,iexcess,imin(0:nproc - 1),imax(0:nproc - 1)
c       n is number of "points" to be distributed among nproc
c       processes.
            n = (b - a)/c + 1
            npts = n/nproc
c       iexcess is the number of extra points at the end
            iexcess = n - nproc * npts
            if (iexcess .eq. 0) then
c               no excess of points
                imin(id) = id * npts + 1
                imax(id) = imin(id) + npts - 1
            else
                if (id .lt. iexcess) then
c                   processes 0,1,..,iexcess - 1 do npts + 1
c                   points.
c                   The remaining processes do npts points
                    imin(id) = id * (npts + 1) + 1
                    imax(id) = imin(id) + npts
                else
                    imin(id) = id * npts + 1 + iexcess
                    imax(id) = imin(id) + npts - 1
                endif
            endif
c       now the work section
            do 1 i = a + (imin(id) - 1) *c,a + (imax(id) - 1) *c,c
            (work)
1           continue
```

Calculating `imin` and `imax` requires each process to execute only four extra statements.

9.7   Special Scheduling

Special scheduling is scheduling which does not fit into the other categories. It is tailored to the particular situation.

CHAPTER 10

Linear Recurrence Relations— Backward Dependencies

10.1 Introduction to Recurrence Relations

This chapter describes the parallel computation of linear recurrence relations. An example of a recurrence relation is the expression in the following loop:

```
        do 1 i = 1,n
              x(i) = a(i) * x(i - 1) + b(i)
1       continue
```

Program 10-1

Each $x(i)$ depends on $x(i - 1)$, and Program 10-1 is an example of a backward dependency. The relation is *linear* because, on the right-hand side of the assignment of 10-1, x alone appears and not a function of x (such as $x(i - 1)**2$ or $\sin(x(i - 1))$).

Recurrence relations appear in the numerical integration of differential equations and in Gaussian elimination of banded matrices.

To parallelize loops like 10-1, the calculation must be reformulated. This chapter explains one way of reformulating recurrence relations so they can be computed in parallel, and it presents programs for doing so.

In general, the calculation of recurrence relations in parallel results in a program considerably more complex than 10-1. In addition, the speedup is always a fraction of the number of processes, frequently $\frac{1}{3}$ or $\frac{1}{4}$ or even less. Even so, the problem can be formulated so that the speedup is linear in the number of processes.

10-1 is only one particular example of a recurrence relation. A more complicated recurrence relation, of level 2, is

$$x(i) = a(1,i) * x(i - 1) + a(2,i) * x(i - 2) + b(i)$$

A general, an *m-level recurrence relation* computes

$$x(i) = a(1,i) * x(i - 1) + a(2,i) * \\ x(i - 2) + ...+ a(m,i) * x(i - m) + b(i)$$

as in the following program:

```
c       m-level recurrence relation, single-stream
        real x(0:1000),a(20,1000),b(1000)
        integer n,i,m,j
        n = 1000
        m = 20
        (initialize a(i,j),b(i))
        (initialize x(0),x(1), . . . ,x(m - 1))
        do 1 i = m,n
             x(i) = b(i)
             do 2 j = 1,m
                  x(i) = x(i) + a(j,i) * x(i - j)
2            continue
1       continue
```

Program 10-2

There are more complex recurrence relations, involving several arrays (the above ones involve only the array x(i) as the unknown). For example, consider the following loop:

```
         do 1 i = 1,n
               x(i) = a(i) * x(i - 1) + b(i) * y(i - 1) + c(i)
               y(i) = d(i) * x(i - 1) + e(i) * y(i - 1) + g(i)
     1         continue
                 .
                 .
                 .
```

Program 10-3

It is not possible to formulate 10-3 as a simple m-level recurrence relation, for any particular m. One can, of course, generalize 10-3 to many more variables and to greater levels of backward dependency.

In this chapter, parallel computation of recurrence relations like 10-2 and 10-3 are both treated. Parts of this chapter require an understanding of elementary matrix algebra.

10.2 x(i) = x(i − 1) + y(i)

In this section, the following simple computation is done in parallel form.

```
c        Recurrence relation x(i) = x(i - 1) + y(i)
c        Single-stream
               real x(0:1000), y(1000)
               integer n,i
               (initialize y(i),x(0),n)
               do 1 i = 1,n
                   x(i) = x(i - 1) + y(i)
     1         continue
               (output results)
               end
```

Program 10-4

In presenting the technique for parallelizing 10-4, it is helpful to rewrite the assignments in a more transparent way. The first iteration of the do 1 loop executes the assignment

$$x(1) = x(0) + y(1) \tag{10-1}$$

The second iteration of the loop executes the statement

$$x(2) = x(1) + y(2) \tag{10-2}$$

x(1) was already determined in (10-1). The value from there can be substituted into (10-2), resulting in

$$x(2) = x(0) + y(1) + y(2) \tag{10-3}$$

The third iteration of the loop executes

$$x(3) = x(2) + y(3) \tag{10-4}$$

Putting the result of (10-3) into (10-4), we get

$$x(3) = x(0) + y(1) + y(2) + y(3) \tag{10-5}$$

We may continue this process so that, for any value of i,

$$x(i) = x(0) + y(1) + y(2) + \ldots + y(i) \tag{10-6}$$

The significance of this equation is that any x(i) is determined only from x(0) and y(1), y(2),..., y(i). The dependence of x(i) on x(i − 1), which appeared in the original recurrence relation, has been eliminated. Because of this, *equation (10-6) no longer contains a backward data dependency*. As a result, we may compute (10-6) in parallel, and this would be equivalent to executing Program 10-4 in parallel.

A crude, unsatisfactory way to evaluate eq. (10-6) in parallel is given by the following program fragment, which is executed by nproc processes simultaneously.

```
c       inefficient parallelization of 10-4,
c       using eq. (10-6) directly.
            .
            .
            .
        id = process_fork(nproc)
        do 1 i = 1 + id,n,nproc
            x(i) = x(0)
            do 2 j = 1,i
                x(i) = x(i) + y(j)
2           continue
1       continue
        call barrier(bar)
            .
            .
            .
```

Program 10-5

Problem: Determine the ideal speedup of Program 10-5, compared to Program 10-4, for n = 100 and nproc = 10.

Answer: Process id = 9 executes the largest number of adds in Program 10-5. The number of adds executed by process 9 is

$$10 + 20 + 30 + \ldots + 100 = 10 * 9/2 = 450$$

That is, when i = 10, process 9 does 10 adds, when i = 20 it does 20 adds, and so forth. On the other hand, the number of adds in the single-stream version, 10-4, is 100. The ideal speedup is then

$$\text{ideal speedup} = 100/450 = .22.$$

In other words, Program 10-5 will run approximately five times slower than 10-4, and so we must try a different algorithm for the parallelization.

A better way to parallelize Program 10-4 is illustrated by considering a specific example. Suppose n = 12 and nproc = 4, so we have 4 processes to calculate the 12 points x(1), ..., x(12). We first divide the 12 points into 4 regions (or intervals), such that process 0 "does" region 0, points 1, 2, 3; process 1 "does" region 1, points 4, 5, 6, and so forth. That is,

region	points
0	1,2,3
1	4,5,6
2	7,8,9
3	10,11,12

This distribution of points is illustrated in Figure 10-1.
The parallel calculation has three stages.

Stage 1

Process 0 computes

$$q(0) = y(1) + y(2) + y(3) \tag{10-7}$$

Process 1 computes

$$q(1) = y(4) + y(5) + y(6) \tag{10-8}$$

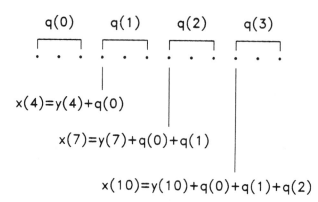

Figure 10-1. Illustration of the distribution of work in Program 10-7.

Process 2 computes

$$q(2) = y(7) + y(8) + y(9) \tag{10-9}$$

Process 3 computes

$$q(3) = y(10) + y(11) + y(12) \tag{10-10}$$

The qs are illustrated in Fig. 10-1.

Stage 2

For stage 2, we calculate $x(1), x(4), x(7), x(10)$, that is, values of x at the smallest point of each region.

Region 1:

$$x(4) = y(4) + q(0) + x(0) \tag{10-11}$$

Region 2:

$$x(7) = y(7) + q(0) + q(1) + x(0) \tag{10-12}$$

Region 3:

$$x(10) = y(10) + q(0) + q(1) + q(2) + x(0) \tag{10-13}$$

This procedure is illustrated in Fig. 10-1.

The equation for x(4) is obtained by combining equations (10-5) and (10-7). The remaining equations are obtained similarly. Note that Stage 2 is sequential and may be implemented in the following fragment (which is executed by a single process only).

```
           .
           .
           .
        m = 1
        s = x(0)
        do 10 i = 0,3
              x(m) = y(m) + s
              m = m + 3
              s = s + q(i)
10      continue
           .
           .
           .
```

Program 10-6

Program 10-6 yields the values of x(1), x(4), x(7), and x(10).

Stage 3

Note that, as if by magic, we have determined x(i) for the ith smallest point for each of the four regions. That is, we have found x(4) without finding x(2) and x(3) beforehand. We determined x(7) without finding x(2), x(3), x(5), and x(6) beforehand, and so forth. We are able to do this because of the formulation of the problem as eq. (10-6), which has no data dependencies.

To find the remaining points of each region, we may use the original relation

$$x(i) = x(i - 1) + y(i). \tag{10-14}$$

Consider, for example, region 2. Since x(7) is known, then x(8) and x(9) can be determined using (10-14). For region 3, since x(10) is known, eq. (10-14) can be used to get x(11) and x(12).

The entire program for this special case then becomes

```
c       Compute x(i) = x(i - 1) + y(i) in parallel, for special
c       case of n = 12, nproc = 4.
           real y(1000),x(0:1000),q(0:19),s
```

```
              integer id,nproc,i,m,bar(4),process_fork,n
              call shared(x,4004)
              call shared(bar,16)
              call shared(q,80)

              (initialize y(i),x(0))
              n = 12
              nproc = 4

              call barrier_init(bar,nproc)
              id = process_fork(nproc)

c       stage 1 - done in parallel
c       q(0) = y(1) + y(2) + y(3)
c       q(1) = y(4) + y(5) + y(6)
c       etc
              q(id) = 0
              do 1 i = 1 + 3 * id, 3 + 3 * id
                   q(id) = q(id) + y(i)
    1         continue
              call barrier(bar)

c       stage 2 - sequential part
c       compute x(1), x(4), x(7) and x(10)
              if (id .eq. 0) then
                   s = x(0)
                   m = 1
                   do 2 i = 0,3
                        x(m) = y(m) + s
                        m = m + 3
                        s = s + q(i)
    2              continue
              endif
              call barrier(bar)

c       stage 3 - done in parallel
c       determine the other two points in each region
              do 3 i = 2 + 3 * id,3 + 3 * id
                   x(i) = x(i - 1) + y(i)
    3         continue
              call process_join()
              (output results)
              end
```

Program 10-7

Note the use of barriers after each stage. The calculations of each stage must
be complete before the next stage begins.

Problem: Calculate the ideal speedup of Program 10-7 compared to Program 10-4.

Answer: For the sequential program, 10-4, there are 12 adds, so the ideal time is 12t, t being the time for a single add, and the loop overhead is neglected. For the parallel version, 10-7, stage 1 requires 2 adds for each process, so the time is 2t. Stage 2 requires 4 adds and is done sequentially, and stage 3 requires 2 adds for each process. The net time is then 2t + 4t + 2t = 8t. The ideal speedup is

$$\text{ideal speedup} = 12/8 = 1.5.$$

The reason that the speedup is so small is that more work is done in the parallel version than in the sequential. That is, the parallel version has a total of 8 adds in stage 1 (each process does 2 adds), 4 adds in stage 2 and 8 adds in stage 3 (each process does 2 adds), giving a total of 20 adds, as compared to 12 in the parallel version. However, for the parallel version, the work can be distributed among the processes in such a way that there is a net speedup. Note that it would be counterproductive to run Program 10-7 on a uniprocessor.

We will now compute the recurrence relation for the general case of any n and any number of processes. The result will be a program analogous to 10-7, but more general.

The algorithm described above uses, in essence, block scheduling. The first step in the general case is to subdivide the n points into nproc intervals, in which the points of region id lie between imin(id) and imax(id) inclusive. This is done by the method of Section 8.4.

Stage 1

Calculate the sum of y's for each region.

$$q(id) = y(imind(id)) + y(imin(id) + 1) + \ldots + \\ y(imax(id)) \tag{10-15}$$

The above expression is analogous to equations (10-7) – (10-10) for the special case. The q's can be calculated in parallel.

Stage 2

For Stage 2, one determines all the x(imin(id)) in a sequential manner. The equation used is

$$x(imin(id)) = y(imin(id)) + q(0) + q(1) + \ldots + q(id - 1) + x(0) \tag{10-16}$$

This is analogous to equations (10-11) − (10-13).

Stage 3

In Stage 3, one determines x(imin(id) + 1), x(imin(id) + 2), ..., x(imax(id)) using (10-14). The program is

```
c       Compute x(i) = x(i - 1) + y(i) in parallel,
c       for any n and nproc.

        real y(1000),x(0:1000),q(0:19),s
        integer id,nproc,i,m,bar(4),process_fork,n
        integer npts,imin(0:19),imax(0:19),iexcess
        call shared(x,4004)
        call shared(bar,16)
        call shared(q,80)
        call shared(imin,80)
        call shared(imax,80)

        (initialize y(i),x(0),n,nproc)
        call barrier_init(bar,nproc)
        id = process_fork(nproc)

c       First subdivide the n points into nproc intervals.
c       Use algorithm of Section 8.4.
        npts = n/nproc
c       iexcess is the number of extra points at the end
        iexcess = n - nproc * npts
        if (iexcess .eq. 0) then
c           no excess of points
            imin(id) = id * npts + 1
            imax(id) = imin(id) + npts - 1
        else
            if (id .lt. iexcess) then
c               processes 0,1,...,iexcess - 1
c               do npts + 1 points
c               the remaining processes do npts points
```

```
                imin(id) = id * (npts + 1) + 1
                imax(id) = imin(id) + npts
            else
                imin(id) = id * npts + 1 + iexcess
                imax(id) = imin(id) + npts - 1
            endif
        endif

c   stage 1 - done in parallel
c   q(id) = y(imin(id)) + y(imin(id) + 1) + ... + y(imax(id))
        q(id) = 0
        do 1 i = imin(id),imax(id)
            q(id) = q(id) + y(i)
1       continue
        call barrier(bar)

c   stage 2 - sequential part
c   compute x(imin(id)) for all id
        if (id .eq. 0) then
            s = x(0)
            do 2 i = 0,nproc - 1
                m = imin(i)
                x(m) = y(m) + s
                s = s + q(i)
2           continue
        endif
        call barrier(bar)

c   stage 3 - done in parallel
c   determine the other points in each region
        do 3 i = imin(id) + 1,imax(id)
            x(i) = x(i - 1) + y(i)
3       continue
        call process_join()
        (output results)
        end
```

Program 10-8

The reader should compare stages 1-3 of Program 10-8 to the equivalent sections of Program 10-7.

Problem: Compute the speedup of Program 10-8 as compared to the speedup of Program 10-4.

Answer: Assume that nproc divides n evenly. Then Stage 1 requires time

$$nt/nproc$$

where t is the time to do a single add. Stage 2 requires time

$$(nproc - 1)t$$

and Stage 3 takes

$$(n/nproc - 1)t$$

On the other hand, the single-stream version, 10-4, takes time n * t. The ideal speedup is then

$$ideal\ speedup = n/((2n/nproc) - 2 + nproc)$$

If n is much larger than nproc, the speedup is

$$ideal\ speedup = nproc/2\ (for\ n\ much\ bigger\ than\ nproc)$$

The ideal speedup is half the number of processes. The parallel version does about twice the amount of work as the serial one (neglecting the sequential Stage 2 and the barrier calls). That is, each process of Stage 1 does n/nproc adds, while each process in Stage 3 does n/nproc adds, leading to the ideal speedup of nproc/2. The overhead will reduce the speedup somewhat, depending on the problem size.

Note that program 10-8 is longer and more complex than Program 10-4. Program 10-8 has 35 noncomment lines, while 10-4 has 5 (excluding the declarations). In addition, 10-8 is much more difficult to follow, and to modify, than 10-4. These general considerations are valid for all programs which compute recurrence relations in parallel.

10.3 x(i) = a(i) * x(i − 1) + y(i)

In this section, the following calculation is done in parallel form:

```
c       Recurrence relation x(i) = a(i) * x(i - 1) + y(i)
c       single-stream
        real x(0:1000),y(1000),a(1000)
        integer n,i
```

```
        (initialize a(i),y(i),n,x(0))
        do 1 i = 1,n
             x(i) = a(i) * x(i - 1) + y(i)
1       continue
        (output results)
        end
```

Program 10-9

This is a more general recurrence relation than was considered in the previous chapter, and Program 10-9 is more difficult to parallelize. In order to understand this section, the reader will have to be familiar with the manipulations of elementary matrix algebra.

To see what is involved, we write out the first few iterations of Program 10-9:

$$x(1) = a(1)x(0) + y(1) \tag{10-17}$$

$$x(2) = a(2)x(1) + y(2) \tag{10-18}$$

$$x(3) = a(3)x(2) + y(3) \tag{10-19}$$

.

.

.

The assignments above can be rewritten using a matrix notation. Equation (10-17) becomes

$$\begin{pmatrix} x(1) \\ 1 \end{pmatrix} = \begin{pmatrix} a(1) & y(1) \\ 0 & 1 \end{pmatrix} \begin{pmatrix} x(0) \\ 1 \end{pmatrix} \tag{10-20}$$

Equation (10-18) is

$$\begin{pmatrix} x(2) \\ 1 \end{pmatrix} = \begin{pmatrix} a(2) & y(2) \\ 0 & 1 \end{pmatrix} \begin{pmatrix} x(1) \\ 1 \end{pmatrix} \tag{10-21}$$

While equation (10-19) is

$$\begin{pmatrix} x(3) \\ 1 \end{pmatrix} = \begin{pmatrix} a(3) & y(3) \\ 0 & 1 \end{pmatrix} \begin{pmatrix} x(2) \\ 1 \end{pmatrix} \tag{10-22}$$

To generalize equations (10-20) − (10-22), define the matrix M(i)

$$\mathbf{M}(i) = \begin{pmatrix} a(i) & y(i) \\ 0 & 1 \end{pmatrix} \tag{10-23}$$

Then the equations (10-20) – (10-22) and the similar equations for $x(4)$, $x(5)$, ..., $x(n)$ can all be written in the simple form

$$\begin{pmatrix} x(i) \\ 1 \end{pmatrix} = \mathbf{M}(i) \begin{pmatrix} x(i-1) \\ 1 \end{pmatrix} \tag{10-24}$$

We can also write a similar equation for $x(i-1)$,

$$\begin{pmatrix} x(i-1) \\ 1 \end{pmatrix} = \mathbf{M}(i-1) \begin{pmatrix} x(i-2) \\ 1 \end{pmatrix} \tag{10-25}$$

If we combine (10-24) and (10-25), so that (10-25) is substituted for the $x(i-1)$ vector of (10-24), we have

$$\begin{pmatrix} x(i) \\ 1 \end{pmatrix} = \mathbf{M}(i)\mathbf{M}(i-1) \begin{pmatrix} x(i-2) \\ 1 \end{pmatrix} \tag{10-26}$$

We may continue this process until we finally get

$$\begin{pmatrix} x(i) \\ 1 \end{pmatrix} = \mathbf{M}(i)\mathbf{M}(i-1)\mathbf{M}(i-2).\ .\ .\ .\ .\mathbf{M}(1) \begin{pmatrix} x(0) \\ 1 \end{pmatrix} \tag{10-27}$$

Equation (10-27) should be compared with equation (10-6) of the previous section. Note that $x(i)$ is determined in terms of $x(0)$, and the $a(1)\ldots a(i)$ and $y(1)\ldots y(i)$ (Each $\mathbf{M}(j)$ depends on $a(j)$ and $y(j)$). Thus *equation (10-27) has no data dependencies*, just as eq. (10-6) of the previous section has no data dependencies. It is because we can eliminate the backward dependency that we are able to perform the computation of Program 10-9 in parallel.

The parallel computation has three stages, which are similar to the three stages of the previous section. Analogous to that section, we first work through the computation for the special case of $n = 12$, nproc $= 4$, and then we present the general argument.

The twelve points are divided into four regions, or groups, where region 0 has points 1, 2, 3, region 1 has points 4, 5, 6, and so forth. In stage 1 we form the 2×2 matrix $q(id)$, for region id $= 0, 1, 2, 3$.

Stage 1

Process 0 computes

$$\mathbf{q}(0) = \mathbf{M}(3)\mathbf{M}(2)\mathbf{M}(1) \tag{10-28}$$

Process 1 computes

$$\mathbf{q}(1) = \mathbf{M}(6)\mathbf{M}(5)\mathbf{M}(4) \tag{10-29}$$

Process 2 computes

$$\mathbf{q}(2) = \mathbf{M}(9)\mathbf{M}(8)\mathbf{M}(7) \tag{10-30}$$

Process 3 computes

$$\mathbf{q}(3) = \mathbf{M}(12)\mathbf{M}(11)\mathbf{M}(10) \tag{10-31}$$

These equations are analogous to equations (10-7) – (10-10) of the previous section. The procedure is schematically illustrated in Fig. 10-1.

If we write the general form of $\mathbf{q}$ as

$$\mathbf{q}(id) = \begin{pmatrix} w1(id) & w2(id) \\ 0 & 1 \end{pmatrix} \tag{10-32}$$

then equations (10-28) – (10-31) can all be computed in parallel by the fragment below (which is executed by all four processes in parallel).

```
        .
        .
        .
     w1(id) = a(1 + 3 * id)
     w2(id) = y(1 + 3 * id)
     do 1 i = 2 + 3 * id,3 + 3 * id
          w1(id) = a(i) * w1(id)
          w2(id) = a(i) * w2(id) + y(i)
  1    continue
        .
        .
        .
```

Program 10-10

Stage 2

For Stage 2, which is the sequential part of the computation, we determine $x(3)$, $x(6)$, $x(9)$, and $x(12)$, that is, the values of x at the largest points of each region. This is similar to what was done in Stage 2 of the previous section, but there the computation concentrated on the smallest points.

Region 0:

$$\begin{pmatrix} x(3) \\ 1 \end{pmatrix} = \mathbf{q}(0) \begin{pmatrix} x(0) \\ 1 \end{pmatrix} \tag{10-33}$$

This equation can be obtained by combining equation (10-27) and equation (10-28).

Region 1:

$$\begin{pmatrix} x(6) \\ 1 \end{pmatrix} = \mathbf{q}(1)\mathbf{q}(0) \begin{pmatrix} x(0) \\ 1 \end{pmatrix} \tag{10-34}$$

This equation follows from combining equations (10-27), (10-28), and (10-29).

Region 2:

$$\begin{pmatrix} x(9) \\ 1 \end{pmatrix} = \mathbf{q}(2)\mathbf{q}(1)\mathbf{q}(0) \begin{pmatrix} x(0) \\ 1 \end{pmatrix} \tag{10-35}$$

This is a combination of (10-27), (10-28), (10-29), and (10-30).

Region 3:

$$\begin{pmatrix} x(12) \\ 1 \end{pmatrix} = \mathbf{q}(3)\mathbf{q}(2)\mathbf{q}(1)\mathbf{q}(0) \begin{pmatrix} x(0) \\ 1 \end{pmatrix} \tag{10-36}$$

This results from combining (10-27), (10-28), (10-29), (10-30), and (10-31). These equations are analogous to equations (10-11) – (10-14) of the previous section.

The values of x(3), x(6), x(9), and x(12) are computed in the following program fragment, which is executed by process 0 only. The product of q's at any iteration is represented by the matrix

$$\begin{pmatrix} tem\_w1 & tem\_w2 \\ 0 & 1 \end{pmatrix}$$

```
      .
      .
      .

      tem_w1 = 1.0
      tem_w2 = 0.
      m = 3
      do 1 i = 0,3
          tem_w1 = tem_w1 * w1(i)
          tem_w2 = w1(i) * tem_w2 + w2(i)
          x(m) = tem_w1 * x(0) + tem_w2
          m = m + 3
  1   continue
      .
      .
      .
```

Program 10-11

Problem: The above calculation can be simplified considerably in the following way. Each of the x's can be computed from

$$x(3) = w1(0)\,x(0) + w2(0) \tag{10-37}$$
$$x(6) = w1(1)\,x(3) + w2(1) \tag{10-38}$$
$$x(9) = w1(2)\,x(6) + w2(2) \tag{10-39}$$
$$x(12) = w1(3)\,x(9) + w2(3) \tag{10-40}$$

Derive the above relations from equations (10-33) – (10-36). (Hint: substitute (10-33) into (10-34). Substitute (10-34) into (10-35) and substitute (10-35) into (10-36).)

Then the calculation of Program 10-11 is done more efficiently in the following fragment, executed only by process 0.

```
      .
      .
      .
```

```
          m = 3
          do 2 i = 0,3
              x(m) = w1(i) * x(m - 3) + w2(i)
              m = m + 3
   2      continue
```

Program 10-12

Stage 3

At this point, we have found $x(3)$, $x(6)$, $x(9)$, and $x(12)$ without finding the other x's. We could do this because of the formulation of equation (10-27), which eliminated the data dependencies.

Finally, Stage 3 uses the original algorithm to get $x(1)$, $x(2)$, $x(4)$, $x(5)$, etc., in exactly the same way as in the previous section. The fragment below is executed by all four processes simultaneously.

```
          .
          .
          .
          do 3 i = 1 + 3 * id,2 + 3 * id
              x(i) = a(i) * x(i - 1) + y(i)
   3      continue
          .
          .
          .
```

Program 10-13

Finally, putting it all together, we have the computation done in parallel.

```
   c      compute x(i) = a(i) * x(i - 1) + y(i) in parallel,
   c      for special case of n = 12,nproc = 4.

          real x(0:1000),y(1000),a(1000)
          real w1(0:19),w2(0:19)
          integer n,nproc,m,i,id,bar(4),process_fork

          call shared(x,4004)
          call shared(bar,16)
          call shared(w1,80)
          call shared(w2,80)

          (initialize a(i),y(i),x(0))
```

```
            n = 12
            nproc = 4

            call barrier_init(bar,nproc)
            id = process_fork(nproc)

c       stage 1 - done in parallel
c       computes matrices, equations (10-28) - (10-31).
            w1(id) = a(1 + 3 * id)
            w2(id) = y(1 + 3 * id)
            do 1 i = 2 + 3 * id,3 + 3 * id
                w1(id) = a(i) * w1(id)
                w2(id) = a(i) * w2(id) + y(i)
    1       continue
            call barrier(bar)

c       stage 2 - sequential part
c       compute x(3),x(6),x(9) and x(12)
            if (id .eq. 0) then
                m = 3
                do 2 i = 0,3
                    x(m) = w1(i) * x(m - 3) + w2(i)
                    m = m + 3
    2           continue
            endif
            call barrier(bar)

c       stage 3 - done in parallel
c       determine the other two points in each region
            do 3 i = 1 + 3 * id,2 + 3 * id
                x(i) = a(i) * x(i - 1) + y(i)
    3       continue
            call process_join()
            (output results)
            end
```

Program 10-14

Problem: Calculate the speedup of 10-14 compared with 10-9.

Answer: The times for 10-14 are (t being the time for an add or multiply):

Stage 1:   Each process, 6t
Stage 2:   Sequential, 8t
Stage 3:   Each process, 4t

The single-stream version has 24 adds and so requires times 24t. The speedup is

ideal speedup = 24t/18t = 1.33

For the parallel calculation of the recursion relation, for any n and any nproc, first subdivide the n points into nproc intervals, such that the points for interval id lie between imin(id) and imax(id), id = 0, 1, ..., nproc − 1.

Stage 1

Determine the matrices q(id) for each region, in parallel.

$$\mathbf{q}(id) = \mathbf{M}(imax(id))\mathbf{M}(imax(id) - 1) \ldots \mathbf{M}(imin(id)) \qquad (10\text{-}41)$$

This equation is analogous to equations (10-28) − (10-31).

Stage 2

In this sequential stage, find x(imax(id)) for each region, using the matrix-vector equation

$$\begin{pmatrix} x(imax(id)) \\ 1 \end{pmatrix} = \mathbf{q}(id) \begin{pmatrix} x(imax(id - 1)) \\ 1 \end{pmatrix} \qquad (10\text{-}42)$$

This equation is analogous to equations (10-37) − (10-40). Note that equation (10-42) for x(imax(0)) must be modified, because imax(−1) is not defined. In that case, one must explicitly use x(0) instead of x(imax(−1)) in (10-42).

Stage 3

Find x(imin(id)), x(imin(id) + 1), ..., x(imax(id) − 1) for each region, in parallel, using

x(i) = a(i) * x(i − 1) + y(i)

The program is

```
c       Compute x(i) = a(i) * x(i - 1) + y(i) in parallel,
c       for any n and nproc.
```

```
      real x(0:1000),y(1000),a(1000)
      real w1(0:19),w2(0:19)
      integer n,nproc,m,i,id,bar(4),process_fork
      integer imin(0:19),imax(0:19),npts,iexcess

      call shared(x,4004)
      call shared(bar,16)
      call shared(w1,80)
      call shared(w2,80)
      call shared(imin,80)
      call shared(imax,80)

      (initialize a(i),y(i),x(0),n,nproc)

      call barrier_init(bar,nproc)
      id = process_fork(nproc)

c     First subdivide the n points into nproc intervals.
c     Use algorithm of section 8.4.
      npts = n/nproc
c     iexcess is the number of extra points at the end
      iexcess = n - nproc * npts
      if (iexcess .eq. 0) then
c         no excess of points
          imin(id) = id * npts + 1
          imax(id) = imin(id) + npts - 1
      else
          if (id .lt. iexcess) then
c             processes 0,1,..,iexcess - 1 do npts + 1
c             points. The remaining processes do npts points
              imin(id) = id * (npts + 1) + 1
              imax(id) = imin(id) + npts
          else
              imin(id) = id * npts + 1 + iexcess
              imax(id) = imin(id) + npts - 1
          endif
      endif

c     stage 1 - done in parallel
c     q(id) = M(imax(id))M(imax(id) - 1)...M(imin(id))
c     Matrix q is
c       w1(id)     w2(id)
c       0          1
c
        w1(id) = a(imin(id))
        w2(id) = y(imin(id))
```

```
                do 1 i = imin(id) + 1,imax(id)
                    w1(id) = a(i) * w1(id)
                    w2(id) = a(i) * w2(id) + y(i)
        1       continue
                call barrier(bar)

c       stage 2 - sequential part, executed by process 0 only
c       In this sequential stage, find x(imax(id)) for each regiom,
c       using the matrix-vector equation
c           |x(imax(id))|                    |x(imax(id - 1))|
c           |           |        = q(id)     |               |
c           |           |                    |               |
c           |1          |                    |1              |
c       x(imax(0)) is handled as a special case.
c
c       This equation is analogous to equations (10-37) - (10-40).
                if (id .eq. 0) then
                        x(imax(0)) = w1(0) * x(0) + w2(0)
                        do 2 i = 1,nproc - 1
                                x(imax(i)) = w1(i) * x(imax(i - 1)) + w2(i)
        2               continue
                endif
                call barrier(bar)

c       stage 3 - done in parallel
c       determine the other points in each region
                do 3 i = imin(id),imax(id) - 1
                    x(i) = a(i) * x(i - 1) + y(i)
        3       continue
                call process_join()
                (output results)
                end
```

Program 10-15

Problem: Calculate the ideal speedup of Program 10-15, assuming nproc evenly divides n.

Answer: The times for the parallel version are (t is the time for a single arithmetic operation, add or multiply):

Stage 1: $3((n/nproc) - 1)t$

Stage 2: $2nproctt$

Stage 3: $2((n/nproc) - 1)t$

The serial version, Program 10-9, requires time 2nt. The ideal speedup is

$$\text{ideal speedup} = 2n/((5n/nproc) - 5 + 2nproc).$$

When n becomes much larger than `nproc`, this expression is approximated by

$$\text{ideal speedup} = (2/5)nproc \text{ (when n much larger than nproc)}$$

Although the speedup increases linearly with the number of processes, it is considerably less than the number of processes.

10.4 x (i) = a (i) * x (i − 1) + b (i) * x (i − 2)

In this section, the following computation is done in parallel:

```
c       Recurrence relation
c              x(i) = a(i) * x(i − 1) + b(i) * x(i − 2)
        real x(0:1000),b(1000),a(1000)
        integer n,i
        (initialize a(i),b(i),x(0),x(1),n)
        do 1 i = 2,n
              x(i) = a(i) * x(i − 1) + b(i) * x(i − 2)
    1       continue
        (output results)
        end
```

Program 10-16

The parallel version is similar to that of the previous section, so we shall present only the three stages for the general case and then the program which does the calculation.

Defining the matrix M(i), in analogy with the previous section,

$$\mathbf{M}(i) = \begin{pmatrix} a(i) & b(i) \\ 1 & 0 \end{pmatrix}. \tag{10-43}$$

Note the different placement of the 1 and 0 in this definition, when compared with (10-23) of the previous section. Then the equation for x(i) is

$$\begin{pmatrix} x(i) \\ x(i-1) \end{pmatrix} = \mathbf{M}(i) \begin{pmatrix} x(i-1) \\ x(i-2) \end{pmatrix} \qquad (10\text{-}44)$$

for i = 2, 3, ..., n. The equation analogous to (10-27) is

$$\begin{pmatrix} x(i) \\ x(i-1) \end{pmatrix} = \mathbf{M}(i)\mathbf{M}(i-1)\mathbf{M}(i-2) \dots \mathbf{M}(2) \begin{pmatrix} x(1) \\ x(0) \end{pmatrix}. \qquad (10\text{-}45)$$

This equation has no data dependencies. Note that, now, both x(1) and x(0) serve as initial conditions, and the calculation starts by finding x(2).
The calculation again has three stages, which are equivalent to those of the previous section. First subdivide the n points into nproc intervals, such that the points for interval id lie between imin(id) and imax(id), id = 0, 1, ..., nproc − 1. In this case, imin(0) = 2 rather than 1.

Stage 1

Determine the matrices q(id) for each region, in parallel. In this case, q(id) has the general form

$$\mathbf{q}(id) = \begin{pmatrix} w1(id) & w2(id) \\ w3(id) & w4(id) \end{pmatrix} \qquad (10\text{-}46)$$

which is slightly different than in the previous section, because of the addition of w3 and w4, but the concept is the same. The matrix equation for the q's is

$$\mathbf{q}(id) = \mathbf{M}(imax(id))\mathbf{M}(imax(id)-1) \dots \mathbf{M}(imin(id)) \qquad (10\text{-}47)$$

Stage 2

In this sequential stage, find x(imax(id)) for each region, using the matrix-vector equation

$$\begin{pmatrix} x(imax(id)) \\ x(imax(id)-1) \end{pmatrix} = \mathbf{q}(id) \begin{pmatrix} x(imax(id-1)) \\ x(imax(id-1)-1) \end{pmatrix} \qquad (10\text{-}48)$$

Note that equation (10-48) for x(imax(0)) must be modified, because imax(−1) is not defined. In that case, one must explicitly use x(1) instead of x(imax(−1)) in (10-48), and x(0) for x(imax(−1) − 1).

Stage 3

Find x(imin(id)), x(imin(id) + 1), ..., x(imax(id) − 1) for each region, in parallel, using

$$x(i) = a(i) * x(i - 1) + b(i) * x(i - 2)$$

The program is

```
c       compute x(i) = a(i) * x(i − 1) + b(i) * x(i − 2) in
c       parallel, for any n and nproc.
        real x(0:1000),b(1000),a(1000)
        real w1(0:19),w2(0:19),w3(0:19),w4(0:19)
        real tem_w1,tem_w2
        integer n,nproc,m,i,id,bar(4),process_fork
        integer imin(0:19),imax(0:19),npts,iexcess

        call shared(x,4004)
        call shared(bar,16)
        call shared(w1,80)
        call shared(w2,80)
        call shared(w3,80)
        call shared(w4,80)
        call shared(imin,80)
        call shared(imax,80)

        (initialize a(i),b(i),x(0),x(1),n,nproc)

        call barrier_init(bar,nproc)
        id = process_fork(nproc)

c       first subdivide the n points into nproc intervals.
c       Use algorithm of section 8.4.
        npts = n/nproc
c       iexcess is the number of extra points at the end
        iexcess = n − nproc * npts
        if (iexcess .eq. 0) then
c           no excess of points
            imin(id) = id * npts + 1
```

```
                     imax(id) = imin(id) + npts - 1
             else
                 if (id .lt. iexcess) then
c                        processes 0,1,...,iexcess - 1
c                        do npts + 1 points.
c                        The remaining processes do npts points
                         imin(id) = id * (npts + 1) + 1
                         imax(id) = imin(id) + npts
                 else
                         imin(id) = id * npts + 1 + iexcess
                         imax(id) = imin(id) + npts - 1
                 endif
             endif
             if (id .eq. 0) imin(0) = 2

c       stage 1 - done in parallel
c       q(id) = M(imax(id))M(id) - 1 ... M(imin(id))
c       Matrix q is
c           wl(id)     w2(id)
c           w3(id)     w4(id)
c
             wl(id) = a(imin(id))
             w2(id) = b(imin(id))
             w3(id) = 1.0
             w4(id) = 0.0
             do 1 i = imin(id) + 1,imax(id)
                 tem_wl = a(i) * wl(id) + b(i) * w3(id)
                 w3(id) = wl(id)
                 wl(id) = tem_wl
                 tem_w2 = a(i) * w2(id) + b(i) * w4(id)
                 w4(id) = w2(id)
                 w2(id) = tem_w2
   1         continue
             call barrier(bar)

c       stage 2 - sequential part, executed by process 0 only
c       In this sequential stage, find x(imax(id))
c       and x(imax(id) - 1) for each region, using the
c       matrix-vector equation
c           |x(imax(id))     |             |x(imax(id - 1))    |
c           |                | = q(id)     |                   |
c           |x(imax(id) - 1)|             |x(imax(id - 1) - 1)|
c       x(imax(0)) and x(imax(0) - 1) is handled as a special case.
c
             if (id .eq. 0) then
                 x(imax(0)) = wl(0) * x(1) + w2(0) * x(0)
```

```
               x(imax(0) - 1) = w3(0) * x(1) + w4(0) * x(0)
               do 2 i = 1,nproc - 1
                  x(imax(i)) = wl(i) * x(imax(i - 1)) + w2(i)
     s             * x(imax(i - 1) - 1)
                  x(imax(i) - 1) = w3(i) * x(imax(i - 1)) + w4(i)
     s             * x(imax(i - 1) - 1)
  2            continue
            endif
            call barrier(bar)

  c      stage 3 - done in parallel
  c      determine the other points in each region
            do 3 i = imin(id),imax(id) - 2
               x(i) = a(i) * x(i - 1) + b(i) * x(i - 2)
  3         continue
            call process_join()
            (output results)
            end
```

Program 10-17

Problem: Compute the ideal speedup of 10-17 compared with 10-16.

10.5   Additional Problems—Other Recurrence Relations

1. A three-level recurrence relation has the form

```
            real x(0:1000),a(1000),b(1000),c(1000)
            integer i,n
            (initialize a,b,c,x(0),x(1),x(2),n)
            do 1 i = 3,n
               x(i) = a(i) * x(i - 1) + b(i) * x(i - 2)
     s           + c(i) * x(i - 3)
  3         continue
            (store results)
            end
```

In this case, a 3×3 array is needed. That is

$$\begin{pmatrix} x(i) \\ x(i-1) \\ x(i-2) \end{pmatrix} = \begin{pmatrix} a(i) & b(i) & c(i) \\ 1 & 0 & 0 \\ 0 & 1 & 0 \end{pmatrix} \begin{pmatrix} x(i-1) \\ x(i-2) \\ x(i-3) \end{pmatrix}$$

Defining

$$M(i) = \begin{pmatrix} a(i) & b(i) & c(i) \\ 1 & 0 & 0 \\ 0 & 1 & 0 \end{pmatrix}$$

we find

$$\begin{pmatrix} x(i) \\ x(i-1) \\ x(i-2) \end{pmatrix} = \mathbf{M}(i)\mathbf{M}(i-1)\mathbf{M}(i-2) \ldots \mathbf{M}(3) \begin{pmatrix} x(2) \\ x(1) \\ x(0) \end{pmatrix}$$

which is equivalent to equation (10-45).

Define the three stages of the calculation of the three-level recurrence relation above, analogous to (10-46), (10-47), and (10-48). Write the program which computes the recurrence relation in parallel and find the speedup.

2. Another recurrence relation which can be handled by a three-dimension matrix is

```
x(i) = a(i) * x(i - 1) + b(i) * x(i - 2) + y(i)
```

Determine the matrix $\mathbf{M}(i)$ for this problem, and write the parallel program to evaluate the recurrence relation. Calculate the speedup.

3. Formulate the m-level recurrence relation, Program 10-2 of the introduction, in array form and write the parallel program. Find the speedup. In the case that m > nproc, a nonarray formulation might be more effective, in which each process does one of the multiplications a(j,i) * x(i - j) for a given i. Write the program in this way, find the speedup, and compare it to the array formulation.

4. Consider the following recurrence relation:

```
real x(0:1000),a,y(1000),b(1000)
integer i,n
n = 1000
do 1 i = 1,n
    x(i) = y(i) + b(i) * a
    a = a - x(i - 1)
1    continue
```

Formulate this recurrence relation as an array multiplication and write the parallel program. (Hint: Make a an array.)

5. The recurrence relation of Program 10-3 of the introduction to this chapter can be formulated in matrix form as

$$\begin{pmatrix} x(i) \\ y(i) \\ 1 \end{pmatrix} = \begin{pmatrix} a(i) & b(i) & c(i) \\ d(i) & e(i) & g(i) \\ 0 & 0 & 1 \end{pmatrix} \begin{pmatrix} x(i-1) \\ y(i-1) \\ 1 \end{pmatrix}$$

Write the program to do this recurrence relation in parallel.

6. Write a parallel program to evaluate the 2m x 2m recurrence relation:

```
x(i) = a(i,1)x(i - 1) + ... + a(i,m) * x(i - m)
+ b(i,1) * y(i - 1) + ... + b(i,m) * y(i - m)
y(i) = c(i,1) * x(i - 1) + ... + c(i,m) * x(i - m)
+ d(i,1) * y(i - 1) + ... + d(i,m) * y(i - m)
```

7. Write a parallel program to integrate the coupled pair of differential equations:

$$dx/dt = a(t)x + b(t)y + c(t)$$
$$dy/dt = d(t)x + e(t)y + f(t)$$

8. A general form of recurrence relations is

$$x(i) = g(i,x(1),x(2), \dots ,x(i))$$

where g is any function. What types of functions lend themselves to a parallel formulation?

9. Consider the pair of ordinary differential equations:

$$dx/dt = f(x,y,t)$$
$$dy/dt = g(x,y,t)$$

What kind of functions f, g will allow efficient parallelization of the program to numerically integrate these equations?

CHAPTER 11

Performance Tuning

11.1 Introduction

In this chapter, issues relevant to performance are considered. Up to now, the issue of performance was addressed by calculating an *ideal speedup*. The ideal speedup assumes that the execution time of the parallel program is determined only by the number of operations performed in the parallelized "core" loop. It ignored all *overhead*, including

1. Time to fork processes,
2. Time for initialization,
3. Time for any sequential stages (such as a consolidation stage),
4. Time for synchronization calls, such as barriers and spin-locks,
5. Time for joins.

The *true speedup* is

$$\text{true speedup} = \frac{\text{execution time for single-stream version}}{\text{execution time for parallel version}}$$

The true speedup is measured directly from execution times, rather than from counting operations in the parallel loop. Even if the "core" loop has been efficiently parallelized, it is still normal for the true speedup to be less than the ideal speedup, because of overhead. If one is not careful, the overhead can require so much time that the true speedup is less than 1, which means that the parallel version runs slower than the single-stream version.

In practical applications, it is the true speedup that is of interest, rather than the ideal speedup. It is the purpose of this chapter to discuss how the true speedup may be estimated when writing a parallel program.

An important influence on overhead is the way in which the `process_fork`, `process_join`, and synchronization functions are implemented. In order for tightly coupled parallel programs (such as parallelized loops) to have significant speedup, it is essential that as little time as possible be spent in synchronization and in creating processes. If synchronization is managed only through operating system calls, then the tightly coupled parallel programs described in this book will not have a performance advantage unless the problem size is enormous (the order of tens of millions of calculations).

The placement of the `process_fork` is also important. If the `process_fork` requires milliseconds, as is the case for the Unix `fork`, then one must fork as infrequently as possible. On the other hand, if the `process_fork` is implemented as a *thread* (discussed later), which can require only a few microseconds, then one can invoke the function freely.

Another factor affecting program performance is whether the program is able to make good use of the cache. Modern microprocessors depend crucially on cache for obtaining high performance, and this topic is addressed at the end of this chapter.

11.2 Parallel Programming and the Structure of Programs

For any but the shortest programs, it is frequently unproductive to arrange for the entire program to be executed as a parallel program. Creating efficient parallel programs can be time consuming. One may not want to invest the energy and time required unless the payoff, in the form of enhanced performance, will be sufficiently great.

It is normal for only a small part of a program to execute in parallel, the remainder of the program running single-stream. Or, if one is parallelizing an existing program, one will normally parallelize only a time-critical portion of it. The criterion that one can use to choose what part of a program to parallelize is described in this chapter.

It is frequently found that, especially for programs doing technical calculations, *over 95% of the execution time occurs in only a few percent of the source-code statements*. That is, most of the time is spent executing a few statements over and over. As a simple example, consider the following program, in which the executable statements are numbered at the left.

```
c       Matrix-vector multiply, single-stream
c       Initialize once, perform multiply many times.
c       This is a toy program to illustrate
c       parallel program structure.
        .
        .
        .
c       initialize
            loop = 1
            do 1 i = 1,n
                c(i) = 0.
                do 2 j = 1,n
                    a(i,j) = float(j)
    2           continue
    1       continue
c       do matrix-vector multiply 10 times
    5       continue
            call matrix_vector_multiply(a,c,c,n)
            loop = loop + 1
            (use result here)
            if (loop .le. 10) goto 5
            end


        subroutine matrix_vector_multiply(a,b,c,n)
c       do a * b = c, a matrix,b,c, vectors
c       b,c can be the same array.
            real a(n,n),b(n),c(n),sum,x(1000)
            integer n,i,j
            do 1 i = 1,n
                sum = 0
                do 2 j = 1,n
                    sum = sum + a(i,j) * b(j)
    2           continue
                x(i) = sum
    1       continue
            do 3 i = 1,n
                c(i) = x(i)
```

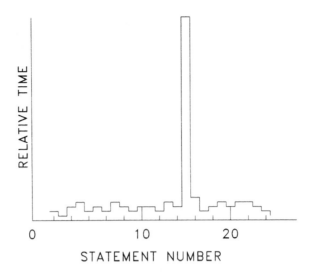

Figure 11-1.   Schematic histogram of the execution time for each statement of Program 11-1.

```
3          continue
           return
           end
```

Program 11-1

A *profile* of a program is a histogram which shows the amount of time spent executing each source statement (which normally is expanded to more than one machine instruction). A profile of Program 11-1 is presented in Figure 11-1.

According to Fig. 11-1, most time is spent on statement 15, which actually performs the matrix-vector multiply and is within a double loop. The initialization is performed only once and does not involve any arithmetic, so that statement 5 of Program 11-1 (also executed within a double loop) requires much less time than statement 15.

In creating the parallel version of 11-1, then, the profile indicates that the effort of parallelizing the initialization portion (do 1 and do 2 loops of main) will yield an insignificant payoff, in the sense that the decrease in execution time of the program would be negligible. Even if the execution time of the initialization loops were reduced to 0, the decrease in execution time of 11-1 would be insignificant.

Similarly, parallelization of the do 3 loop of the subroutine will not decrease execution time significantly.

On the other hand, parallelizing the do 1 and do 2 loops of subroutine matrix_vector_multiply would yield a much higher payoff in the form of decreased execution time. It is here, then, that the parallel programming effort should be concentrated.

The parallel version of 11-1 is (taking the simplest approach)

```
c       Matrix-vector multiply, parallel version
c       Initialize once, perform multiply many times.
c       Parallelize matrix-vector multiply, not initialization.
        .
        .
        .
        call shared(bar,16)
        .
        .
        .
        call barrier_init(bar)
        id = process_fork(nproc)

c       initialize
        loop = 1
        if (id .ne. 0) goto 6
        do 1 i = 1,n
            c(i) = 0.
            do 2 j = 1,n
                a(i,j) = float(j)
2           continue
1       continue
6       continue

c       barrier for initialization
        call barrier(bar)

5       continue
        call matrix_vector_multiply(a,c,c,n,id,nproc,bar)
        loop = loop + 1
        (use results)
        if (loop .le. 10) goto 5
        call process_join()
        end

        subroutine matrix_vector_multiply(a,b,c,n,id,nproc,bar)
c       do a * b = c, a matrix, b,c, vectors
c       parallel version
        real a(n,n),b(n),c(n),sum,x(1000)
        integer n,i,j,bar(1),id,nproc
```

```
        do 1 i = 1 + id,n,nproc
            sum = 0
            do 2 j = 1,n
                sum = sum + a(i,j) * b(j)
2           continue
            x(i) = sum
1       continue

        call barrier(bar)

        if (id .eq. 0) then
            do 3 i = 1,n
                c(i) = x(i)
3           continue
        endif

        call barrier(bar)

        return
        end
```

Program 11-2

Note that process_fork and process_join are called only once each, thus minimizing the overhead of these functions. (See the discussion in the next section.) In addition, the iterations over the variable loop can only be done sequentially, because of the data dependency involving c(i).

A more abstract view of the execution of a single-stream program is illustrated in Fig. 11-2. There, the looping line depicts the sequence in which program statements are executed. The vertical axis of the figure is the statement number of the source code. No assumptions are made about the program, which can include subroutine and function calls and gotos.

Normally, for programs doing technical calculations, the vast majority of time is spent in loops. (We neglect recursive calls, which should not be used in the time-critical parts of programs unless the compiler can convert the recursion to loops.) This situation is illustrated in Fig. 11-2 by the sections, denoted A, B, C, D, and E. It is clear that the most time is spent in section A, followed by B. Very little time is spent in sections C, D, or E or the other portions of the program which are executed only a few times.

One would obtain the most effective payback from parallelization by writ-

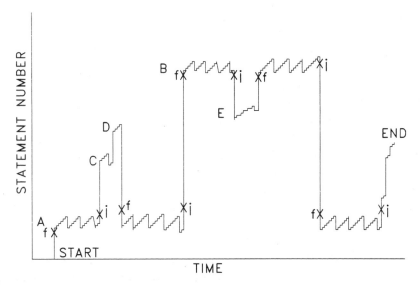

Figure 11-2. Schematic illustration of the execution of a hypothetical program in which most of the time is spent executing only a few statements.

ing sections A and B in parallel, leaving the rest of the program to execute single-stream.

11.3   Positioning the process_fork

The nature of the process_fork is more complex than has been indicated by the discussion of the previous chapters. Depending on the implementation, the time required for the process_fork, or for an operation which is logically equivalent to the process_fork, can range from microseconds to tens of milliseconds, and even longer.

The time required for the process_fork and the effect of this time on performance has an important influence on where the process_fork is placed in the program. This, in turn, affects the structure of the program—how easy the program is to understand, to modify, and to support.

The issues can be illustrated by referring to Program 11-2. In 11-2, the process_fork occurs at the beginning of the program. Since the initialization section is not done in parallel, it was necessary to redirect the children to bypass the initialization, so that they only execute the subroutine doing the matrix-vector multiply. Within this subroutine, the children were shunted around the do 3 loop. (In this toy case, it would have been easier to parallelize the do 3 loop directly. The reader should attend to the spirit of the example, rather than to the letter of it.)

A more logical place for the process_fork would be at the beginning of the subroutine matrix_vector_multiply. The join would follow statement label 1. In this case, new processes would be process_forked and joined 10 times, each time the matrix−vector_multiply subroutine was invoked. If the process_fork required a relatively long execution time (compared to the time spent in the remainder of the subroutine), then the execution time required for the entire program might be greatly increased by this latter arrangement.

While 11-2 is an artificial example, it does illustrate the trade-off between performance and program modifiability which is frequently encountered in any real application. If executing the process_fork is time consuming, the best thing from the performance point of view is to execute it once, at the beginning of the program, and then to manipulate the children in such a way that they bypass the single-stream sections of the program. This, however, introduces greater program complexity in the form of logic to manipulate the children. If, on the other hand, the process_fork is not time consuming (or will not cause a significant performance degradation if called repeatedly), then it is best to place it as close as possible to the parallel parts of the program and to destroy the children (or idle them somehow) when the parallel section is complete. This allows much simpler program structure.

The principle is illustrated in a more abstract way in Fig. 11-2. The simplest, most logical thing to do is to process_fork everywhere that an "f" appears in the figure and to join where there is a "j." If this introduces too much overhead, then one must process_fork once, when the program starts, and then manipulate the children, which may greatly increase the complexity of the program.

As a further illustration of this point, consider the following simple program fragment (which is similar to one that the author actually encountered but did not create):

```
          .
          .
          .
   10     continue
          call sub1(kxt)
          if (kxt .eq. 1) goto 5
    6     continue
          call sub2(a,b,c)
```

```
5    continue
     call sub3(w)
     call sub1(kxz)
     if (kxz .ne. 4) goto 6
     call sub5(x)
     loop = loop + 1
     if (loop .le. n) goto 10
        .
        .
        .
```

Program 11-3

Suppose that the majority of time is taken in sub1, so that sub1 is the only routine that needs to be written in parallel. If the overhead for the pro-cess_fork is large, so that one is forced to process_fork once only, at the start, the parallel version of 11-3 would look like the following:

```
        .
        .
        .
     id = process_fork(nproc)
10   continue
     call sub1(kxt)
     call barrier(bar)
     if (kxt .eq. 1) goto 5
6    continue
     if (id .eq. 0) call sub2(a,b,c)
     call barrier(bar)
5    continue
     if (id .eq. 0) call sub3(w)
     call barrier(bar)
     call sub1(kxz)
     call barrier(bar)
     if (kxz .ne. 4) goto 6
     if (id .eq. 0) call sub5(x)
     call barrier(bar)
     loop = loop + 1
     if (loop .ne. n) goto 10
        .
        .
        .
```

Program 11-4

If, on the other hand, the process_fork did not introduce much overhead, then the process_forks could be placed in subroutine sub1 itself, and parallelization would leave 11-3 untouched.

Regardless of one's opinions about the use of gotos in 11-3 (and 11-3 is reasonably well written by the standards of technical computing), 11-4 is far more difficult to follow than 11-3.

Up to now, it has been assumed that the consequence of calling the process_fork is that the region of memory occupied by the parent is copied en masse (except for the shared area) and that the copies become the children. The time required for such an implementation is then *at least* the time required for the copying. If a program has four MByte of instructions and data, and if very little of the data is shared, and a four byte copy requires a microsecond (which is reasonable performance), then the process_fork would take a full second of real time, a considerable performance penalty.

It turns out that this copying is in fact an implementation issue and is not necessarily a fundamental part of the process_fork concept. The logical nature of the process_fork is this: *a* process_fork *starts up a number of additional, identical (except for process-id number) processes, which run concurrently with the process which called the* process_fork. Note the use of *starts up* rather than creates in the above description. This start-up may involve a complete copy of the parent, but it need not. One new approach utilizing *threads* allows an operation logically equivalent to the fork to be executed very rapidly. The thread can be considered, conceptually, a "lightweight" process, which can be manipulated rapidly, as is now discussed. There are many different ways of implementing a threadlike concept, and the description below is just one possibility. The discussion of threads presented here is superficial and is meant to convey the general idea of what happens.

In the thread approach, the desired number of processes are created only once, when the program is loaded into memory from disk, by copying the parent. Normally, as many processes are created as there are available processors. Most of the variables in the program would be shared, and the instructions are shared, so that the children do not occupy much extra memory.

Following the load, only the parent process is allowed to execute. The children are held in abeyance. That is, the children occupy memory but are not actually running on a processor. They are idle, in a kind of suspended animation.

When the parent calls the process_fork, the children begin executing *from that place in the program*. Since the children have already been created, the only overhead required is to get the children running from the appropriate place in the program. This can take tens of microseconds.

When a child arrives at a `process_join`, it is put back in suspended animation rather than destroyed and can be restarted rapidly with the next `process_fork` call.

In this implementation, then, the function call

```
id = process_fork(nproc)
```

does not initiate a Unix-like fork (in which new processes are created by making copies of the parent) but merely starts up preexisting threads. Logically (from the point of view of the operation of the program rather than its performance) the user cannot tell if a Unix-like fork occurred or a thread was started up.

If the parallel programming library being used has a threadlike implementation, there will normally be separate subroutine calls to create the processes, define the threads, and start up the threads. However, from a logical point of view, the use of the `process_fork` will serve as well.

In summary, then, the `process_fork` function may represent either a Unix-like fork, in which multiple copies of the parent are made and which can require tens of milliseconds or longer, or it can represent the start-up of preexisting threads, which can take only a few tens of microseconds. Both operations—fork and threads—are *logically* equivalent, and the functionality available to the user will depend upon his particular hardware and software. The implementation and the performance goals will then affect the structure of the program. One consequence of this is that, at least for the present, creating programs which have the combined attributes of being efficient, simply structured, and portable may not be possible.

11.4   The Effect of the Number of Processes on Overhead

Typically, the execution times of synchronization functions, and of the sequential parts of a parallel program, increase with the number of processes. This is illustrated by the familiar fragment below, which sums the elements of an array in parallel.

```
c       Sum elements of array. Variable sum is shared.
c       This program illustrates performance issues
        .
        .
        .
        sum = 0
        call barrier_init(bar)
        id = process_fork(nproc)
c       start timing here
            tem = 0
c       this is the core loop
            do 1 i = 1 + id,n,nproc
                tem = tem + a(i)
  1         continue
c       this part is overhead
            call spin_lock(lok)
                sum = sum + tem
            call spin_unlock(lok)
            call barrier(bar)
c       end of timed section
        .
        .
        .
```

Program 11-5

The timed section of the program is indicated by the comments. The part of the program from do 1 to 1 continue is the "core" parallelized part, and the time to execute it is

$$n * t_L/nproc \tag{11-1}$$

(assuming that n is a multiple of nproc) where t_L is the time to execute one iteration of the loop (hence the L), including the loop overhead. This time decreases with the number of processes and increases with n, the size of the problem. *The performance gain of parallelization is entirely summed up in expression (11-1), giving a decreased execution time with increasing number of processes.*

After executing the loop the appropriate number of times, each process carries out four "overhead" steps: calls the spin-lock, updates the shared variable sum, unlocks the spin-lock, and calls the barrier. If the time for one process to execute these four statements is t_0 (0 for overhead), then for the worst case, the overhead is done sequentially, and the total amount of time required for the overhead is approximately

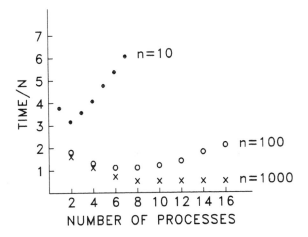

Figure 11-3.   Graph of equation (11-3).

$$nproc * t_0 \tag{11-2}$$

This time is independent of n, the size of the problem, but it increases with the number of processes. This works against the decrease in execution time of the loop part with increasing number of processes.

The time to execute the entire timed section of 11-5 is then

$$execution\ time = n * t_L/nproc + nproc * t_0 \tag{11-3}$$

Figure 11-3 shows the magnitude of this execution time. In this figure, we have chosen values of t_L and t_0 which are characteristic of current multiprocessor computers. We have selected

t_L = 3 microseconds
t_0 = 8 microseconds

Consider first the case for n = 10 and n = 100 in Fig. 11-3. For these cases, the execution time for a small number of processes is long. As the number of processes increases from 2, the execution time decreases. However, as more and more processes are added, the execution time goes through a minimum and then begins to actually increase.

This changeover, from decrease to increase, is a consequence of the fact that, as nproc increases, the amount of overhead increases to the extent where it dominates the execution time of the calculation.

As n, the size of the problem, increases, the curves of Fig. 11-3 shift to the right. More and more time is spent in the "core" part of the program. The amount of time spent on overhead stays the same and becomes *relatively* less significant. Finally, when n becomes very large, the overhead time is negligible, and adding processes always results in a decrease of execution time.

The moral of this story is that *increasing the number of processes which execute a parallel program may result in a performance degradation, particularly if the size of the problem is small.*

Whether or not the total release time of a barrier increases with the number of processes being released depends on the implementation. If the hardware is such that processes must be released at a barrier one by one, then the time to execute a barrier will increase with increasing number of processes. If the implementation is such that all processes can be released simultaneously, then the time for the barrier will be independent of the number of processes.

In summary, for a calculation being done in parallel, it is possible that increasing the number of processes does not always lead to a decrease in execution time. This effect is most pronounced when the problem size is relatively small. A programming project which creates a "souped-up" Gaussian elimination, and which must take into account the behavior described in this section, is given in Chapter 16.

Problem: Estimate the overhead, and the speedup when overhead is taken into account, for the several versions of the "histogram" and "max value" programs of previous chapters. Assume that each call to a spin-lock takes 5 microseconds. Assume that the time to execute the barrier is 20 + 5 * nproc microseconds. Do not include the times for the process_fork and process_join in the overhead times. Calculate the speedup for nproc = 2, 10, 20 and n = 10, 20, 50, 100, 500, 1000, 10000.

11.5   Using Cache Effectively

Minicomputers and microcomputers depend upon effective use of cache memory to achieve high performance. Normally, one does not take cache into account when creating programs, but some elementary considerations can make a difference of more than a factor of two in execution time. This is particularly true of computers which run at more than 10 MIPS (million

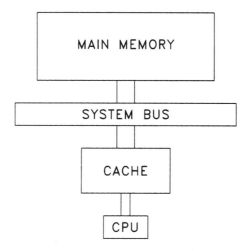

Figure 11-4.   Schematic illustration of the logical position of cache memory. Memory accesses by the CPU are first referred to cache, and then, if the location is not there, to main memory.

instructions per second) and which can execute more than 2 million floating point operations per second.

A schematic illustration of the place of cache in minicomputer hardware is illustrated in Fig. 11-4. The main memory is relatively inexpensive random-access memory. The amount of main memory typically varies from .5 to 2 Mbytes in microcomputers to more than 100 MBytes in multiuser minicomputers. The access time for any 32 bit word from main memory is normally a few hundred nanoseconds. Adding in the time for the bus transactions increases the time for a memory access to .5 to 1 microsecond. If this were the only computer memory, it would limit the rate of executing integer machine instructions to less than two million per second.

The size of cache memory is typically 32 to 256 KByte, and a 32 bit word in cache can normally be accessed in a few tens of nanoseconds. This memory is considerably more expensive than main memory, and consequently it is used sparingly.

The importance of the cache is that *the cache memory contains a copy of the data in main memory*. If the CPU could do all its calculations by utilizing only cache memory, then the memory access rate would allow some 50 million integer machine instructions a second, a performance considerably greater than that obtained if only main memory were available.

Normally, some of the data or instructions a program needs is located in cache, and some is not located there. (The cache is too small to hold every-

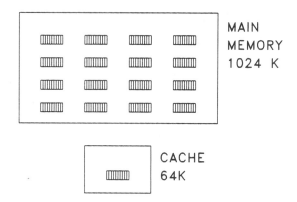

Figure 11-5. Illustration of direct-mapping of main memory to cache.

thing.) For computers with cache, a memory access occurs as follows. The CPU requests a word at a particular main memory address. If a copy of the word is located in cache, it is delivered immediately to the CPU, in a time appropriate for the cache (tens of nanoseconds for most minicomputers). If a copy of the word is not found in the cache, then the request must go out on the bus and the CPU must halt until the data becomes available. The data is transferred from main memory to the cache, where it updates the appropriate cache location. The CPU then accesses the data from the cache, as it tried to do in the first place, and this time the attempt is successful.

One of the consequences of cache, then, is that if the instructions and/or data are available in cache, and do not have to be transferred from main memory (over the bus), the calculation can proceed at a greater rate than if they are not in the cache.

The problem with cache is that there is so little of it, so that the entire process—instructions, data, and administrative area—cannot all fit into the cache at one time. What is normally done is that many different locations of main memory correspond to a single location of cache. This is known as *mapping* the main memory to cache. There are many ways to arrange this mapping, and these are beyond the scope of this book. One common arrangement, called *direct mapping*, is illustrated in Fig. 11-5.

Suppose in Fig. 11-5 that the cache is 64K. Then main memory is imagined as being divided into 64K blocks, and the byte that is offset by w from the start of any 64K block in main memory corresponds to the wth byte of cache. The cache holds instructions, data and anything else. Every time the CPU reads from or writes to main memory, for any reason, the appropriate cache location is updated. On a write, the most common implementations update main memory simultaneously with updating the cache, although this is not necessary.

The effectiveness of the cache depends on the behavior of the program. As discussed in Section 11.2, and shown in Fig. 11-2, many programs spend most of their time looping through a small number of statements. If the amount of data accessed in these loops is also relatively small, then once the cache is set up with instructions and data, the calculation can proceed rapidly, doing virtually all reads from cache. On the other hand, if the program jumps around, or if it accesses a large amount of data in a random fashion, then the cache will not help performance very much, because the chances are that the data will not be there.

Of course, a program also writes data, altering the values in main memory. In the simplest caching algorithms, writes always go onto the bus, updating both main memory and cache simultaneously. This takes $\frac{1}{2}$ to 1 microseconds normally and so could be a bottleneck. However, on the average, most programs write only once for every six reads (a program rarely writes its instructions). Also, modern caching algorithms allow for writes that do not go onto the bus. These issues are beyond the scope of this book.

In the case of multiprocessor computers, the cache has another function besides providing a performance enhancement for each processor. Many commercial multiprocessor computers have the bus design of Figure 3-2(a), and the cache helps minimize bus traffic. All the processors must access memory through the common bus, which could become a bottleneck. If a processor can do its reads from cache, and if all its writes need not go onto the bus and into main memory, then bus traffic is minimized and performance is enhanced.

To make effective use of cache, one should try to arrange data so that the processors can work out of cache. This normally involves paying attention to the dimension of arrays and grouping the data into blocks, depending on how the data is accessed. These considerations are valid for both uniprocessor and multiprocessor computers.

In the case of multiprocessors, the general principle to adhere to is as follows: *if each process is to access some subset of a data pool repeatedly, have each process always access the same subset.* Once the cache of a processor is loaded, that processor will be able to work out of cache. In this way, the data is not constantly being transferred between the caches of different processors via main memory.

There is flexibility here which is not present in uniprocessors. The idea is illustrated by considering a fragment similar to a portion of Gaussian elimination. (The algorithm for Gaussian elimination is presented in Chapter 13, where the ideas described below are incorporated.) The single stream fragment is

```
c       Gaussian elimination fragment-single stream
        real a(100,101),...
             .
             .
             .
        do 1 krow = 1,n - 1
            do 2 jrow = krow + 1,n
                t = -a(jrow,krow)/a(krow,krow)
                do 3 m = krow + 1,n + 1
                    a(jrow,m) = a(jrow,m) + t * a(krow,m)
3               continue
2           continue
1       continue
```

Program 11-6

Program 11-6 processes array a(i,j) row by row. The do 1 loop picks out the row number krow to be processed. For each krow, all the rows jrow below krow are manipulated. The do 2 loop processes rows jrow which lie below row krow. The do 3 loop manipulates the individual elements of row jrow.

It may be useful to consider some sample iterations. If krow = 1, then rows 2, 3, 4, ..., n are processed in the do 2 and do 3 loops. If krow = 2, then rows 3, 4, 5, ..., n are processed by the two inner loops. If krow = 3, then rows 4, 5, 6,..., n are processed. It is seen that many rows are processed more than once. For example, row 3 is processed twice, row 4 three times, and so forth.

One possible parallelized version of this program, using loop splitting, is

```
c       Gaussian elimination fragment-parallel version
c       uses loop splitting. Backward iteration of "do 2"
c       loop allows processors to work out of cache as
c       much as possible.

        real a(100,101),...
        integer bar(4)
c       a, bar shared
             .
             .
             .
        call barrier_init(bar,nproc)
```

```
        id = process_fork(nproc)
        do 1 krow = 1,n - 1
            do 2 jrow = n - id,krow + 1,-nproc
                t = -a(jrow,krow)/a(krow,krow)
                do 3 m = krow + 1,n
                    a(jrow,m) = a(jrow,m) + t * a(krow,m)
3               continue
2           continue
            call barrier(bar)
1       continue
```

Program 11-7

The important feature is the loop

```
        do 2 jrow = n - id,krow + 1,-nproc
```

which *iterates over the rows in reverse order*, from the bottom up. This makes sure that, as krow advances, each process always executes the same values of jrow, time after time. Thus process 0 manipulates rows n, n − nproc, n − 2 * nproc, etc. Process 1 executes rows n − 1, n − nproc − 1, n − 2 * nproc − 1 and so forth. After the appropriate data a(jrow,1), a(jrow,2),... is loaded into cache, the same data is accessed over and over again from cache rather than from main memory. If the program is run on a high-performance multiprocessor computer, this trick can result in more than a factor of two enhancement in performance.

CHAPTER 12

Discrete Event, Discrete Time Simulation

12.1 Introduction

In this chapter, the subjects of data dependency and contention for data structures are illustrated by examining a relatively simple discrete event, discrete time simulation. Contention refers to a situation in which more than one process tries to alter a data structure at the same time, as described in Chapter 5. Data dependencies were introduced in Chapter 8. Data dependencies and contention in discrete event simulation are more complex than in the relatively simple examples discussed up to now. This chapter should give the reader a flavor for how hindrances to parallel performance are circumvented in a real application.

Discrete event simulators are used to simulate systems which can be modeled as a collection of discrete components interacting with each other, and whose actions are, or can be modeled as, a sequence of well-defined, atomic *events*. An event is an action taken by a component, and normally results in the alteration of the contents of data structures.

Discrete event simulators can model computers, antimissile systems, military battles, factories, and physical systems, among other things. For example, in modeling a computer, the components can be the individual gates. In the case of an antimissile system, the discrete components may be radar installations, missiles, command posts, targets, defense weapons, and whatever else is required. For battle simulation, the components are those individual subgroups deemed useful, such as individual tanks, platoons, etc. For modeling a factory, the components include portions of the assembly line, control center, inventory delivery systems (trucks), shipping room, warehouse, and so forth. Each component of the system can do the equivalent of reading from and writing to other components, which can alter the state of behavior of both components.

The example presented here is a model of a physical system, namely a collection of billiard balls constrained to move in one dimension. Although simulating this system is not trivial, the example is chosen for its relative simplicity.

In a discrete time simulation, the passage of time occurs in discrete intervals. This is either an approximation to the actual situation, or, as in the present case, the problem lends itself to this treatment. At the start of each time interval, each component can ascertain the state of the other components, either in the immediate past or for all previous time, and act accordingly. One component can send other components data directly, if desired, and components can share memory.

In the type of event simulator described here, the central data structure is a queue of *possible* events, called an *event queue*. Events are placed on the event queue and are ordered according to the times that the events will occur. These events will not *necessarily* happen in the future, but they will occur if there is no interference from the consequences of other events.

The simulator loops through the following sequence of actions:

1. Get the next events, i.e., the events that will occur at the earliest time.
2. Execute the events. That is, carry out the action of the events.
3. Compute alterations to the event queue, because the execution of the events may have affected other events occurring later.

One way to parallelize an event simulator is to have each process execute different events at the same time. (If it is possible to execute a single event in parallel in an efficient manner, then few of the problems described below will arise.) Since different events may occur at different times, it frequently happens that, while one process executes an event, another process will, at the same real (i.e. programmer's) time, execute an event which takes place later in simulation time. There are data dependencies between events because the occurrence of an event at one time can alter the nature, and even the existence, of an event at a later time (as occurs in the example described below). This means that the processes executing events in parallel cannot proceed in isolation but must interact.

Interaction among processes can occur in many ways, two of which are (a) a process can alter the nature, or existence, of a later event, at the same time that another process is executing that (the later) event, and (b) processes may try to update the event queue in parallel, so that this queue requires protection. Both types of interaction tend to serialize the simulation and decrease the speedup obtainable by parallelization. Both of these categories are relevant to the simulation described in this chapter.

12.2   Description of the Model

The system to be simulated is a collection of billiard balls which are restricted to move in one dimension only—say along the x-axis. One can imagine the balls as being in a long, narrow box, of length L, whose width is just slightly greater than the diameter of the balls. The balls move without friction, and the ends of the box are closed.

Initially, the balls are placed in some positions and start out with some distribution of velocities, whose details do not concern us here. As time passes, adjacent balls collide, as in Figure 12-1. The time duration of a collision is so small that any collision involves exactly two balls. If two pairs

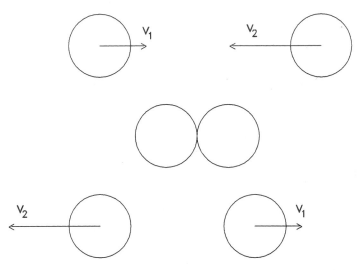

Figure 12-1.   Illustration of a billiard ball collision, in which the colliding balls interchange velocities.

happen to collide at exactly the same time, the events can be executed one after another, as if one collision took place an instant after the other.

According to Newton's laws of physics, the two balls involved in a collision interchange velocities, so that after collision each ball has the velocity which the other had before the collision (see Fig. 12-1). When a ball collides with a wall at the end of the box, its velocity is reversed. Between collisions, each ball moves in a straight line at constant velocity.

The activity of the system is then a sequence of *events*, each event being a collision between two of the balls. Between events, nothing happens except that the balls move in a straight line at constant velocity. Every time there is an event, two balls interchange velocities. The system is then modeled as proceeding from event to event.

Each neighboring pair of balls can be characterized by a *time-to-collision*, which is the time at which the next collision between those balls occurs, assuming that neither ball undergoes a collision with its other neighbor. The time-to-collision is a time at which a collision would potentially occur if the pair of balls did not collide with anything else. Some neighboring pairs of balls may not be on a potential collision path. (For example, they may be moving away from each other.)

The *event queue* is an ordered, doubly linked list of the times-to-collision, along with the pair of balls that will be involved in the collision. The next event of importance is then the collision occurring the soonest.

A simple illustration of the way in which the system proceeds from one event to another is given in Fig. 12-2. There, four balls are in the one-dimensional box, with left wall at 0, the right wall at 10 cm, and each ball has a diameter of 1 cm (these are small billiard balls). The arrows on the balls show the direction of motion, and the numbers on the arrows give the velocity in cm/sec. The vertical lines below the horizontal axis label the position of the balls, in cm.

The variable tnow is the time, which starts at 0 seconds. Figure 12-2(a) shows the initial positions of the balls. Initially, balls 2 and 3 potentially will be involved in two collisions each, while balls 1 and 4 are potentially involved in only one. For the (3,4) collision, ball 4 will catch up with ball 3. The same is true for (2,3).

The event queue, also shown in Fig. 12-2, holds the colliding pair and the time in seconds at which that pair will collide (the *time-to-collision*). The collisions on the event queue need not definitely take place. They are potential collisions and will occur only if no other balls interfere. This will become clear as the example unfolds.

According to the event queue, the first collision occurs at time 1/2 seconds

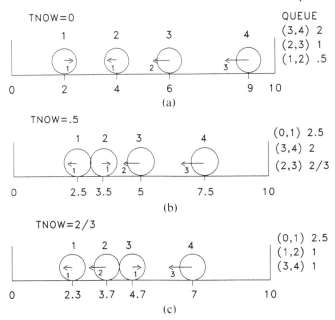

Figure 12.2 Illustration of the event queue for the first two collisions of a system of four balls.

and will involve balls 1 and 2. The time tnow can then be updated to 1/2 seconds, and each ball moved in a straight line at its velocity for a time of 1/2. (The unit of seconds for time will be assumed.) The state of the system at the instant following this collision is shown in Fig. 12-2(b). At a collision, the balls interchange velocities. (Because the balls have equal velocities, the new velocities are the same as the old. Note the change of direction of motion of balls 1 and 2.)

The event queue has also been updated in Fig. 12-2(b). Balls 1 and 2 will no longer collide, so this pair doesn't appear on the updated queue. The collision between balls 2 and 3 has been altered. After the (1,2) collision, ball 2 is traveling in the opposite direction and will collide with ball 3 earlier than the time that was indicated on the event queue initially (Fig. 12-2(a)). This is an example in which one event alters another event on the event queue. In addition, at time 5/2, there is an additional collision between ball 1 and the left wall (denoted by a 0). Ball 1, having reversed direction because of the (1,2) collision, will now collide with the left wall. This is an example of one event causing another event to be added to the event queue.

According to the event queue, the next event will occur at a time of 2/3. The system at a time just after the event is shown in Fig. 12-2(c), as is the updated event queue. In this case, the (3,4) collision has been altered by the event, in that it will occur sooner than was indicated in the event queue in Fig. 12-2(b). As a consequence of the (2,3) collision, a potential (1,2) collision will now occur, and this is added to the event queue.

The fact that collisions (1,2) and (3,4) will both occur at time 1 is an accident of the fact that simple round numbers are used in this example. This will be a very rare case in a realistic simulation, where positions and velocities will be characterized by random numbers with 32 or 64 bit accuracy. Another way of looking at this is that the two collisions occur nearly at the same time. They can still be handled separately.

We point out that, if the billiard balls were in a three-dimensional box (rather than a one-dimensional one), the model becomes what is called the hard-sphere liquid, which is a common and accurate model for many kinds of liquids, particularly liquid metals. It is not uncommon for simulations of this type to contain several thousand balls. For the one-dimensional system, the calculation can proceed so efficiently that tens of thousands of balls may be simulated with a 5 to 20 MIP computer.

12.3   Single-Stream Algorithm and Data Structures

A simple algorithm for simulating this system single-stream is

Initialize—get ball positions and initialize the event queue.

do nstep times

1. Find the pair of balls (i, i + 1) which have the smallest time-to-collision. This time-to-collision is the smallest time on the event queue. Let dt be the time interval at the end of which the pair collide. (That is, if tnow is the current time, and tcol is the time-to-collision of the pair, then

    dt = tcol − tnow

2. Move all balls in a straight line. If the velocity of the ith ball is v(i), then move the ith ball a distance v(i)*dt. Do the same for ball i + 1. After this, balls i and i + 1 will be just touching.

3. Interchange the velocities of the two colliding balls (or, if the ball is bouncing off the wall, reverse its velocity).

4. Remove all collisions involving balls i and i + 1 from the event queue. (Because i and i + 1 collided, the time-to-collision of ball i with ball i − 1, and of ball i + 1 with ball i + 2, will be different than the times on the event queue. Note that i and i + 1 can no longer collide with each other.)

5. Compute the new times-to-collision of i and i + 1 with their neighbors, and put the new times-to-collision on the event queue.

endo

While this algorithm will do the job, there is a performance penalty in the fact that, at each collision, the positions of *all* the balls must be updated, even for the balls not involved in the collision. (There may be thousands of balls, and only two of them are involved in any collision.) Since balls move in a straight line between collisions, it is not necessary to actually update the position of a ball if it is not involved in a collision. All that is necessary is to keep track of the last time that the ball was involved in a collision. Then step 2 is replaced by steps 2 and 2a below:

2. Move colliding balls i and i + 1 in a straight line. Let the time at which the last collision of ball i occurred be last_update_time(i). Then, if tnow is the current time, and if the velocity of the ith ball is v(i), then move the ith ball a distance

```
v(i) * (tnow - last_update_time(i) + dt),
```

and move ball i + 1 a distance

```
v(i+i) * (tnow - last_update_time(i + 1) + dt).
```

After this, balls i and i + 1 will be just touching.

2a. Update last_update_time, i.e.,

```
last_update_time(i) = last_update_time(i + 1) = tnow + dt.
```

In the introduction to this chapter, the three major steps of an event simulator had been outlined. One can now see how this particular example follows this general scheme.

1. Get the next event. In this case, find the smallest time-to-collision on the event queue, and get the associated pair of particles.
2. Carry out the action of the event. In this case, execute the collision.
3. Compute alterations to the event queue. In this case, this involves steps 4 and 5 of the algorithm, which is to remove all collisions involving the colliding pair from the event queue and replace them with the new times-to-collision of each colliding pair.

The implementation of the algorithm described above depends on the structure of the event queue. The structure to be used is chosen with an eye on the parallelization of this algorithm. To jump ahead a bit, if there are many more balls than processors (for example, 5000 balls and 10 processors), then it is likely that successive collisions will involve balls relatively far from each other. This means that, if there are nproc processes, we can execute nproc collisions simultaneously. An important consideration is the time required to find the next nproc collisions on the queue. If this is to be done in parallel, then the event queue should be divided into sections, such that each section holds only a few collisions, and processes can skip rapidly over sections to get the appropriate times.

The basic idea, then, is to subdivide the event queue into *bins*, such that each bin holds times-to-collision that occur within a narrow range of times. Each bin holds a small number of times. It is necessary that the event queue be a circular queue, as discussed below.

The modular structure of the event queue will also tend to reduce contention when the event queue must be updated in parallel by different processes.

The *logical* structure of the event queue, and its associated data structure, are illustrated in Fig. 12-3, for two bins. There are two doubly-linked lists, one for each bin. The first bin holds times-to-collision between 0 and 5, while the second holds times between 5 and 10. (A third bin would hold times between 10 and 15 and has its own doubly linked list, and so forth.) The start of the list for bin number ibin is pointed to by the array start_ time(ibin). Each member of the list holds the time-to-collision (t), one of the pair of balls involved in the collision (see below), and pointers to the next and previous members of the list. The pointers are labeled p and q.

It is necessary to keep a record of which balls are involved in a collision. Each ball can be involved in a collision with at most its two neighboring balls to the right and left. Thus, ball i can potentially collide with balls i − 1 and i + 1. (Balls i = 0 and i = n + 1 represent the walls and

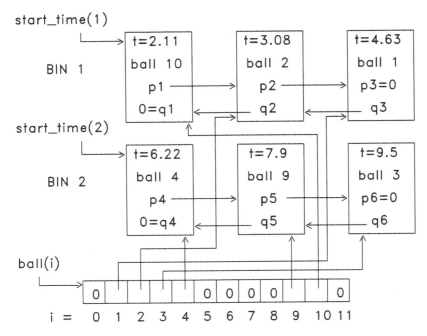

start_time(1)

Figure 12-3.   Illustration of the logical structure of the event queue.

are always stationary.) The code used is as follows: *if a collision is said to involve ball* i, *it means that the collision is between balls* i *and* i+1. Thus, in Fig. 12-3, in bin 1 the colliding pairs are (10,11), (2,3), and (1,2). In bin 2, the pairs of colliding balls are (4,5), (9,10), and (3,4).

The fact that the list is doubly linked expedites adding and removing events from the queue (step 4 of the algorithm).

To insert a time-to-collision tcol into the linked list, first its bin number is found from

$$\texttt{ibin = mod((tcol - tbase)/tbin, float(num\_bins)) + 1}$$

where tbase is a fixed past time and num_bins is the total number of bins in the queue. (The mod function mod(a,b) returns the remainder of a/b. This mod(10,2) = 0, while mod(11,2) = 1.) The above expression means that the list of bins is circular. For example, a time-to-collision tcol is stored in bin number 1 whenever the following are true:

```
0 < tcol - tbase < tbin
tbin * num_bins < tcol - tbase < tbin * num_bins + tbin
2 * tbin * num_bins < tcol - tbase < 2 * tbin *
num_bins + tbin
.
.
.
```

This means that there is a threshold time-to-collision such that if the actual `tcol` is larger than the threshold, it cannot be inserted into the queue (because it would possibly overwrite the part of the queue holding smaller times). At any instant `tnow`, the threshold time is

```
threshold = tnow + tbin * (num_bins - 1)
```

The variable `num_bins` is decremented by 1 in the above expression because, otherwise, a time just slightly less than `tnow + tbin * num_bins` would overlap the threshold bin.

Finally, the array `num_times(ibin)` equals the number of times-to-collision stored in bin number `ibin`. This array is used in the parallel version as follows: Process number `id` will process the `(id + 1)` smallest time-to-collision on the event queue. The process may use the array `num_times` to bypass a particular bin, so it does not have to follow all the pointers in the bin. For example, for the case of Fig. 12-3, the process with `id = 4` will execute the fifth smallest collision, and because

```
num_times(1) = 3,
```

the process need not sift through the times in the first bin. Because

```
num_times(2) = 3,
```

it must look for the second time in the second bin.

At this point, the reader should be sure he understands how the algorithm for the simulation of the system of billiard balls makes use of the data structures of Fig. 12-3.

12.4   Single-Stream Program

Implementing the linked-list structure in Fortran is not as straightforward as it would be in C or Pascal, where Fig. 12-3 would translate directly into the data structures. Rather, the data structures are explained below. They

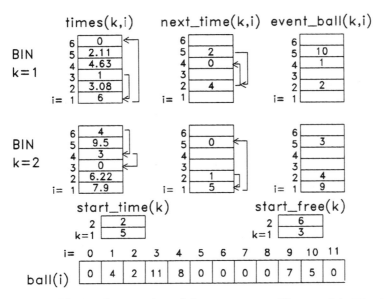

Figure 12-4.   The implementation of the event queue illustrated in Fig. 12-3.

are shown in Fig. 12-4, which describes the same situation as Fig. 12-3.

n—the number of balls.

L—the length of the "box" holding the balls.

x(i)—the position of the ith ball, i = 0, 1, 2, ..., n + 1. The "ball" at x(0) is the left wall, while the "ball" at x(n + 1) is the right wall. It is always the case that x(0) = −R and x(n + 1) = L + R, where R is the radius of a ball.

v(i)—the velocity of the ith ball, i = 0, 1, 2, ..., n + 1. It is always the case that v(0) = v(n + 1) = 0.

diameter—diameter of each ball.

num_bins—the total number of bins.

tbin—the collision time interval of a bin.

tnow—the current time.

max_slots—the maximum number of slots in any bin

times(ibin, k)—the collision times for bin number ibin. The integer k = 1, 2, ... indexes the times, but the times are not ordered in terms of k. (The variable k labels the *slots*.) For example, it is possible that `times(ibin,1) > times(ibin,2)`, but the reverse is also possible. If the time-to-collision is `tcol`, the time-to-collision is stored in bin number `ibin`, where

$$\text{ibin = mod((tcol - tbase)/tbin,num\_bins) + 1}$$

where `tbase` is some past time which has been chosen as a base point. The array `times` also contains the free-list pointers, as explained below.

`start_time(ibin)`—the smallest time in bin number `ibin` is

$$\text{times(ibin,start\_time(ibin)).}$$

If `start_time(ibin) = 0`, the bin is empty.

`next_time(ibin, k)`—in bin number `ibin`, the time-to-collision which is the next largest after `times(ibin,k)` is

$$\text{times(ibin,next\_time(ibin,k))}$$

If `next_time(ibin,k) = 0`, then `times(ibin,k)` is the largest time in the bin. This array is used to create the forward-linked list for bin number `ibin`.

`prev_time(ibin,k)`—like `next_time`, but for previous times. if `prev_time(ibin,k) = 0`, then `times(ibin,k)` is the smallest time in the bin. This array is used to create the backward-linked list for bin number `ibin`.

`num_times(ibin)`—the number of times-to-collision stored in bin number `ibin`.

`start_free(ibin)`—there is a linked list of free slots in each bin. The first slot in each list is `start_free(ibin)`. That is, `times(ibin,start_free(ibin))` is free to be assigned a time-to-collision. The position of the next free slot is stored in `times(ibin,k)` itself, for simplicity. Thus, if the first free slot is at

$$\text{kl = start\_free(ibin)}$$

then the next free slot is at

$$\text{k2 = int(times(ibin,kl))}$$

if k2 > 0. If k2 = 0, there is no next free slot. This mechanism is illustrated in Fig. 12-4, where the arrows delineate the free list.

`last_update_time(i)`—the last time that the position of ball i was updated. At time tnow, the true position of ball i is

$$v(i) * (tnow - last\_update\_time(i)).$$

`event_ball(ibin,k)`—the pair of balls involved in the collision whose time-to-collision is stored in `times(ibin,k)` is given by this array. If

$$i = event\_ball(ibin,k),$$

then the pair of balls (i, i + 1) are involved in the collision.

`ball(i)`—if `ball(i) > 0`, it means that balls i and i + 1 will potentially be involved in a future collision. If the time-to-collision is stored in `times(ibin,k)` then

$$ball(i) = (ibin - 1) * num\_slots + k$$

The time-to-collision of balls i and i + 1 is calculated from the formula

$$time\_to\_col = tnow + dt$$

where

$$dt = -(x(i) - x(i + 1) + 2 * radius)/(v(i) - v(i + 1))$$

for x(i) < x(i + 1). If dt is negative, the balls will not collide (they are moving away from each other).

The single-stream simulation is done in subroutine `time_steps`, which is

```
      subroutine time_steps(x,v,n,L,nstep,tbin,tnow,diameter,
     s                      num_slots,num_bins,times,next_time,
     s                      prev_time,start_time,start_free,
     s                      num_times,event_ball,ball,
     s                      last_update_time)
c
c     Follow motion of n billiard balls restrained to move in one
c     dimension for nstep collisions. All balls have unit mass
c     and the same diameter.
c     Balls 0 and n + 1 are the end walls. Balls have unit mass.
c     Single-stream program.
c     On entry, x(i), v(i) are true positions and velocities of
```

```
c       balls at time tnow. On exit, tnow has been updated and
c       x(i), v(i) are new true positions and velocities at the
c       new time tnow.
c       It is assumed that x(i) < x(i + 1). x(0) is the left
c       wall, and x(n + 1) is the right wall.
c       At the end of nsteps, the total kinetic energy and speed
c       are printed out. The energy and speed are unchanged during
c       the entire course of the simulation.


        integer n,nstep,num_slots,num_bins
        integer next_time(num_bins,1),prev_time(num_bins,1)
        integer start_time(1),start_free(1),ball(0:1)
        integer event_ball(num_bins,1),num_times(1)
        real x(0:1),v(0:1),diameter,L,tnow,tbase,tbin
        real times(num_bins,1),last_update_time(0:1)


        real queue_length,dt,radius,vtem,abs
        real tcol,get_time_to_col,energy,speed
        integer ibin,iplace,icol,i,j,k,mod,m

c       first executable statement
        queue_length = tbin * (num_bins - 1)
        tbase = 0.
        radius = .5 * diameter


c       ********************************************************
c       BEGIN INITIALIZATION SECTION
c       initialize the event queue and other arrays
        do 2 ibin = 1,num_bins
            num_times(ibin) = 0
            start_free(ibin) = 1
            start_time(ibin) = 0
            do 3 iplace = 1,num_slots
                next_time(ibin,iplace) = 0
                prev_time(ibin,iplace) = 0
c               initialize free list
                times(ibin,iplace) = iplace + 1 + .001
3           continue
c           last member of free list
            times(ibin,num_slots) = .001
2       continue

        do 4 i = 0,n + 1
            ball(i) = 0
            last_update_time(i) = tnow
4       continue
```

```
c       initialize the walls
        x(0) = 0. - radius
        v(0) = 0.
        x(n + 1) = L + radius
        v(n + 1) = 0.
c       add times to event queue
        do 6 i = 0,n
c               For each pair, (i,i + 1), get the time-to-collision
                tcol = get_time_to_col(i,queue_length,
     s          diameter,x,v,tnow,last_update_time)


c               Add this pair to the event queue if
c               tcol is positive.

                if (tcol .gt. 0.) then
                    call add_time_to_queue(i,tcol,tbase,tbin,
     s                      num_bins,num_times,num_slots,
     s                      start_free,times,ball,event_ball,
     s                      start_time,next_time,prev_time)
                endif
   6    continue


c               END OF INITIALIZATION SECTION
c       ********************************************************


c       Now do nstep collision
        do 100 icol = 1,nstep


c       -------------- get the next event to process --------------
c               Find pair i,j which have smallest time-to-collision
c               by getting the smallest time on the event queue.

c               smallest time should be in this bin.
                ibin = mod((tnow - tbase)/tbin,float(num_bins)) + 1


c               If ibin has no entries, move onto the next bin.
                do 11 m = 1,num_bins
                    if (num_times(ibin) .ne. 0) goto 12
                    ibin = ibin + 1
                    if (ibin .gt. num_bins) then
                        ibin = 1
                    endif
  11            continue
```

```
c                      if this error is found, try a larger value of
c                      tbin or increase the value of num_bins.
                       print *,'no times no event queue'
                       call exit()


  12                   continue


c                      find the slot k
                       k = start_time(ibin)


c                      find pair i,i + 1 of colliding balls
                       i = event_ball(ibin,k)
                       j = i+1
c
c                      recalculate the time-to-collision to correct
c                      for roundoff error. Roundoff error should not
c                      affect the order of times on the event_queue.
                       tcol = get_time_to_col(i,queue_length,
      s                diameter,x,v,tnow,last_update_time)


c                      update tnow.
c                      This next statement is the expression of the
c                      discrete-time nature of the simulator.
                       tnow = tcol

c      ------------- execute the event   -------------------------

c                      move balls i,j in straight line until they just
c                      touch. This is moment of collision.
                       x(i) = x(i) + v(i) * (tnow - last_update_time(i))
                       x(j) = x(j) + v(j) * (tnow - last_update_time(j))
                       last_update_time(i) = tnow
                       last_update_time(j) = tnow

c      find new velocities. Check for wall
                       if (i .eq. 0) then
c                          j hits wall
                           v(j) = -v(j)
                       elseif (i .eq. n) then
c                          i hits wall
                           v(i) = -v(i)
                       else
c                          no wall
                           vtem = v(i)
```

```
                      v(i) = v(j)
                      v(j) = vtem
              endif


c       ----------  update the event queue  ------------------------


c       remove all collisions involving balls i and j from the
c       event queue
            call remove_from_queue(i,ball,num_slots,times,
     s                             start_free,num_times,start_time,
     s                             next_time,prev_time,num_bins)


c       Add new collisions with balls i - 1, i + 1 to event queue.
c       Note - balls i, i + 1 cannot collide with each
c       other again until one of them collides with something else.
            j = i - 1
            do 60 m = 1,2
            tcol = get_time_to_col(j,queue_length,diameter,x,v,
     s                             tnow,last_update_time)
            if (tcol .gt. 0) then
                call add_time_to_queue(j,tcol,tbase,tbin,
     s                          num_bins,num_times,num_slots,
     s                          start_free,times,ball,event_ball,
     s                          start_time,next_time,prev_time)
            endif


            j = j + 2
 60         continue


 100        continue


c       Total energy and speed must be conserved.
            energy = 0.
            speed = 0.
            do 50 i = 1,n
                energy = energy +.5 * (v(i)**2)
                speed = speed + abs(v(i))
 50         continue
            print *,'energy =',energy


c       restore true positions of balls
            do 55 i = 1,n
                x(i) = x(i) + v(i) * (tnow - last_update_time(i))
```

```
55        continue

          return
          end
c         ***************************    get_time_to_col

          real function get_time_to_col(i,queue_length,
     s    diameter,x,v,tnow,last_update_time)

          integer i
          real queue_length,diameter,x(0:1),v(0:1),tnow
          real last_update_time(0:1)

          real delt,abs,small
          real x_tem_i,x_tem_il

c     delt is amount of time remaining before collision
c     will occur.
          small = 1.e - 36
          if (abs(v(i) - v(i + 1)) .lt. small) then
              delt = -1.
          elseif (v(i) - v(i + 1) .le. 0.) then
c             balls can't collide under this condition,
c             if x(i) < x(i + 1)
              delt = -1.
          else
              x_tem_i=x(i) + v(i) *
     s        (tnow - last_update_time(i))
              x_tem_il=x(i + 1)+v(i + 1) *
     s        (tnow - last_update_time(i + 1))
              delt = -(x_tem_i - x_tem_il + diameter)/
     s        (v(i) - v(i+1))
          endif
c     if delt < 0, particles will not collide
c     if delt > queue_length, time is greater than threshold
          if (( delt .lt. 0.) .or. (delt .gt. queue_length)) then
              get_time_to_col = -1.
          else
              get_time_to_col = tnow + delt
          endif

          return
          end


c         ***********************************  add_time_to_queue

          subroutine add_time_to_queue(i,tcol,tbase,tbin,
     s                        num_bins,num_times,num_slots,
```

```
     s                           start_free,times,ball,event_ball,
     s                           start_time,next_time,prev_time)

          integer i,num_bins,num_slots,num_times(1)
          integer ball(0:1),event_ball(num_bins,1)
          integer next_time(num_bins,1),prev_time(num_bins,1)
          integer start_time(1),start_free(1)
          real times(num_bins,1),tcol,tbase,tbin

          integer prev,k1,ktime
          integer mod,int,ibin,i,j,k

c     pair i,i + 1 will collide at time tcol. Add this time
c     and pair to the event queue.

c     find bin number
          ibin = mod((tcol - tbase)/tbin,float(num_bins)) + 1

          if (num_times(ibin) .eq. num_slots) then
              print *,'no more room on queue,bin # ',ibin
              call exit()
          endif

c     The following bookkeeping takes place no matter what
c     the situation. Put new time-to-collision in slot k1.

          k1 = start_free(ibin)
c     next free slot is given by contents of times(ibin,k1).
          start_free(ibin) = int(times(ibin,k1))
          times(ibin,k1) = tcol
          ball(i) = (ibin - 1) * num_slots + k1
          event_ball(ibin,k1) = i

c     check if bin number ibin is empty
          if (num_times(ibin) .eq. 0) then
              start_time(ibin) = k1
              next_time(ibin,k1) = 0
              num_times(ibin) = 1
              prev_time(ibin,k1) = 0
              return
          endif

          num_times(ibin) = num_times(ibin) + 1
c     now find the position of tcol in the linked
c     list of times
```

```
            ktime = start_time(ibin)
            if (tcol .lt. times(ibin,ktime)) then
c                  now tcol becomes the smallest time in the bin
                   start_time(ibin) = kl
                   next_time(ibin,kl) = ktime
                   prev_time(ibin,ktime) = kl
                   prev_time(ibin,kl) = 0
                   return
            else
c                  now tcol is greater than the smallest time in
c                  the bin.
 100               continue
                   prev = ktime
                   ktime = next_time(ibin,ktime)
                   if (ktime .gt. 0) then
                       if (tcol .lt. times (ibin,ktime)) then
c                              now tcol comes after the time in slot
c                              prev and before the time in slot ktime.
                               next_time(ibin,prev) = kl
                               prev_time(ibin,kl) = prev
                               next_time(ibin,kl) = ktime
                               prev_time(ibin,ktime) = kl
                               return
                       else
                           goto 100
                       endif
                   else
c                      now tcol will become the largest time
c                      in the bin. times(ibin,prev) becomes the
c                      second-to-largest time.
                       next_time(ibin,prev) = kl
                       next_time(ibin,kl) = 0
                       prev_time(ibin,kl) = prev
                       return
                   endif
            endif

            return
            end


c     ********************************* remove_from_queue

        subroutine remove_from_queue (i,ball,num_slots,times,
     s                         start_free,num_times,start_time,
     s                         next_time,prev_time,num_bins)

        integer i,ball(0:1),num_slots,start_free(1)
```

```
            integer start_time(1),next_time(num_bins,1)
            integer prev_time(num_bins,1),num_times(1)
            real times(num_bins,1)

            integer j,ibin,k,knext,kprev

c     Remove all collision involving balls i,i + 1 from the
c     event queue.

            do 1 j = i - 1,i + 1
c                 first ascertain if pair j,j + 1 is in queue, and then
c                 find the bin number ibin and slot k for the pair
                  if (ball(j) .eq. 0) then
                        goto 1
                  else
                        k = mod(ball(j) - 1,num_slots) + 1
                        ibin = ((ball(j) - 1)/num_slots) + 1
                  endif

c                 make slot k head of the free list
                  times(ibin,k) = start_free(ibin) + .001
                  start_free(ibin) = k
c                 remove pair
                  ball(j) = 0

c                 redirect list of times
                  num_times(ibin) = num_times(ibin) - 1
                  if (start_time(ibin) .eq. k) then
c                       slot k holds smallest time
                        start_time(ibin) = next_time(ibin,k)
                        if (start_time(ibin) .ne. 0) then
                              prev_time(ibin,start_time(ibin)) = 0
                        endif

                  elseif (next_time(ibin,k) .eq. 0) then
c                       slot k holds largest time and
c                       there must be at least one other
c                       smaller time, which now becomes the
c                       largest time.
                        next_time(ibin,prev_time(ibin,k)) = 0

                  else
c                       slot k is in the middle of list somewhere.
c                       pull it out.
                        knext = next_time(ibin,k)
                        kprev = prev_time(ibin,k)
                        next_time(ibin,kprev) = knext
                        prev_time(ibin,knext) = kprev
```

```
              endif
   1      continue

          return
          end
```

12.5   Introduction to the Parallel Version

The event simulator will be executed in parallel by having, as much as possible, all processes execute different collisions simultaneously. If the number of balls is muich larger than the number of processes, it is probable that collisions will be isolated from each other. If the collisions were truly isolated, and if the maintenance of the event queue required no synchronization, then the ideal speedup would be equal to the number of processes.

Unfortunately, there are several characteristics of the system which act to restrict the speedup. These include both *data dependencies* among the collisions and *contention* when more than one process updates the event queue at the same time. These topics are treated in the next two sections.

Data dependencies and contention are expected to be important in all event simulators. In general, data dependencies will restrict the ability to execute events in parallel, while contention will limit the ability to update the event queue in parallel. The way in which these interfere with parallel execution and how they can be circumvented in practice (if, indeed, they can be circumvented), depends on the details of the event simulator. Each case has its own peculiar data dependencies and event queue implementation. Therefore, while the details of parallelization of a particular model may not be appropriate for other simulators, it may still be useful to see how it is done in a particular case. In addition, the handling of contention can be generalized to other linked-list managers, and so has been explained in a separate section.

12.6   Data Dependencies in the Parallel Algorithm

The basic approach to parallelization is to attempt to execute as many events in parallel as possible. *The criterion for executing collisions in parallel is that the collisions must be executed independently.* Data dependencies among collisions can limit the number of collisions which can be executed independently.

There are two important types of data dependencies for the colliding-balls

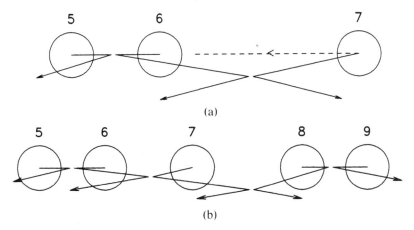

Figure 12-5. Two pairs of collisions showing overlap. (a) Collisions 5-6 and 6-7 overlap. (b) Collisions (5,6) and (8,9) overlap.

problem—*overlap* and *early recollisions*. In the case of overlap, the same ball will be involved in two collisions that are being executed in parallel. In the case of early recollisions, a collision creates a new collision which occurs at an earlier time than some of the collisions being executed in parallel.

As a matter of terminology, the event with the smallest time-to-collision on the event queue will be referred to as the *first collision* or *collision number 1*. The one with the next smallest time-to-collision will be the *second collision* or *collision number 2*, and in general the collision with the kth smallest time will be referred to as the *kth collision* or *collision number k*.

When executing events in parallel with nproc processes, then, the first nproc collisions are executed simultaneously.

Overlap is defined as follows. Let balls $(i, i + 1)$ and $(j, j + 1)$ be among the pairs involved in the first nproc collisions. The two events *overlap* if one or more of the four balls $i - 1 \rightarrow i + 2$ is the same as one or more of the four balls $j - 1 \rightarrow j + 2$.

The simplest case of overlap occurs when the same ball is involved in two of the first nproc collisions, as illustrated in Fig. 12-5(a). Collisions (5,6) and (6,7) are among the first nproc collisions on the event queue, with (6,7) occurring at a later time than (5,6). The solid line in Fig. 12-5(a) shows the actual path of the balls, while the dashed line indicates the original (6,7) collision as it would occur without interference from ball 5. The (5,6) collision will in general alter the nature, or even the existence, of the (6,7) collision. Note that the new (6,7) collision can occur either earlier or later than the original (6,7) collision (the one originally on the event queue).

If overlap exists, the two collisions cannot be executed in parallel, because the time-to-collision of the second collision cannot be computed until the consequences of the first collision are computed. It is left as a problem to show that overlap corresponds to the definition of data dependency of Chapter 8. Overlap can also cause other inconveniences, such as the fact that two processes will be updating the positions of the same ball in parallel.

The definition of overlap given above is more restrictive than disallowing two collisions which have one ball in common. According to this definition, the (5,6) and (8,9) collisions shown in Fig. 12-5(b) also overlap. The reason for this more stringent restriction is related to the requirement to calculate recollisions in parallel, as discussed below.

If balls $(i, i + 1)$ are involved in one of the first $nproc$ collisions, then *recollisions* are the subsequent collisions by pairs $(i - 1, i)$ and $(i + 1, i + 2)$ (if the collisions occur). The problem with *recollisions* among overlapping balls arises as follows. Suppose that $tmax$ is the time-to-collision of the $nproc$th collision. (That is, it is the largest time-to-collision of all the $nproc$ collisions being executed in parallel.) Let the first $nproc$ collisions be executed, and now find $tnew(i - 1)$ and $tnew(i + 1)$, the times-to-*recollision* of pairs $(i - 1, i)$ and $(i +, i + 2)$, for all the pairs $(i, i + 1)$ involved in the first $nproc$ collisions. A recollision such that

$$tnew(j) < tmax$$

will be termed an *early recollision* of balls $(j, j + 1)$. *The existence of an early recollision means that a new collision occurs at an earlier time than one or more of the nproc collisions just processed.* It is a new event occurring out of turn, and disrupts the independent execution of the first $nproc$ events.

The parallel algorithm must include a check for early recollisions, and it is most efficient if this check can be carried out in parallel. That is, the process which executed a collision between balls $(i, i + 1)$ also finds the recollisions between $(i - 1, i)$ and $(i + 1, i + 2)$. Different processes should be able to calculate these new collisions in parallel. This cannot happen if an overlap such as that shown in Fig. 12-5(b) occurs. In this case, the collisions (5,6) and (8,9) are executed in parallel. Then both balls 6 and 8 will recollide with 7. Suppose that the (6,7) recollision occurs earlier. Then the (7,8) collision cannot be processed until the (6,7) collision is processed, which means that the recollisions cannot be processed in parallel. It is for this reason that the (5,6) and (7,8) collisions are said to overlap.

Problem: Why is it expected that the number of early recollisions decreases as the number of balls increases (for a fixed number of processes)?

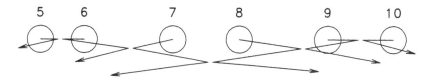

Figure 12-6. Collision used in a problem.

The way in which overlap and early recollisions restrict the number of collisions that can be executed in parallel is described in the section following the next one.

In general, one can expect the analogs of overlap and early collision to exist in other event simulators that are executing in parallel. From an abstract point of view, overlap refers to a situation in which executing one event alters the nature of one or more events occurring at a later time but which are being executed in parallel with the first. Early recollision describes the situation in which the occurrence of an event produces a second event that will occur earlier than one or more events already being processed in parallel. This new event can then act to alter the nature or existence of the ones already executed in parallel.

Problem: Show that overlap and early recollisions are consistent with the definition of data dependency of Chapter 8.

Problem: Consider the chain of collisions of Fig. 12-6. Pairs (5,6) and (9,10) are among the first `nproc` colliding pairs. After these two collisions, pairs (6,7) and (8,9) collide, followed by a (7,8) collision. Why is it not necessary to treat the (5,6) and (9,10) collisions as overlapping? (If it were, then all collisions would overlap, and no parallelization would be possible.)

12.7   Updating Linked Lists—Contention and Deadlock

Updating the event queue requires two steps: (1) Events involving balls whose collisions were executed in parallel must be removed from the event queue, and (2) new or revised events must be added to the event queue.

Removing an element from the event queue and adding that element to the free list is illustrated in Fig. 12-7. The event queue is represented by the doubly linked list, with list elements 1–4. The free list is singly linked, with elements 5, 6. The pointer start_time points to the beginning of the doubly linked list, while the pointer start_free points to the beginning of the free list.

The goal is for one process to remove the second element of the doubly linked list and insert it into the free list in such a way that, if another process wants to simultaneously remove another element (say element 3), the operation will proceed correctly. The dashed lines of Fig. 12-7 show the pointers after the removal of the second list element. The pointers p1, q3, p2, must be rearranged, while start_free now points to the list element which has been removed (which becomes the head of the free list).

A serious problem that can occur in removing the item from a singly or doubly linked list is *deadlock*. *A deadlock arises when a process is waiting at a locked lock that cannot possibly be unlocked.*

Deadlock is illustrated by a simple algorithm to remove the second list element from the doubly linked list of Fig. 12-7. Assume that each list element can be locked independently. If a process *locks a list element*, it means that no other process can either read or alter the pointers of that list element. That is, the process which locks the list element *owns* the element, and doesn't let any process access that list element.

Consider the following algorithm to remove the second element from the linked list of Fig. 12-7 and put that element into the free list.

1. Lock list element number 2.

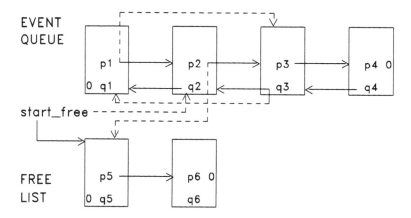

Figure 12-7.   Illustration of removal of a member of the event queue.

2. Read the backward and forward pointers p2, q2 of list element number 2.

3. Lock list element 1, then lock 3 (pointed to by pointers read in step 2 above.)

4. Redirect the pointers p1, q3.

5. Lock the entire free list. (No other process can now access the free list.)

6. Redirect p2 to point to the element which is pointed to by start_free.

7. Make start_free point to list element 2.

8. Unlock everything.

The subroutine which implements the above algorithm, using the event queue, is given below. A list element is also referred to as a *slot*.

```
         subroutine remove_in_parallel(ibin,k0,times,next_time,
   s                lok_slot,lok_free,num_bins,start_free,
   s                prev_time)

         integer num_bins,lok_free(1),ibin,start_free(1)
         integer k0,next_time(num_bins,1),lok_slot(num_bins,1)
         integer prev_time(num_bins,1)
         real times(num_bins,1)

         integer kn,kp

c        Illustrative subroutine to remove slot k0 from the
c        event queue, bin number ibin.
c        This procedure can undergo deadlock.
c        Assume k0 is not the first or last element of the
c        list, and that list has at least 4 elements.
c        Array lok_slot(ibin,k) locks slot number k of
c        bin number ibin. The array is shared.
c        Shared variable lok_free locks the free list.
c        Variables times, next_time,prev_time,start_free
c        are shared.

c        lock slot k0
         call spin_lock(lok_slot(ibin,k0))

c        get forward pointer kn and backward pointer kp. ("n" for
c        "next," "p" for "previous.")
         kn = next_(ibin,k0)
         kp = prev_time(ibin,k0)
```

```
c       lock slots kn,kp in bin number ibin
        call spin_lock(lok_slot(ibin,kn))
        call spin_lock(lok_slot(ibin,kp))

c       redirect pointers
        next_time(ibin,kp) = kn
        prev_time(ibin,kn) = kp

c       add slot to free list
        call spin_lock(lok_free(ibin))
            times(ibin,k0) = start_free(ibin) + .001
            start_free(ibin) = k0

c       unlock all slots.
        call spin_unlock(lok_free(ibin))
        call spin_unlock(lok_slot(ibin,kp))
        call spin_unlock(lok_slot(ibin,k0))
        call spin_unlock(lok_slot(ibin,kn))

        return
        end
```

To see the problem with this algorithm, suppose that two processes, A and B, each try to remove an element from the doubly linked list at the same time. Suppose process A tries to remove the second list element, while process B tries to remove the third. The two processes execute the previous subroutine simultaneously. The value of the private variable k0 will be 2 for process A and 3 for process B, while ibin is the same for both.

Consider the following chain of events:

1. Process A locks the second list element (its k0).
2. Process B locks the third list element (its k0).
3. Process A gets the forward and backward pointers kn, kp from the second list element. For process A, kn = 3 and kp = 1. Process A then tries to lock element kn. Since element 3 has been locked by process B (in step 2 above), process A must spin at this lock until process B unlocks it.
4. Process B gets its forward and backward pointers kn, kp from the third list element. For process B, kn = 4, kp = 2. Process B locks the fourth element (its kn) and then tries to lock the second element (its kp). But process A has locked that element (in step 1 above), so process B must spin at this lock, waiting for process A to release it.

The timeline for this sequence of events is illustrated in Fig. 12-8. Process

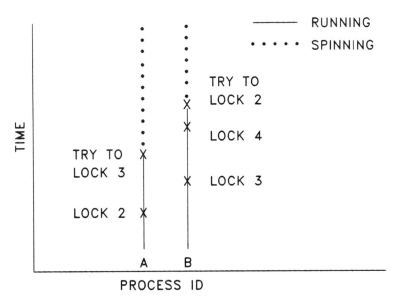

Figure 12-8.   Possible timeline illustrating deadlock among two processes trying to simultaneously remove elements from the list of Fig. 12-7.

A is waiting for B to unlock element 3 and process B is waiting for A to unlock element 2. The processes can never continue, and this is an example of *deadlock*. The locks are dead, incapable of being unlocked.

In order to avoid such a situation, it is necessary for each process to *test* the locks of the elements, without actually calling the spin_lock function. If the lock is unavailable, the process should not spin (thus keeping all its other locks locked) but should unlock all the locks that it has acquired and then try all over again from the beginning. In this way, either a process gets all three of the locks or it gets none of them.

One way to implement this idea is to associate with each list element an integer test(ibin,k). The variable test is initialized to 0, but whenever test(ibin,k) is 1, it means that a process "owns" the list element and no other process should try to acquire it or access it in any way. By *own* we mean essentially the same thing as acquiring a lock (so the process can enter the protected region), except that the ownership is not acquired by means of a spin_lock.

The subroutine above then becomes

```
       subroutine remove_in_parallel(ibin,k0,times,next_time,
  s                  lok_slot,lok_free,num_bins,start_free,
  s                  prev_time,test)
```

```
      integer num_bins,lok_free(1),ibin,start_free(1)
      integer k0,next_time(num_bins,1),lok_slot(num_bins,1)
      integer test(num_bins,1),prev_time(num_bins,1)
      real times(num_bins,1)
      integer kn,kp

c     Illustrative subroutine to remove slot k0 from the
c     event queue, bin number ibin.
c     Assume k0 is not the first or last element of the
c     list, and that list has at least 4 elements.
c     Array lok_slot(ibin,k) locks slot number k of
c     bin number ibin. The array is shared.
c     Shared variable lok_free locks the free list.
c     Variables times, next_time,prev_time,start_free
c     are shared.
c
c     This uses an algorithm which cannot deadlock.
c     Shared array test(ibin,k) must be initialized to 0
c     before this routine is called by any process.
c     The element test(ibin,k) is read and written only when
c     the kth list element (bin ibin) is locked by a spin-lock.
c     When a process sets test(ibin,k) to 1, that process
c     "owns" the slot k, and no other process may access it.
c
c     processes come back here when they fail to own all
c     three list elements
 100      continue

c     try to own element k0
          call spin_lock(lok_slot(ibin,k0))
              if (test(ibin,k0) .eq. 1) then
c                 element owned by someone else
                  call spin_unlock(lok_slot(ibin,k0))
                  goto 100
              else
c                 this process now owns slot k0.
                  test(ibin,k0) = 1
              endif
          call spin_unlock(lok_slot(ibin,k0))

c     The process owns slot k0.
c     get forward pointer kn and backward pointer kp. ("n" for
c     "next," "p" for "previous.")
          kn = next_time(ibin,k0)
          kp = prev_time(ibin,k0)

c     Try to own slot kn
```

```
            call spin_lock(lok_slot(ibin,kn))
                if (test(ibin,kn) .eq. 1) then
c                   element owned by someone else
                    call spin_unlock(lok_slot(ibin,kn))
c                   release element k0
                    call spin_lock(lok_slot(ibin,k0))
                        test(ibin,k0) = 0
                    call spin_unlock(lok_slot(ibin,k0))
                    goto 100
                else
c                   now this process owns slot kn
                    test(ibin,kn) = 1
                endif
            call spin_unlock(lok_slot(ibin,kn))

c       The process owns slots k,kn.
c       Try to own slot kp
            call spin_lock(lok_slot(ibin,kp))
                if (test(ibin,kp) .eq. 1) then
c                   element owned by someone else
                    call spin_unlock(lok_slot(ibin,kp))
c                   release elements k0, kn
                    call spin_lock(lok_slot(ibin,k0))
                        test(ibin,k0) = 0
                    call spin_unlock(lok_slot(ibin,k0))
                    call spin_lock(lok_slot(ibin,kn))
                        test(ibin,kn) = 0
                    call spin_unlock(lok_slot(ibin,kn))
                    goto 100
                else
c                   now this process owns slot kp
                    test(ibin,kp) = 1
                endif
            call spin_unlock(lok_slot(ibin,kp))

c       Now this process owns slots k,kn,kp.
c       Note that none of the slots are locked by spin-locks,
c       but are owned because of the fact that test = 1.

c       redirect pointers
            next_time(ibin,kp) = kn
            prev_time(ibin,kn) = kp

c       add element to free list
            call spin_lock(lok_free(ibin))
                times(ibin,k0) = start_free(ibin) + .001
                start_free(ibin) = k0
```

```
           call spin_unlock(lok_free(ibin))
c      Release all three elements
           call spin_lock(lok_slot(ibin,k0))
                test(ibin,k0) = 0
           call spin_unlock(lok_slot(ibin,k0))
           call spin_lock(lok_slot(ibin,kn))
                test(ibin,kn) = 0
           call spin_unlock(lok_slot(ibin,kn))
           call spin_lock(lok_slot(ibin,kp))
                test(ibin,kp) = 0
           call spin_unlock(lok_slot(ibin,kp))

           return
           end
```

The important feature of this routine is that, if a process successfully acquires a lock, it does not call `spin_lock` again until it unlocks the first lock. Therefore, no process will ever hold two spin-locks at the same time, and a deadlock cannot occur. If a process cannot get exclusive access to a list element (because `test = 1` for that element), it releases all the list elements which it owns and goes back to the beginning. It does not keep the elements which it already owns, hoping to get more.

Implicit in this subroutine is the assumption that no two processes will ever try to remove the same list element in parallel. (Why?)

Ownership of a list element is different from locking the element. Ownershp is a mutually agreed upon convention among processes that, if the variable test is 1, the element is owned by some other process and cannot be accessed. The spinning (`goto 100`) is done in the subroutine itself and is not managed by a `spin_lock` subroutine. For this reason, when the process fails to get ownership, it can try again.

Problem: Why can't kn and kp be determined before the process gets ownership of slot k0?

Problem: The problem with the algorithm is that, if both processes are proceeding at the same rate, the processes may have to make many tries before one of them actually succeeds in gaining ownership of the three elements it needs. This interaction is a "collision" (of processes, not balls—no pun intended). Develop a way to minimize the number of tries.

Problem: Some parallel programming implementations have a built-in function which can test whether a spin-lock is locked or unlocked. Suppose we have the function

```
integer test_lock,lok_condition,lok
lok_condition = test_lock(lok)
```

The function returns 1 if the lock is unlocked and 0 if it is locked. Also, if the lock was found to be unlocked, the lock is locked, so the inquiring process owns the lock. Rewrite the previous subroutine using this function.

Problem: Enhance the routine so that the element to be removed can be also be the first or last element of the list.

Problem: One possible algorithm to reduce contention when removing events from the event queue is as follows. A process locks k0, reads kp, kn from the element k0, then unlocks k0. It then locks kp, then locks k0, and then locks kn. This "left-to-right" order of locking will eliminate the possibility of deadlock. (Why?) However, there is a serious problem because slot k0 is unlocked and then relocked later. What is this problem? Can this problem be overcome without using a strategy of testing the lock?

Now consider adding an element in parallel to an ordered doubly linked list, like the event queue. If the list is unindexed (as is the event queue used in this chapter), then the list must first be searched for the place at which the element is to be added. In this search, one tests each element k to see if the time-to-collision of the list element k is smaller than the time-to-collision to be added to the list, and if it is not, one goes on to the next list element.

It is necessary to lock both list elements before testing the time-to-collision, otherwise some other process can interfere with the process. The problem that can arise is illustrated in Figure 12-9. The chain of events in this figure is as follows:

1. Process A decides to insert the new element between elements 2 and 3. It has not locked element 2 (Fig. 12-9(a)). It then becomes idle.
2. Procedure B now inserts an element between list elements 2 and 3, to get Fig. 12-9(b).
3. Procedure A restarts, locks the elements, and does its insertion, producing Fig. 12-9(c). The list is now corrupt.

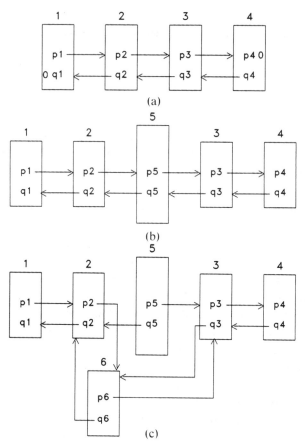

Figure 12-9. Illustration of improper insertion of an element into a doubly linked list.

Locking the list elements will avoid situations like that discussed above. If, at step (1), process A locked element 2, then B could not perform step (2). It is the order of locking that is important. So long as the previous list element is locked before the later one, there can be no deadlock. The procedure to add an element to the doubly linked list is

1. Lock the entire free list, extract a free slot, then unlock the free list.
2. Lock the first list element.
3. If the time to be inserted is smaller than the time of the first list element, insert it, release lock, and return.
4. If the time to be inserted is greater than the time of the currently locked list element, lock the next list element if there is one. If there is not, insert the time at the end of the list and return.

5. If the time to be inserted is less than the next list element, insert it, release the locks, and return.

6. If the time to be inserted is larger than the next list element, unlock the first list element and goto 4.

The algorithm assumes that a process will not try to remove an element from the list at the same time that an element is being added.

Problem: Write a program implementing the above algorithm.

Problem: Show that no deadlock can result from this algorithm.

12.8 The Parallel Algorithm

The parallel algorithm attempts to execute as many collisions in parallel as possible. Process 0 executes the first collision on the event queue, process 1 executes the second, process 2 the third, and so forth. A variable idmax is defined such that, at any stage, processes 0 through idmax execute collisions in parallel. It is possible for idmax to be smaller than nproc − 1 because of data dependencies.

The algorithm executes approximately nstep collisions. Because of the possibility that overlap or early recollision will restrict the number of collisions that can be executed in parallel to less than nproc, the variable num_steps keeps track of the number of collisions actually executed. When this variable becomes greater than nstep, the simulation ends.

The algorithm is

```
Initialize
num_steps = 0
do while num_steps <= nstep
```

1. Process number id gets from the event queue the balls involved in the (id + 1)th collision. Let the time-to-collision be tcol(id).

2. Set idmax = nproc − 1.

3. Ascertain if there is an overlap among the nproc collisions. If there is, then reassign idmax to be the largest process-id such that the first idmax + 1 collisions do not have any overlap.

4. Execute the first idmax + 1 collisions. (Then nproc−idmax processes

are idle.) Positions, velocities and last-update-times of the balls involved are first stored, then updated. (Storage is for possible rollback later.)

5. Assign `old_idmax = idmax`. Find new times-to-collision for all balls involved in the collisions (4). These are the recollisions. Let `tnew(i)` be the time-to-recollision for the pair (i, i + 1). If, for any i,

        tnew(k) < tcol(idmax),

then *reassign idmax* to be the largest process-id such that all the times-to-recollision for processes 0, 1, ..., idmax (the new idmax) are greater than `tcol(idmax)`—the new idmax. Now idmax + 1 collisions are executed in parallel, and there is no overlap or early recollisions among these processes.

6. Process `idmax + 1` through `old_idmax` inclusive have altered the positions, velocities and last-update-times of balls. These new values must be *rolled back* to the original values. At the same time, processes 0 through idmax inclusive update the event queue with the recollisions.

7. Set `num_steps = num_steps + (idmax + 1)`.

endo

12.9 Parallel Program

```
          subroutine time_steps(x,v,n,L,nstep,tbin,tnow,diameter,
    s                           num_slots,num_bins,times,
    s                           next_time, prev_time,start_time,
    s                           start_free,num_times,event_ball,
    s                           ball,last_update_time,
    s                           lok_idmax,test,lok_slot,lok_free,
    s                           lok_start,lok_idmax,lok_recol,
    s                           xold,vold,last_old,tnew,used,
    s                           used_id,id,nproc,trecol,idmax,
    s                           old_idmax,first_bin,recollide,
    s                           tmax,tnow,new_tmax,lok_used,
    s                           is_time)
    c
    c     Follow motion of n billiard balls constrained to move in one
    c     dimension for nstep collisions.
    c     Balls 0 and n + 1 are the end walls. Balls have unit mass.
    c     Parallel program. Each process calls this routine.
    c     On entry, x(i), v(i) are true positions and velocities of
    c     balls at time tnow. On exit, tnow has been updated and
```

```
c       x(i), v(i) are new true positions and velocities at the
c       new time tnow.
c       During the simulation, the "current time" tnow is
c       different for each process.
c       is_time - used for error detection. is_time = 0 normally.
c       If it is set to 1, all processes exit.
c       At the end of nsteps, the total kinetic energy and speed
c       are printed out. The energy and speed are unchanged during
c       the entire course of the simulation.
c
c       All spin-locks must be initialized to be unlocked before
c       the first call to this routine. Variables starting in
c       "lok_" are spin-locks.
c       bar_array(l,k) is a barrier for k processes, for
c       l <= k <= nproc. These barriers must be initialized before
c       the first call to this routine.
c       Spin-locks and barriers are shared.
c
c       The following variables are shared:
c       x,v,times,next_time,prev_time,start_time,start_free
c       num_times,event_ball,ball,last_update_time,test,
c       used,used_id,xold,vold,last_old,tnew,trecol,
c       idmax,old_idmax,first_bin,recollide,tmax,new_tmax
c       num_steps,is_time.

        integer n,nstep,num_slots,num_bins,id,nproc
        integer next_time(num_bins,1),prev_time(num_bins,1)
        integer start_time(1),start_free(1),ball(0:1)
        integer event_ball(num_bins,1),test(num_bins,1)
        integer lok_slot(num_bins,1),lok_free(1)
        integer lok_start(1),lok_idmax,lok_recol,lok_used(0:1)
        integer used(0:1),bar_array(4,1),used_id(0:1),is_time
        integer xold(0:1),vold(0:1),last_old(0:1),tnew(0:1)
        real x(0:1),v(0:1),L,diameter,tnow,tbase,tbin
        real times(num_bins,1),last_update_time(0:1)
        real last_old(0:1)
        real queue_length,diameter,dt
        real tcol,get_time_to_col,energy,speed
        integer ibin,iplace,icol,i,j,k,mod,m
        integer idpl,ntot,idtem,num_steps
        integer idmax,old_idmax,first_bin,recollide,max,min
        real tnow,new_tmax,tmax,radius,abs

c       first executable statement

        if (id .eq. 0) then
            queue_length = tbin * (num_bins - 1)
```

```
                        radius = .5 * diameter
                        tbase = 0.
                 endif

c        ********************************************************
c             BEGIN INITIALIZATION SECTION

c        initialize the event queue and other arrays in parallel
                 do 2 ibin = 1 + id,num_bins,nproc
                        num_times(ibin) = 0
                        start_free(ibin) = 1
                        start_time(ibin) = 0
                        do 3 iplace = 1,num_slots
                             next_time(ibin,iplace) = 0
                             prev_time(ibin,iplace) = 0
                             test(ibin,iplace) = 0
c                            initialize free list
                             times(ibin,iplace) = iplace + 1 + .001
    3                   continue
c                       last member of free list
                        times(ibin,num_slots) = .001
    2            continue

                 do 4 i = id,n + 1,nproc
                        ball(i) = 0
                        used(i) = 0
                        last_update_time(i) = tnow
    4            continue

c        initialize the walls,num_steps,is_time
                 if (id .eq. 0) then
                        x(0) = -radius
                        v(0) = 0.
                        x(n + 1) = L + radius
                        v(n + 1) = 0.
                        num_steps = 0
                        is_time = 0
                 endif

                 call barrier (bar_array(1,nproc))
c        add times to event queue
                 do 6 i = id,n,nproc
c                       for each pair, (i,i + 1), get the time-to-collision

                        tcol = get_time_to_col(i,queue_length,
    s                   diameter,x,v,tnow,last_update_time)
```

```
c               add this pair to the event queue if
c               tcol is positive.

                if (tcol .gt. 0.) then

                    call add_time_to_queue(i,tcol,tbase,tbin,
     s                     num_bins,num_times,num_slots,
     s                     start_free,times,ball,event_ball,
     s                     start_time,next_time,prev_time,
     s                     lok_slot,lok_start,lok_free)

                endif
    6       continue

            call barrier(bar_array(1,nproc))


c               END OF INITIALIZATION SECTION
c       ****************************************************
c       Now do at least nstep collisions
  150       continue
            if (num_steps .gt. nstep) goto 100

c       -------------- get the next event to process --------------

c       find pair i,j which has smallest time-to-collision
c       by getting the smallest time on the event queue.
c       initialize idmax.

c       smallest time should be in bin number first_bin.
            if (id .eq. 0) then
                idmax = nproc - 1
                first_bin = mod((tnow - tbase)/tbin,
     s          float(num_bins)) + 1
c               if first_bin has no entries, move to next bin.
                do 11 m = 1,num_bins
                    if (num_times(first_bin) .ne. 0) goto 12
                    first_bin = first_bin + 1
                    if (first_bin .gt. num_bins) then
                        first_bin = 1
                    endif
   11           continue
            else
                goto 12
            endif
```

```
c        If this error is found, try a larger value of
c        ibin or increase the value of num_bins.
c        Process cannot exit here, else program will hang
c        at the barrier.
             print *,'no times on event queue'
             is_time = 1

12           continue

             call barrier(bar_array(1,nproc))

c        check for no time on queue
             if (is_time .eq. 1)call exit()

c        Process id executes collision number id + 1.
c        Each process checks the bins in succession.
c        If the number of times in the bin is such that
c        the collision to be executed by the process is
c        not in the bin, the process goes on to the next bin.
c        ntot = total number of times in all bins <= ibin.
             ipdl = id + 1
             ibin = first_bin
             ntot = num_times(ibin)
             do 101 i = 1,num_bins
                 if (idpl .gt. ntot) goto 102
c                go on to next bin
                 ibin = ibin + 1
                 if (ibin .gt. num_bins) ibin = 1
                 ntot = ntot + num_times(ibin)
101          continue

c        Error if arrive here. Process cannot exit here else
c        program will hang at barrier
             is_time = 1
             print *,'not enough times in bins'
             goto 103

102          continue
c            find slot k
             k = start_time(ibin)
             do 70 i = ntot - num_times(ibin) + 1,id
                 k = next_time(ibin,k)
                 if (k .eq. 0) then
                     print *,'error,k = 0'
                     is_time = 1
                     goto 103
                 endif
```

```
 70        continue

c     Find pair i,i + 1 of colliding balls from slot k, bin ibin
          i = event_ball(ibin,k)
          j = i + 1
c     Set value of private variable tnow. After
c     executing the statement below, each process
c     will have a different "current time."
          tnow = tcol

c     Recalculate the time-to-collision to correct
c     for roundoff error. Roundoff error should not
c     affect the order of times on the event_queue.
          tcol = get_time_to_col(i,queue_length,diameter,x,v,
     s                           tnow,last_update_time)

          if (id .eq. idmax)tmax = tcol
 103      continue

          call barrier(bar_array(1,nproc))

          if (is_time .eq. 1)call exit()


c     -------------- check for overlap    ----------------------

c     In a double overlap, at most two collisions overlap.
c     In a triple overlap, three collisions overlap. If
c     there is a triple overlap, set idmax = 0, so only a single
c     collision is processed. For double overlaps, if user_id is
c     the maximum value of the id involved in any particular double
c     overlap, then idmax is set to be the minimum of all the user_id
c     for all double overlaps, minus 1. Then processes 0 thru
c     idmax will have no overlap.
c
c     To check for overlap, increment used(i) by 1 for each
c     collision involving ball i. If any used(i) = 3, it means
c     there is a triple overlap. If used(i) = 1, set used_id(i)
c     equal to the id of the process handling the collision.

          do 71 m = i - 1,i + 2
              call spin_lock(lok_used(m))
                  used(m) = used(m) + 1

                  if (used(m) .eq. 3) then

c                     triple overlap
                      call spin_lock(lok_idmax)
```

```
                                idmax = 0
                         call spin_unlock(lok_idmax)
                         call spin_unlock(lok_used(m))
                         goto 73

                  elseif (used(m) .eq. 2) then

c                        double overlap
                         used_id(m) = max(id,used_id(m))
                         call spin_lock(lok_idmax)
                            if (idmax .eq. 0) then
                                 call spin_unlock(lok_idmax)
                                 call spin_unlock(lok_used(m))
                                 goto 73
                            else
                                 idmax=min(idmax,used_id(m)-1)
                            endidf
                         call spin_unlock(lok_idmax)

                  else

c                        no overlap yet
                         used_id(m) = id

                  endif
               call spin_unlock(lok_used(m))
 71      continue
 73      continue

         call barrier(bar_array(1,nproc))

         if (idmax .lt. 0) then
              print *,'ERROR, idmax < 0'
              call exit()
         endif

c     reinitialize used(m) for next cycle
         do 72 m = i - 1,i + 2
              used(m) = 0
 72      continue

c     Processes 0 through idmax execute their collisions.
         if (id .gt. idmax) goto 400
         if (idmax .eq. 0) goto 201

c     Execute the following only if idmax is not 0
```

```
          if (id .eq. idmax) then
              tmax = tcol
              trecol = tmax
              recollide = 0
              old_idmax = idmax
          endif

c     save old values for rollback (processes 0 → idmax)
          do 76 m = i,i + 1
              xold(m) = x(m)
              vold(m) = v(m)
              last_old(m) = last_update_time(m)
 76       continue

c     barrier for idmax + 1 processes
          call barrier(bar_array(1,idmax + 1))
 201      continue

c     ------------- execute the event  -------------------------

c     Execute the first idmax + 1 collisions.
c     Move balls i,j in straight line until they just touch
c     this is moment of collision.
          x(i) = x(i) + v(i) * (tnow - last_update_time(i))
          x(j) = x(j) + v(j) * (tnow - last_update_time(j))
          last_update_time(i) = tnow
          last_update_time(j) = tnow

c     find new velocities. Check for wall
          if (i .eq. 0) then
c             j hits wall
              v(j) = -v(j)
          elseif (i .eq. n) then
c             i hits wall
              v(i) = -v(i)
          else
c             no wall
              vtem = v(i)
              v(i) = v(j)
              v(j) = vtem
          endif
          call barrier(bar_array(1,idmax + 1))

c     ---------------- find early recollisions  --------------

c     Let tnew(i) be the time-to-recollision for pairs (i,i + 1),
c     If any tnew(i) < tmax, there must be a rollback, and idmax
```

```
c       must be reassigned.
c       execute this only if idmax > 0.

        if (idmax .eq. 0) goto 210

c       First find the smallest time-to-recollision, if it
c       is less than tmax.
        do 78 m = i - 1,i + 1,2
            tnew(m) = get_time_to_col(m,queue_length,
  s         diameter,x,v,tnow,last_update_time)
            if (tnew(m) .lt. trecol) then
                recollide = 1
                call spin_lock(lok_recol)
                    if (tnew(m) .lt. trecol) then
                        trecol = tnew(m)
                    endif
                call spin_unlock(lok_recol)
            endif
 78     continue
        call barrier(bar_array(1,idmax + 1))

c       If recollide = 1, it means there is at least one
c       early recollision. In this case,
c       all processes for which tcol < trecol can be executed in
c       parallel. Set idmax to be the largest process-id such that
c       tcol for process idmax is < trecol.

        if (recollide .eq. 1) then
            do 77 m = i - 1,i + 1,2
                if (tnew(m) .ge. trecol) then
                    call spin_lock(lok_idmax)
                        if (idmax .gt. id - 1)idmax =
  s                     max(0,id - 1)
                    call spin_unlock(lok_idmax)
                endif
 77         continue
            call barrier(bar_array(1,old_idmax + 1))
        endif

c       rollback for idmax + 1 → old_idmax
        if ((id .ge. idmax + 1) .and. (id .le. old_idmax))then
            do 79 m = i,i + 1
                x(i) = xold(i)
                v(i) = vold(i)
                last_update_time(i) = last_old(i)
 79         continue
```

```
               goto 400
           endif

c      The rest of the processes update the event queue. This can
c      proceed in parallel with the rollback.

           call barrier(bar_array(1,idmax + 1))

 210       continue

c      ----------  update the event queue  -----------------------

c      Remove all collisions involving balls i and i + 1 from the
c      event queue

           call remove_from_queue(i,ball,num_slots,times,
     s                          start_free,num_times,start_time,
     s                          next_time,prev_time,num_bins,test,
     s                          lok_slot,lok_start,lok_free)

c      Add new collisions with balls i - 1, i + 1 to event queue.
c      collision times are tnew(m)
           do 60 m = i - 1,i + 1,2
               if (idmax .eq. 0) then
                   tnew(m) = get_time_to_col(m,queue_length,
     s                 diameter,x,v,tnow,last_update_time)
               endif

c              add this pair to the event queue if tnew(m) > 0
               if (tnew(m) .gt. 0.) then
                   call add_time_to_queue(m,tnew(m),tbase,tbin,
     s                          num_bins,num_times,num_slots,
     s                          start_free,times,ball,event_ball,
     s                          start_time,next_time,prev_time,
     s                          lok_slot,lok_start,lok_free)
               endif
 60        continue

 400       continue

           call barrier(bar_array(1,nproc))

c      Cycle back to do more collisions.
           goto 150
 100       continue
```

```
c       total energy and speed must be conserved.
        if (id .ne. 0) goto 65
        energy = 0.
        speed = 0.
        do 50 i = 1,n
             energy = energy + .5 * (v(i)**2)
             speed = speed + abs(v(i))
50      continue
        print *,'energy = ',energy, 'speed = ',speed

c       restore true positions of balls
        do 55 i = 1,n
             x(i) = x(i) + v(i) * (tnow - last_update_time(i))
55      continue
65      continue
        call process_join

        return
        end

c       *****************************  get_time_to_col

        real function get_time_to_col(i,queue_length,
     s  diameter,x,v,tnow,last_update_time)

        integer i
        real queue_length,diameter,x(0:1),v(0:1),tnow
        real last_update_time(0:1)

        real delt,abs,small
        real x_tem_i,x_tem_il
c       delt is amount of time remaining before collision
c       will occur.
        small = 1.e - 36
        if (abs(v(i) - v(i + 1)) .lt. small) then
             delt = -1.
        elseif (v(i) - v(i + 1) .le. 0.) then
c            balls can't collide under this condition,
c            if x(i) < x(i + 1)
             delt = -1.
        else
             x_tem_i = x (i) + v(i) * (tnow -
     s       last_update_time(i))
             x_tem_il = x(i + 1) + v(i + 1) *
     s       (tnow - last_update_ time(i + 1))
             delt = -(x_tem_i - x_tem_il + diameter)/
     s       (v(i) - v(i + 1))
        endif
```

```
c      if delt < 0, particles will not collide
c      if delt > queue_length, time is greater than threshold
           if (( delt .lt. 0.) .or. (delt .gt. queue_length)) then
               get_time_to_col = -1.
           else
               get_time_to_col = tnow + delt
           endif

           return
           end

c      *************************************  add_time_to_queue

           subroutine add_time_to_queue(i,tcol,tbase,tbin,
     s                     num_bins,num_times,num_slots,
     s                     start_free,times,ball,event_ball,
     s                     start_time,next_time,prev_time,
     s                     lok_slot,lok_start,lok_free)

           integer i,num_bins,num_slots,num_times(1)
           integer ball(0:1),event_ball(num_bins,1)
           integer next_time(num_bins,1),prev_time(num_bins,1)
           integer start_time(1)
           integer lok_slot(num_bins,1),lok_start(1)
           integer lok_free(1),start_free(1)
           real times(num_bins,1),tcol,tbase,tbin

           integer prev,kl,ktime
           integer mod,int,ibin,i,j,k

c      Pair i,i + 1 will collide at time tcol. Add this time
c      and pair to the event queue.
c      Routine can be called in parallel.
c      Assume no process will remove an element in parallel
c      with this routine. Assume no other process will add
c      the (i,i + 1) pair in parallel.
c      find bin number
           ibin = mod((tcol - tbase)/tbin,float(num_bins)) + 1

           if (num_times(ibin) .eq. num_slots) then
               print *,'no more room on queue, bin # ',ibin
               call exit()
           endif

c      Get new slot kl, remove kl from free list.
```

```
c       Put new time-to-collision in slot kl.
            call spin_lock(lok_free(ibin))
                kl = start_free(ibin)
                start_free(ibin) = int(times(ibin,kl))
            call spin_unlock(lok_free(ibin))
            times(ibin,kl) = tcol
            ball(i) = (ibin - 1) * num_slots + kl
            event_ball(ibin,kl) = i
c       No other process can access kl during this procedure.

c       Check if bin number ibin is empty
c       lock start_time and num_times together
            call spin_lock(lok_start(ibin))
            if (num_times(ibin) .eq. 0) then
                start_time(ibin) = kl
                next_time(ibin,kl) = 0
                num_times(ibin) = 1
                prev_time(ibin,kl) = 0
                call spin_unlock(lok_start(ibin))
                return
            else
                num_times(ibin) = num_times(ibin) + 1
c               now find the position of tcol in the linked
c               list of times.
                ktime = start_time(ibin)
c               lock head of list
                call spin_lock(lok_slot(ibin,ktime))
                if (tcol .lt. times(ibin,ktime)) then
c                   tcol becomes the
c                   smallest time in the bin
c                   both start_time and slot ktime
c                   are locked.
                    start_time(ibin) = kl
                    next_time(ibin,kl) = ktime
                    prev_time(ibin,ktime) = kl
                    prev_time(ibin,kl) = 0
                    call spin_unlock(lok_start(ibin))
                    call spin_unlock(lok_slot(ibin,ktime))
                    return
                else
c                   tcol is greater than the smallest time in
c                   the bin. Unlock start_time,
c                   lock the next member of queue.
                    call spin_unlock(lok_start(ibin))
100                 continue
                    prev = ktime
c                   this process owns slot # prev
```

```
                        ktime = next_time(ibin,ktime)
                        if (ktime .gt. 0) then
                            call spin_lock(lok_slot(ibin,ktime))
                            if (tcol .lt. times(ibin,ktime)) then
c                               insert kl between prev and ktime
                                next_time(ibin,prev) = kl
                                prev_time(ibin,kl) = prev
                                next_time(ibin,kl) = ktime
                                prev_time(ibin,ktime) = kl
c                               release both locks
                                call spin_unlock
     s                              (lok_slot(ibin,prev))
                                call spin_unlock
     s                              (lok_slot(ibin,ktime))
                                return
                            else
c                               unlock prev
                                call spin_unlock
     s                              (lok_slot(ibin, prev))
                                goto 100
                            endif
                        else
c                           tcol becomes the largest time
c                           in the bin. times(ibin,prev) becomes the
c                           second-to-largest time.
                            next_time(ibin,prev) = kl
                            next_time(ibin,kl) = 0
                            prev_time(ibin,kl) = prev
                            call spin_unlock(lok_slot(ibin,prev))
                            return
                        endif
                    endif
                endif

                return
                end

c       ***************************************** remove_from_queue

                subroutine remove_from_queue(i,ball,num_slots,times,
     s                        start_free,num_times,start_time,
     s                        next_time,prev_time,num_bins,test,
     s                        lok_slot,lok_start,lok_free)

                integer i,ball(0:1),num_slots,start_free(1)
                integer start_time(1),next_time(num_bins,1)
                integer prev_time(num_bins,1),test(num_bins,1)
                integer lok_slot(num_bins,1),lok_start(1),lok_free(1)
```

```
            integer num_bins,test_lock,num_times(1)
            real times(num_bins,1)
            integer j,ibin,k,knext,kprev,kn,kp

c      Remove all collision involving balls i,i + 1 from the
c      event queue.

c      done in parallel. Assume no other process will remove the
c      same balls in parallel, and that no process tries to add
c      balls to queue in parallel with this routine.

            do 1 j = i - 1,i + 1
            if (j .lt. 0) goto 1
c              first ascertain if pair j,j + 1 is in queue, and
c              then find the bin number ibin and slot k
c              for the pair
               if (ball(j) .eq. 0) then
                   goto 1
               else
                   k = mod(ball(j) - 1,num_slots) + 1
                   ibin = ((ball(j) - 1)/num_slots) + 1
               endif

c              remove pair
               ball(j) = 0
c              try to own slot k and two slots on either side.
 100           continue
c              try for slot k
               if (test_lock(test,ibin,k,lok_slot,num_bins)
     s             .lt. 0) then
                   goto 100
               endif

c              Process now owns slot k. try for next slot, if this
c              is not the last slot in the bin.
               kn = next_time(ibin,k)
               kp = prev_time(ibin,k)
c              Break if-statement into 2 parts because Fortran
c              does not guarantee order of execution of connected
c              expressions.
               if (kn .gt. 0) then
                if (test_lock(test,ibin,kn,lok_slot,num_bins)
     s             .lt. 0) then
c                   release k, start again
                    call release_slot(test,ibin,k,
     s              lok_slot,num_bins)
                    goto 100
                endif
               endif
```

```
              endif

c             process now owns kn and k. Try for kp.
              if (kp .gt. 0) then
               if (test_lock(test,ibin,kp,lok_slot,num_bins)
     s          .lt. 0) then
c                 release k,kn start again
                  call release_slot(test,ibin,k,
     s            lok_slot,num_bins)
                  call release_slot(test,ibin,kn,
     s            lok_slot,num_bins)
                  goto 100
                 endif
               endif

c             now the process owns all three slots. Remove
c             slot k from the queue.

c             redirect list of times
              if (start_time(ibin) .eq. k) then
c                 slot k holds smallest time
                  start_time(ibin) = next_time(ibin,k)
                  if (start_time(ibin) .ne. 0) then
                      prev_time(ibin,start_time(ibin))=0
                  endif

              elseif (next_time(ibin,k) .eq. 0) then
c                 slot k holds largest time and
c                 there must be at least one other
c                 smaller time, which now becomes the
c                 largest time.
                  next_time(ibin,prev_time(ibin,k)) = 0

              else
c                 slot k is in the middle of list somewhere.
c                 pull it out.
                  knext = next_time(ibin,k)
                  kprev = prev_time(ibin,k)
                  next_time(ibin,kprev) = knext
                  prev_time(ibin,knext) = kprev
              endif

c             make slot k head of the free list
              call spin_lock(lok_free(ibin))
                  times(ibin,k) = start_free(ibin) + .001
```

```
                              num_times(ibin) = num_times(ibin) - 1
                              start_free(ibin) = k
                        call spin_unlock(lok_free(ibin))

c
c                       release everybody

                        call release_slot(test,ibin,k,
     s                  lok_slot,num_bins)
                        call release_slot(test,ibin,kn,
     s                  lok_slot,num_bins)
                        call release_slot(test,ibin,kp,
     s                  lok_slot,num_bins)

     1      continue

            return
            end


c       ************************************************** test_lock

            integer function test_lock(test,ibin,k,
     s      lok_slot,num_bins)
c
            integer test(num_bins,1),lok_slot(num_bins,1),num_bins
            integer ibin,k,test_lock

c       If test(ibin,k) = 1 on entry, return -1. It means the slot
c       (ibin,k) is owned by a different process.
c       If test(ibin,k) is 0 on entry, set it to 1 and return 1.
c       This means the process owns the slot (ibin,k).
c       The variable test is read and set in a locked region.
c       Unlock locks before returning.

            call spin_lock(lok_slot(ibin,k))
                if (test(ibin,k) .eq. 1) then
                    test_lock = -1
                else
                    test(ibin,k) = 1
                    test_lock = 1
                endif
            call spin_unlock(lok_slot(ibin,k))

            return
            end
```

```
c        ***********************************************release_slot

         subroutine release_slot(test,ibin,k,lok_slot,num_bins)

         integer test(num_bins,1),lok_slot(num_bins,1),num_bins
         integer ibin,k,test_lock

c        set test(ibin,k) = 0 in locked region, if k > 0.

         if (k .gt. 0) then
             call spin_lock(lok_slot(ibin,k))
                 test(ibin,k) = 0
             call spin_unlock(lok_slot(ibin,k))
         endif

         return
         end


c        ************     END OF PROGRAM     **************************
```

Problem: Why does subroutine release_slot set test = 0 in a protected region?

Problem: In main program, have the do 11 loop execute in parallel. (This is similar to Section 8.6.)

Problem: Show that the do 71 loop of the main program cannot deadlock, even though two locks are taken. Show that the do 78 loop is correct.

Problem: Assuming no overlap or early recollision occurs, how much overhead is in the parallel version compared to the single-stream version?

Problem: Show that routines add_time_to_queue and remove_from_queue will not deadlock.

Problem: It is possible to speed up the process of removing the first nproc collisions from the event queue, by removing them in a block. Write the removal in a more efficient form.

12.10   Summary

In this chapter, the parallelization of a relatively simple discrete time, discrete event simulator has been described. The nature of data dependencies and contention in the event simulator has been described, and it was shown how these inhibitors to parallelism are expected to affect other event simulators.

Perhaps the most striking aspect of the parallel program is how complex it is, compared with the single-stream version. This complexity seems to belie the qualitative perscription for parallelizing the single-stream program: Execute `nproc` processes in parallel, where `nproc` is the number of processes. The additional complexity is simply the extra logic needed to test for mishaps (for "collisions" among events) and to manage such mishaps effectively.

While parallelizing event simulators may be a bit difficult, there is no other way of attaining significantly improved performance from such programs. Event simulators will not normally benefit from running on vector processors.

CHAPTER 13

Some Applications

13.1 Introduction

This chapter presents applications which make use of the techniques developed in the previous chapters. Each application is a subroutine which is called by each process. It is assumed that, before the subroutine is called, nproc processes have been forked, that barriers and locks have been initialized, and that variables which must be shared have been shared. The requirements will be listed in the comment section of each subroutine. A maximum of 20 processors are presumed available.

It is a useful exercise for the reader to estimate the true speedup and ideal speedup of each of the programs and to write the programs in different forms.

13.2 Average and Mean Squared Deviation

The average <a> of an array a is

$$\langle a \rangle = (1/n)sum(i)\ a(i)$$

where i is summed between i1 and i2 inclusive in steps of istep, and the number of points n is

$$n = (i1 - i2)/istep + 1$$

The mean squared deviation is

$$MS(a) = [(1/n)sum(i)(a(i)**2)] - \langle a \rangle**2$$

where, again, i is summed as described above.
The parallel calculation is

```
              subroutine stat(a,il,i2,istep,id,nproc,bar,lok
     s                        average,deviation)
c
c       Find average and mean-squared deviation of array a(i),
c       for i between il and i2 inclusive, in steps of istep.
c       The values are returned in shared variables
c       average and deviation.
c       Variables bar and lok, for barrier and spin-lock
c       respectively, are shared.
c       bar is barrier for nproc processes.
c       Other variables are private, but a,il,i2,istep,n
c       may be shared if desired.

        real a(1),average,deviation
        integer il,i2,istep,id,nproc,lok,bar(1),i
        real tem_average,tem_deviation,n
c
c       initialize variables.
        if (id .eq. 0) then
            average = 0.
            deviation = 0.
        endif
        tem_average = 0.
        tem_deviation = 0.
        n = float((i2 - il)/istep + 1)

        call barrier(bar)

c       partial sums
        do 1 i = il + id * istep,i2,istep * nproc
            tem_average = tem_average + a(i)
            tem_deviation = tem_deviation + a(i)**2
    1       continue
```

```
c       accumulation
        call spin_lock(lok)
             average = average + tem_average
             deviation = deviation + tem_deviation
        call spin_unlock(lok)

c       make sure all processes have completed before continuing
        call barrier(bar)

c       final results computed by process 0 only
        if (id .eq. 0) then
             average = average/n
             deviation = (deviation/n) - average**2
        endif

        call barrier(bar)

        return
        end
```

Problem: Why are variables `average` and `deviation` initialized by process 0 alone? What is the purpose of the barrier above the do 1 loop? What would happen if variables `average` and `deviation` were initialized following the 1 `continue` statement? What is the purpose of the barrier directly above the `return` statement?

Problem: How would you alter the program so that `average` and `deviation` were not shared? Could you eliminate the first and last barriers? Write the program so that the accumulation stage is done by process 0, without spin-locks.

13.3   Fitting a Line to Points

Given a set of n points in a plane

$$(x(i), y(i)),$$

the line which forms the best fit to the data, in the sense of the minimum least squares difference, has the form

$$y = a * x + b$$

where

```
a = (h(0) * w(1) - h(1) * w(0))/(h(0) * h(2) - h(1)**2)
b = (h(2) * w(0) - h(1) * w(1))/(h(0) * h(2) - h(1)**2)
```

and

```
h(m) = sum(i) x(i)**m
w(m) = sum(i) y(i) * (x(i)**m)
```

with i going from 1 to n inclusive.

The parallel program to calculate the values of a and b is

```
c            subroutine fit_line(x,y,n,a,b,id,nproc,bar)

c      fit a line a * x + b to n points (x(i),y(i)).
c      variables a,b are shared
c      Bar is barrier for nproc processes and is shared.
c      All other variables are private. However, the
c      variables x,y,n may be shared if desired.

            real x(1),y(1),a,b
            integer n,id,nproc,bar(1)
            integer i
            real tem_h1(0:19),tem_h2(0:19)
            real tem_w0(0:19),tem_w1(0:19),tem_w2(0:19)
            real sum_h0,sum_h1,sum_h2,sum_w0,sum_w1,sum_w2
            real denom,temp

c      initialize variables
            tem_h1(id) = 0.
            tem_h2(id) = 0.
            tem_w0(id) = 0.
            tem_w1(id) = 0.
            tem_w2(id) = 0.

c                                        ******* point A

c      each process accumulates temporary sums for h(m), w(m)
            do 1 i = 1 + id,n,nproc
                  sum_h1 = sum_h1 + x(i)
                  temp = x(i) * x(i)
                  sum_h2 = sum_h2 + temp
                  sum_w0 = sum_w0 + y(i)
                  sum_w1 = sum_w1 + y(i) * x(i)
```

```
                  sum_w2 = sum_w2 + y(i) * temp
    1         continue
              tem_h1(id) = sum_h1
              tem_h2(id) = sum_h2
              tem_w0(id) = sum_w0
              tem_w1(id) = sum_w1
              tem_w2(id) = sum_w2

c     When all processes have finished, process 0 accumulates
c     the final sum
              call barrier(bar)
              if (id .eq. 0) then
                  sum_h0 = float(n)
                  do 2 i = 1,nproc - 1
                      sum_h1 = sum_h1 + tem_h1(i)
                      sum_h2 = sum_h2 + tem_h2(i)
                      sum_w0 = sum_w0 + tem_w0(i)
                      sum_w1 = sum_w1 + tem_w1(i)
                      sum_w2 = sum_w2 + tem_w2(i)
    2             continue
                  denom = 1./(sum_h0 * sum_h2 - sum_h1**2)
                  a = (sum_h0 * sum_w1 - sum_h1 * sum_w0) * denom
                  b = (sum_h2 * sum_w0 - sum_h1 * sum_w1) * denom
              endif

              call barrier(bar)

              return
              end
```

Problem: Make this program robust by including an option for denom as undefined (i.e., sum_h0 * sum_h2 - sum_h1**2 is zero).

Problem: In the do 2 loop, why don't the variables sum_h1, ..., sum_w2 have to be explicitly initialized before the loop? (Hint: Why does the loop start with i = 1?)

Problem: What is the purpose of the final barrier call? Why is no barrier needed at point A?

Problem: Minimize the overhead by accumulating each sum_h1, ..., sum_w2 in a protected region, with a different spin-lock for each sum.

13.4 Numerical Integration

This routine calculates the numerical integration of a function using Simpson's rule. The integral is

$$integral = \int_b^a funct(x)\ dx.$$

The numerical integration uses step size `step`, and the algorithm is

```
integral = (step/3)[funct(a) + 4 * funct(a + step) +
        2 * funct(a + 2 * step) + 4 * funct(a + 3 * step) +
        2 * funct(a + 4 * step) + ... + 4 * funct(a+ (n - 1) * step)+
        funct(b)]
```

where n must be even and

```
step = (b - a)/float(n).
```

The parallel subroutine is

```
          subroutine intgrt(a,b,n,integral,id,nproc,bar,lok)

c         Integrate funct(x) between a and b inclusive, using
c         Simpson's rule, subdividing interval into n points.
c         Result is returned in "integral."
c         barrier bar for nproc processes is shared.
c         lok is spin-lock and is shared.
c         Variable integral is shared. Other variables are private.
c         a,b may be shared if desired.

          real a,b,integral
          integer n,id,nproc,bar(1),i,lok
          real funct,tem_integral,x,step

c         check that n is even
          if ((mod(n,2) .ne. 0) .or. (n .eq. 0)) then
              print *, 'ERROR, n must be even and non-zero'
              call exit(-1)
          endif

c         initialize variables
```

```
            if (id .eq. 0)integral = funct(a) + funct(b)
            step = (b - a)/float(n)
            tem_integral = 0.

            call barrier(bar)

c       Each process computes a portion of
c       the sum, stored in tem_integral. Note that the
c       contribution of funct(b - step) is not included.
            do 1 i = 1 + 2 * id,n - 3,2 * nproc
                x = a + i * step
                tem_integral = tem_integral + 4. * funct(x)
    s                               +2. * funct(x + step)
  1         continue

c       accumulation stage.
c       Each process accumulates its partial value
            call spin_lock(lok)
                integral = integral + tem_integral
            call spin_unlock(lok)

c       Make sure all processes have finished before continuing
            call barrier(bar)

c       process 0 creates final value
            if (id .eq. 0) then
                integral = (step/3.) * (integral + 4. *
    s           funct(b - step))
            endif

            call barrier(bar)

            return
            end
```

Problem: Rewrite the above program using block scheduling. Is this more efficient?

13.5   Exploring a Maze

In this section, a simulation of an explorer traversing a maze is described. The maze is in the form of rooms connected to each other by doors. The explorer starts out in one of the rooms, and the goal is to reach the "outside,"

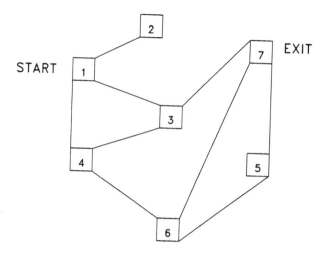

Figure 13-1.   A possible maze.

that is, to reach a particular other room. An example of the maze is shown in Figure 13-1.

The goal is to compute *any* path that leads from the start to the exit. It need not be the most direct path. (In general, it will not be the most direct route.)

For the single-stream version of the program, it will be assumed that the Fortran implementation allows recursion. While standard Fortran 77 is not recursive, most modern implementations of the language are stack based and allow recursion. The parallel version is not recursive, and when run with only one process, it provides an alternative single-stream version.

The following variables are used:

num_of_rooms—the total number of rooms.

num_of_doors(i)—the number of doors in room i.

room_connect(i, k)—the room number to which one passes if one takes door k of room i.

taken(i)—0 if the explorer has not yet been in room i. 1 if the explorer has already been in room i.

done—0 normally. Set to 1 when the explorer has found the exit.

start_room—the room number in which the explorer begins

exit_room—the room number in which the exit is located.

The explorer starts in room number start_room and explores until he or she arrives at room number exit_room. Each time the explorer enters a room i, he or she sets taken(i) to 1, so as to not enter the room a second time, from a different doorway. In this way, the explorer passes through each room once, trying each door in each room, until arriving at the exit.

The result of the computation is the path through the maze. This is returned in the one-dimensional array path, so that path(i) is the room number from which the explorer entered room i. This array is all that is necessary to trace the path to the exit. Because the explorer can enter a room only once, the path is merely a succession of room numbers, path(start_room) = 0.

The computation is carried out in subroutine explore.

```
explore(room_number,path,taken,room_connect,
num_of_rooms,num_of_doors,exit_room,done)
```

and room_number is the number of the room that the explorer is in. This subroutine acts as follows:

```
If room_number = exit_room, then
    set done = 1 and return.
else
    for each door in the room
        if the room to which the door leads has not
            yet been explored, explore that room
endif
```

Each time the explorer passes to a new room, the explore subroutine is invoked.

```
*******************************************************get-path
        subroutine get_path(num_of_rooms,num_of_doors,
    s      room_connect,taken,exit_room,start_room,path)
c    driver subroutine.
c    single-stream version.
c    Explore the maze which is described by arguments. These
c    arrays are presumed to have been initialized by the calling
c    program.

        integer num_of_doors(1),room_connect(num_of_rooms, 1)
        integer taken(1),path(1)
        integer exit_room,start_room,num_of_rooms
        integer done
```

```
c       initialize variables
        do 1 i = 1,num_of_rooms
            taken(i) = 0
            path(i) = 0
 1      continue
        done = 0

c       explore the maze.
        call explore(start_room,path,taken,room_connect,
 s          num_of_rooms,num_of_doors,exit_room,done)

        if (done .eq. 0) then
            print *, MAZE HAS NO EXIT'
            call exit()
        endif

c       print the path
        print *, 'path to exit,in reverse order'
        print *, 'exit room = ',exit_room
        prev_room = path(exit_room)
 10     continue
            print *, 'room = ',prev_room
            if (prev_room .ne. start_room) then
                prev_room = path(prev_room)
                goto 10
            endif
c       end of print loop

        return
        end

******************************************************explore
        subroutine explore(room_number,path,taken,room_connect,
 s          num_of_rooms,num_of_doors,exit_room,done)

c    The explorer is in room with number room_number.
c    He explores each door, entering the next room
c    if it has not yet been explored. If he enters the next
c    room, he updates the path appropriately.

        integer room_number,path(1),taken(1)
        integer room_connect(num_of_rooms,1)
        integer exit_room,done
        integer next_room,i

        if (room_number .eq. exit_room) then
            done = 1
            return
```

```
              endif

              do 1 k = 1,num_of_doors(room_number)
                  next_room = room_connect(room_number,k)
                  if (taken(next_room) .eq. 1) goto 1
c                 The next room is free. Update path.
c                 Explore the next room.
                  path(next_room) = room_number
                  taken(next_room) = 1
                  call explore(next_room,path,taken,room_connect,
     s                num_of_rooms,num_of_doors,exit_room,done)
                  if (done .eq. 1) return
1             continue
              return
              end
```

There are several ways of implementing the search in parallel. The general idea is that many processes explore simultaneously, each updating the "path" array and each searching for exit_room.

For example, each time a process enters a new room, it can spawn a new process for each door, and the new processes explore the next rooms. When a process can go no further, it is destroyed. However, this is not efficient because of the overhead of creating and destroying processes.

Another possibility is to spawn nproc processes and have each explore independently. One of the processes must arrive at the exit. This algorithm is likely to be inefficient because, in all probability, one or more processes will become boxed in, either at a dead end, or because other processes have explored all the rooms to which a given process can proceed. In such a case, the boxed-in processes will become idle while other processes continue the search, thus leading to poor distribution of work.

A third possibility is to have a global stack of the rooms which are available for processes to enter. Whenever a process enters a new room, it adds to the stack those rooms to which the room provides access and which have not already been added to the stack or visited. The exploration proceeds by having each process pop a room from this stack, enter the room, and then push onto the stack the rooms which are accessible from the new room (and which are not already on the stack and which have not already been visited). It also updates the path array. This process continues until one process arrives at the exit room. The problem with this algorithm is that the single stack becomes a bottleneck. Since rooms are always pushed onto or popped from the top of the stack, every time a process adds or subtracts from this stack, it must lock the entire stack. This will force the exploration to be nearly sequential.

The algorithm to be used is a combination of the second and third methods described above. nproc processes are spawned, and these explore independently. Rather than accessing a single stack, each process keeps its own stack of rooms which it can enter, and whenever it can go no farther, it starts a new path from this stack. If a process uses up all the rooms on its own stack, it can take rooms from the stack of another process. It is only when this happens that the processes become synchronized, and in general this synchronization is expected to be relatively infrequent.

The stack used to keep track of the available rooms is

```
room_stack(id,k)
```

where id identifies the process which "owns" the stack, and k denotes the amount of space on the stack, 1 <= k <= stack_length. The variable top_of_stack(id) points to the top of the stack (the next free space). If top_of_stack = 1, the stack is empty.

The parallel version is

```
            subroutine get_path(num_of_rooms,num_of_doors,
     s               room_connect,nproc,id,taken,
     s               exit_room,start_room,path,lok_stack,
     s               bar_array,lok_taken,room_stack,
     s               stack_length,top_of_stack,done)

c      driver subroutine.
c      Parallel version.
c      If nproc = 1, this is valid as a single-stream version as
c      well. Explore the maze which is described by dummy
c      arguments. nproc processes call this subroutine.
c      The locks and barriers have been initialized before entry.
c      The following variables are shared: taken, path, lok_stack,
c      bar_array, lok_taken, room_stack, stack_length,done
c      top_of_stack.
c      The other variables are private.
c      Variables num_of_rooms,num_of_doors,room_connect,
c      exit_room,start_room,stack_length may be shared if
c      desired.

        integer num_of_doors(1),room_connect(num_of_rooms,1)
        integer taken(1),path(1),nproc,id,done
```

```
      integer exit_room,start_room,num_of_rooms
      integer done,lok_stack(0:1),bar_array(1)
      integer room_stack(0:19,1),top_of_stack(0:1)
      integer lok_taken(1),stack_length

      integer new_id,i,j,next_room,current_room,new_room
      integer mod,available,k,prev_room

c     initialize variables
      do 1 i = 1 + id,num_of_rooms,nproc
            taken(i) = 0
            path(i) = 0
  1      continue
      if (id .eq. 0) done = 0
c     initialize stack
      top_of_stack(id) = 1
c     Process 0 starts off in start_room. Push this room onto
c     the stack of process 0.
      if (id .eq. 0) then
            top_of_stack(0) = 2
            room_stack(0,1) = start_room
      endif

      call barrier(bar_array)

c     Explore the maze.
c     Each process gets a room from a stack, preferably
c     its own.
 20      continue
      if (done .eq. 1) goto 50
      next_room = 0

      do 3 j = id,nproc + id
            new_id = mod(j,nproc)
            call spin_lock(lok_stack(new_id))
                  if (top_of_stack(new_id) .ne. 1) then
                        next_room = room_stack(new_id,
     s                        top_of_stack(new_id) - 1)
                        top_of_stack(new_id) =
     s                        top_of_stack(new_id) - 1
                  endif
            call spin_unlock(lok_stack(new_id))
            if (next_room .ne. 0) goto 4
 3       continue
c     If process gets here, it was unable to get a new room.
c     try again
```

```
              goto 20
    4         continue
c         If process gets here, it obtained next_room from a stack.
c         Now put all rooms reachable from next_room onto the
c         room_stack. Sum over all doors k.
              current_room = next_room
              do 5 k = 1,num_of_doors(current_room)
                  new_room = room_connect(current_room,k)
                  available = 0
                  call spin_lock(lok_taken(new_room))
                      if (taken(new_room) .ne. 1) then
                          taken(new_room) = 1
                          available = 1
                          path(new_room) = current_room
                      endif
                  call spin_unlock(lok_taken(new_room))
                  if (available .eq. 1) then
c                     check that new_room is exit_room
                      if (new_room .eq. exit_room) then
                          done = 1
                          goto 50
                      else
c                         put room on stack
                          call spin_lock(lok_stack(id))
                              top_of_stack(id) =
    s                             top_of_stack(id) + 1
                              room_stack(id,top_of_stack(id) - 1)=
    s                             new_room
                          call spin_unlock(lok_stack(id))
                      endif
                  endif
    5         continue
              goto 20
   50         continue

              if (id .ne. 0) return

c     print the path
              print *, 'path to exit,in reverse order'
              print *, 'exit room = ',exit_room
              prev_room = path(exit_room)
   10         continue
                  print *, 'room = ',prev_room
                  if (prev_room .ne. start_room) then
                      prev_room = path(prev_room)
                      goto 10
                  endif
```

```
c          end of print loop
           return
           end
```

Problem: Why must room_stack(id,k) be locked whenever it is accessed, even if process id is accessing it?

Problem: What is the purpose of setting taken(i) to 1 when room i is added to the stack of a process (even though the room is not visited immediately)?

Problem: Before a process adds a new room i to its room_stack, it first locks taken(i), then checks that taken(i) is not 1, sets taken(i) to 1, then adds the room i to its stack. Explain the logic behind this. Why does taken(i) have to be locked in order to determine its value? Why is each element of taken locked separately?

Problem: Could one lock each element of each stack separately?

Problem: Why is it not necessary to set done = 1 in a locked region?

Problem: The program above is not robust. No check is made that top_of_stack does not get too large. If the maze has no exit, the program will never exit. If path does not contain start_room, the print statement at the end of the subroutine will never terminate. Make the program more robust.

Problem: Rewrite the program so as to compute the shortest path through the maze (i.e., the path entering the fewest number of rooms). If there is more than one shortest path, return the first one.

Problem: Write a parallel program to approximate the shortest path by eliminating all loops of length <= L. A loop of length L is a path between any two rooms, say i, j, which passes through a total of L rooms (including i, j), and such that there exists a shorter path between i, j passing through k rooms, k < L. A loop is illustrated by the dashed line in Fig. 13-2. The dotted line in that figure is a shorter path between rooms i, j and is not a loop (because there is no shorter path connecting the same two rooms).

Problem: When subroutine get_path is used to explore a maze in the

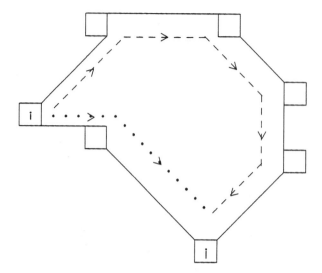

Figure 13-2.   The dashed path between rooms i and j is a loop of length 6, which can be replaced by the path represented by the dotted line.

form of a checkerboard (a square two-dimensional grid), then for small nproc, the final path tends to be long and meandering, while for larger nproc, the path tends to be short and direct. Why should this be the case?

13.6   Traveling Salesman Problem

There are n cities. A salesman starts at city number 1, visits all the other cities exactly once each, and then returns to city number 1. Find a route which minimizes the distance travelled.

Both the single-stream and parallel programs which solve this problem are presented. The algorithm used is complete enumeration. All possible itineraries are generated, one by one, the travel distance of each itinerary is computed, and the final result is the itinerary which has the minimum travel distance.

This problem readily lends itself to a recursive formulation, which is now described. The procedure can then be implemented either using recursive function calls or nonrecursive calls.

The following notation will be useful. Consider, as an example, six cities. The notation

1 2 3 {4 5 6} 1

is used to describe a *set of itineraries*. The itineraries in the set are generated as follows: The salesman starts at city number 1, then visits 2, and then 3. He then visits cities 4, 5, and 6 in all possible orders. Each itinerary of the set ends with a visit to city 1. Thus 1 2 3 {4 5 6} 1 is a shorthand for all the itineraries

        1 2 3 4 5 6 1
        1 2 3 4 6 5 1
        1 2 3 5 4 6 1
        1 2 3 5 6 4 1
        1 2 3 6 4 5 1
        1 2 3 6 5 4 1

It is possible to consider subpaths, so that for example

        3 6 {2 4 5} 1

means a set of itineraries which start at city 3, passes through 6, and then visits 2, 4, and 5 in all possible orders, each one returning finally to city 1.

The traveling salesman problem, formulated in terms of the above notation is as follows: Find the itinerary which has the minimum travel distances of all the itineraries

        1 {2 3 4 . . . n} 1.

The recursive formulation follows.
The path with the minimum travel distance, out of all paths

        1 {2 3 4 . . . n} 1

is the path with the minimum distance from among all the paths

        1 2 {3 4 . . . n} 1
        1 3 {2 4 . . . n} 1
        1 4 {2 3 5 . . . n} 1
        .
        .
        .
        .
        .
        .

        1 n {2 3 . . . n − 1} 1.

The recursive formulation is fleshed out as follows. Suppose the array `istops(i)` describes some path

```
istops(1) istops(2) istops(3) istops(4) ... istops(k) 1
```

always ending at city 1. That is, the salesman first stops at city `istops(1)`, then at `istops(2)`, and so forth through `istops(k)`, finally stopping at city 1. (It is not necessary here that `istops(1) = 1`. The array `istops` may contain a smaller subpath.)

We may create a function

```
find_minimum_distance(istops,k, ...)
```

where ... indicates other arguments which don't concern us here. Upon entry to this function, `istops(i)` contains k cities, `istops(1)`, `istops(2)`, ..., `istops(k)`. The purpose of the function is to determine the minimum travel distance for all the itineraries

```
istops(1) {istops(2) istops(3) ... istops(k)} 1
```

On return, `istops` has the itinerary with the minimum travel distance, and the function returns the travel distance for that itinerary.

The basis of the algorithm can be expressed as follows:

```
c     ******* pseudocode for solving traveling salesman problem
c     recursive solution

c     MAIN
          Assign itin(i) = i, i = 1,2,...,n. This is the initial
              itinerary.
          dist = find_minimum_distance(itin,n,....)
          end

          real function find_minimum_distance(istops,k,....)
          assign dtem = travel distance for the itinerary
              istops(1) - istops(2) - .... istops(k) - 1.
          if (k .eq. 2) then
              find_minimum_distance = dtem
              return
          endif
          store array istops(i) into integer array best_itin(i)
```

```
        do 1 j =2,n
                if j .ne. 2, then interchange cities istops(2) and
                        istops(j)
                new_dtem = find_minimum_distance(istops(2),k - 1,
                ....)
                if (new_dtem .lt. dtem) then
                        dtem = new_dtem
                        store array istops into
                                integer array best_itin
                endif
                Restore array istops(i) to the form it had on entry
                        to this function.
1               continue

        copy array best_itin into istops
        find_minimum_distance = dtem
        return
        end

c       ****************  end of pseudocode
```

The function find_minimum_distance works as follows. When it is
called, it must find the minimum distance of the set of itineraries

```
        istops(1) {istops(2) ... istops(k)} 1
```

It does this by finding the minimum travel distance of the itineraries

```
        istops(1) istops(2) {istops(3) ... istops(k)} 1
        istops(1) istops(3) {istops(2) istops(4) ... istops(k)} 1
        istops(1) istops(4) {istops(2) istops(3) istops(5) ...} 1
        .
        .
        .
        .
        .
        .
```

It does this by calling itself recursively. The whole process is ended when
$k = 2$, at which point there is only a single possibility and the minimum
travel distance can be returned directly.

The algorithm is a way of turning the n-city traveling salesman problem
into an $(n - 1)$-city problem in a recursive way. A nonrecursive solution
may be easily constructed from the recursive one.

The single-stream version is presented below. First, the recursive form of find_minimum_distance is used, and then a nonrecursive form is used. (Some implementations of Fortran77 allow recursion). The nonrecursive version is derived directly from the recursive one.

```
c       Traveling salesman problem, single-stream version.
c       Assume a maximum of 30 cities.
c       n - the number of cities.
c       x(i), y(i) - the x and y positions of city number i.
c       Assume that city number 1 is always at the origin,
c       so x(1) = y(1) = 0.0.
c       itin(i) - the itinerary for the trip with the
c       minimum distance travelled. Each itin(i) is a city,
c       so the cities are visited in the order
c       itin(1),itin(2),...,itin(n), itin(1) where itin(1) = 1.
c       For any i and j, i .ne. j, itin(i) .ne. itin(j), so no
c       city is visited twice.
c       dmin - the minimum distance of all paths enumerated.
c       This is the distance travelled for the path in itin(i).
c       separation(i,j) - the distance between cities i and j.
c       Note that separation(i,j) = separation(j,i).

        real x(30),y(30),separation(30,30),dmin,dstart
        real get_travel_distance,find_minimum_distance
        integer n,itin(30),i,j

c       first executable statement.
c       initialize
        (enter n,x(i),y(i))
        do 1 i = 1,n
            itin(i) = i
1       continue
c       form separation(i,j)
        do 10 i = 1,n
            do 11 j = i,n
                if (i .eq. j) then
                    separation(i,j) = 0.
                else
                    separation(i,j) =
     s                  sqrt((x(i) - x(j))**2 + (y(i) - y(j))**2)
                    separation(j,i) = separation(i,j)
                endif
11          continue
10      continue

c       dstart - travel distance for the path in itin(i)
```

```
          dstart = get_travel_distance(itin,n,separation)

c     find the minimum distance for all n cities
          dmin = find_minimum_distance(itin,n,dstart,separation)

c     output result
          print *, 'minimum travel distance = ', dmin
          print *, 'path of least travel distance is'
          print *, 'stop #      city #'
          do 2 i = 1,n
              print *,i,itin(i)
  2       continue
          end

c         ********************************get_travel_distance
          real function get_travel_distance(istops,k,separation)
          integer istops(1),k
          real sum,separation(30,30)

c     The salesman stops at cities istops(1),istops(2),...,
c     istops(k) and then returns to city 1.
c     Return the total distance travelled.

          sum = 0.
          do 2 i = 1,k - 1
              sum = sum + separation(istops(i),istops(i + 1))
  2       continue
          get_travel_distance = sum + separation(istops(k),1)

          return
          end

c         ***************************************find_minimum_distance
          real function find_minimum_distance(istops,k,
     s          dis0,separation)
          integer istops(1),k,j,i
          real dis0,dis,separation(30,30),dmin,dtem,dnew
          integer smin(30),istore(30)

c     Recursive version of the routine.
c     Return the minimum distance travelled for the salesman
c     starting at city istops(1), then traveling to all
c     the cities istops(2),...,istops(k), and returning to
c     city 1. The cities istops(2)...istops(k) may be visited
c     in any order. On return, istops(i) contains the itinerary
c     for minimum travel distance, where istops(i) contains the
c     itinerary for minimum travel distance, where istops(1) is
c     unaltered.
```

```
c       (The salesman must start at city istops(1).)
c       dis0 = travel distance for the itinerary istops when
c       this function is called. This value is meaningless on
c       return. smin(i) - temporary array, contains the
c       itinerary for the trip covering the least distance.
c       dmin - the minimum distance.
c       dtem, dnew are temporary variables holding travel distances.
c       istore(i) is temporary storage for the itinerary.
c       Successively interchange istops(2) with istops(3),
c       istops(4),..., istops(k), find the minimum path
c       for each of these arrangements.

c       first executable statement

c       If k = 2, the minimum distance must be dis0, as there is
c       no alternative route.
        if (k .eq. 2) then
             find_minimum_distance = dis0
             return
        endif

c       initialize - istore saves itinerary for later restoration.
        do 1 i = 1,k
             istore(i) = istops(i)
             smin(i) = istops(i)
  1         continue

        dmin = dis0

c       Modify dis0 to be the travel distance of itinerary
c       istops(i), starting from city istops(3), and visiting
c       istops(4),...,istops(k), 1, in that order.
        dis0 = dis0 - separation(istops(1),istops(2))
     s                  - separation(istops(2),istops(3))

c       Find the minimum distance for an itinerary which
c       starts at istops(1), then goes to istops(j), then
c       covers the other cities istops(3),..., istops(j - 1),
c       istops(2), istops(j + 1),..., istops(k),
c       in any order, then returns to city 1. j successively
c       takes on values 2,3,4,...,n.

        do 2 j = 2,k

c               dtem = the travel distance for the
c               itinerary which visits cities in the order
```

```
c                   istops(j), istops(3),..., istops(j - l),
c                   istops(2), istops(j + l),...,istops(k), l. The case
c                   of j = 3 and/or j = k must be handled specially.
c                   Subroutine interchange interchanges istops(2) and
c                   istops(j) in array istops and returns dtem.

                    if (j .ne. 2) then
                        call interchange(dis0,istops,dtem,j,k,
     s                   separation)
                    else
                        dtem = dis0 + separation(istops(2),istops(3))
                    endif

c                   get the minimum distance for the itinerary that
c                   starts at istops(2), goes thru istops(3),...,
c                   istops(k) in any order, and returns to city l.
                    dnew = find_minimum_distance(istops(2),k - l,
     s                   dtem,separation)

c                   Compare the travel distance of the new itinerary
c                   in istops(i) with the distance dmin.
c                   If travel distance has been decreased, save new
c                   itinerary.

                    dnew = dnew + separation(istops(l),istops(2))
                    if (dnew .lt. dmin) then
                        dmin = dnew
                        do 3 i = 2,k
                            smin(i) = istops(i)
    3                   continue
                    endif
c                   restore istops(i) for next iteration
                    do 30 i = 2,k
                        istops(i) = istore(i)
   30               continue

    2       continue

c       return minimum distance and new itinerary
            find_minimum_distance = dmin
            do 4 i = l,k
                istops(i) = smin(i)
    4       continue

            return
            end
```

```
c           ***************************************************interchange
            subroutine interchange(dis0,istops,dtem,j,k,separation)
            real dis0,dtem,separation(30,30)
            integer j,k,istops(1)
            integer item

c           On entry, dis0 = travel distance for itinerary
c           in istops(i), starting at istops(3) and proceeding
c           in order to istops(k) and then to 1.
c           dtem = the travel distance for the
c           itinerary which visits cities in the order
c           istops(j), istops(3),..., istops(j - 1),
c           istops(2), istops(j + 1),...,istops(k), 1. The case
c           of j = 3 and/or j = k must be handled specially.
c           Subroutine interchange interchanges istops(2) and
c           istops(j) in array istops and returns dtem.

            dtem = dis0
            if (j .ne. 3) then
                dtem = dtem - separation(istops(j),istops(j - 1))
            endif

            if (j .ne. k) then
                dtem = dtem - separation(istops(j),istops(j + 1))
            else
                dtem = dtem - separation(istops(j),1)
            endif

c           interchange cities istops(2) with istops(j)
            item = istops(2)
            istops(2) = istops(j)
            istops(j) = item

            dtem = dtem + separation(istops(2),istops(3))
            if (j .ne. 3) then
                dtem = dtem + separation(istops(j),istops(j - 1))
            endif
            if (j .ne. k) then
                dtem = dtem + separation(istops(j),istops(j + 1))
            else
                dtem = dtem + separation(istops(j),1)
            endif

            return
            end
```

Now the nonrecursive version of find_minimum_distance is presented.

The nonrecursive version is essentially the same as the recursive one, with some slight alterations. To make the subroutine nonrecursive, we must alter the flow of control of the subroutine and replace many of the scalars by arrays and some of the arrays by arrays of larger dimensionality.

For the control fow, the nonrecursive version is obtained directly from the recursive one by replacing the recursive call to find_minimum_distance with a branch to the beginning of the subroutine, and the subroutine returns by a branch to the statement directly following the recursive subroutine call or by an exit to the caller. The variable k has the addition function of keeping track of the level of recursive call being mimicked. Each recursive call passes a pointer to within array istops(i). This pointer is implemented explicitly as ibegin(k).

```
            real function find_minimum_distance(istops,n,
       s          dis00,separation)
            integer istops(1),k,j(30)
            real dis00,dis,separation(30,30),dmin(30),dtem,dnew(30)
            real dis0(30),dis(30)
            integer smin(30,30),istore(30,30),ibegin(30),n,m

c     Nonrecursive version of the routine.
c     Return the minimum distance travelled for the salesman
c     starting at city istops(1), then traveling to all
c     the cites istops(2),...,istops(n), and returning to
c     city 1. The cities istops(2)...istops(n) may be visited
c     in any order, On return, istops(i) contains the itinerary
c     for minimum travel distance, where istops(1) is unaltered.
c     (The salesman must start at city istops(1).)
c     dis00 = travel distance for the itinerary istops when
c     this function is called. This value is meaningless on
c     return. smin(i) - temporary array, contains the
c     itinerary for the trip covering the least distance.
c     dmin - the minimum distance
c     dtem, dnew are temporary variables holding travel distances.
c     istore(i) is temporary storage for the itinerary
c     ibegin(k) - a pointer to within array istops(i)
c     m = ibegin(k) is frequently used.

c     first executable statement
c     initialize variables - this section is executed
c     only once
            k = n
            dis0(k) = dis00
            ibegin(k) = 0
```

```
              do 40 i = k - 1,2, - 1
                    ibegin(i) = ibegin(i + 1) + 1
  40          continue


c       entry point for "recursive" calls.
  100         continue


c       If k = 2, the minimum distance must be dis0(k), as there is
c       no alternative route. Simulate return
              if (k .eq. 2) then
                    k = k + 1
                    dnew(k) = dis0(k - 1)
                    if (k .le. n) then
                          goto 200
                    else
                          find_minimum_distance = dis0(k - 1)
                          return
                    endif
              endif
c       initialize - istore saves itinerary for later restoration.
              m = ibegin(k)
              do 1 i = 1,k
                    istore(k,i) = istops(m + i)
                    smin(k,i) = istops(m + i)
   1          continue


              dmin(k) = dis0(k)


c       Modify dis0 to be the travel distance of itinerary
c       istops(i), starting from city istops(3), and visiting
c       istops(4),...,istops(k), 1, in that order.
              m = ibegin(k)
              dis0(k) = dis0(k) - separation(istops(m + 1),istops(m + 2))
     s                          - separation (istops(m + 2),istops(m + 3))


c       Find the minimum distance for an itinerary which
c       starts at istops(m + 1), then goes to istops(m + j), then
c       covers the other cities istops(m + 3),..., istops(m + k),
c       istops(m + 2) in any order, then returns to city 1.
c       m = ibegin(k).
c       j successively takes on values 2,3,4,...,n.


              j(k) = 1
  150         continue
              j(k) = j(k) + 1
```

```
          if (j(k) .gt. k)goto 2
c     *********do 2 j = 2,k
c              dtem = the travel distance for the
c              itinerary which visits cities in the order
c              istops(m + j), istops(m + 3),..., istops(m + j - 1),
c              istops(m + 2), istops(m + j + 1),...,istops(m + k),
c              1. The case of j = 3 and/or j = k must be handled
c              specially. Subroutine interchange interchanges
c              istops(m + 2) and istops(m + j) in array istops and
c              returns dtem. m = ibegin(k).


               if (j(k) .ne. 2) then
                    call interchange(dis0(k),istops(ibegin(k) +
     s              1),dtem,j(k),k,separation)
               else
                    dtem = dis0(k) +
     s              separation(istops(m + 2),istops(m + 3))
               endif


c              get the minimum distance for the itinerary that
c              starts at istops(m + 2), goes thru
c              istops(m + 3),..., istops(m + k)
c              in any order, and returns to city 1, m = ibegin(k).


               k = k - 1
               dis0(k) = dtem
               goto 100
c     ******** dnew = find_minimum_distance(istops(2),k - 1,
c     ********    dtem,separation)


 200           continue


c              Compare the travel distance of the new itinerary
c              in istops(i) with the distance dmin.
c              If travel distance has been decreased, save new
c              itinerary.


               m = ibegin(k)
               dnew(k) = dnew(k) +
     s         separation(istops(m + 1),istops(m + 2))
               if (dnew(k) .lt. dmin(k)) then
                    dmin(k) = dnew(k)
```

```
                          do 3 i = 2,k
                              smin(k,i) = istops(m + i)
   3                      continue
                      endif

c                     restore istops(i) for next iteration
                      do 30 i = 2,k
                          istops(m + i) = istore(k,i)
   30                 continue

              goto 150
   2          continue
c         return minimum distance and new itinerary
              m = ibegin(k)
              do 4 i = 1,k
                  istops(m + i) = smin(k,i)
   4          continue
              k = k + 1
              if (k .le. n) then
                  dnew(k) = dmin(k - 1)
                  goto 200
              else
                  find_minimum_distance = dmin(k - 1)
                  return
              endif

c     error if the instruction below is executed.
              print *, '******** error, executing end of function'
              print *, 'find_minimum_distance.'
              call exit(-1)

              return
              end
```

To execute this algorithm in parallel, different processes will determine the minimum distances of different sets of paths. The scheduling is essentially *self-scheduling* and is illustrated by an example. Consider six cities and three processes. Process 1 will find the minimum distance for all paths that pass through cities 2 and 3, that is, for itineraries

1 2 3 {4 5 6} 1.

Then process 2 evaluates the paths

1 2 4 {3 5 6} 1.

Process 3 evaluates

   1 2 5 {3 4 6} 1.

Process 1, when it is finished, next evaluates

   1 2 6 {3 4 5} 1.

Process 2, when it is done, carries on with

   1 3 2 {4 5 6} 1.

Process 3, the second time around, does

   1 3 4 {2 5 6} 1.

Process 1, on its third pass, does

   1 3 5 {2 4 6} 1

and so forth.

In the general case, a variable num is introduced, such that the subset of itineraries is characterized by the first num cities in the itinerary. Each process gets a different set of num cities and then goes off to find the minimum travel distance for all possible itineraries consistent with having these num cities as the first num stops. (In the example above, num = 3.) To find the minimum distance, the process can make use of the function find_minimum_distance (either the recursive or nonrecursive form) unchanged.

The function schedule_cities is used to determine the first num cities in the itinerary of a given process. The call is

```
call schedule_cities(new_sched,num,...)
```

where new_sched(i) contains the previous schedule, and num is the number of cities to be scheduled. (The ellipses means that the subroutine has other parameters, which are not detailed here.)

In terms of the above example, on the first call, we pass num = 3 and

```
new_sched(1) = 1
new_sched(2) = 2
new_sched(3) = 3
```

The first call returns new_sched unchanged. This is an initialization. On the second call, schedule_cities returns

```
new_sched(1) = 1
new_sched(2) = 2
new_sched(3) = 4
```

On the third call, the new values of new_sched are passed, and on return we have

```
new_sched(1) = 1
new_sched(2) = 2
new_sched(3) = 5
```

On the fourth call, the array new_sched(i) = 1 2 6, on the fifth call it is 1 3 2, on the sixth call it is 1 3 4, and so forth. Each call to schedule_cities is made by a process that has finished its work and needs a new set of itineraries to evaluate. The cities in new_sched then provide the first num stops. After each call to schedule_cities, the process goes off and finds the minimum distance for all possible itineraries consistent with these first num stops, by calling find_minimum_distance in the usual way.

This is self-scheduling. The call to schedule_cities must be made in a protected region so that the scheduling is sequential. As will be seen, the time required for scheduling is expected to be minuscule compared to the time to solve the problem, even in parallel. This is discussed at the end of the section.

The subroutine is

```
      subroutine schedule_cities(new_sched,
s     num,n,call_num,used)
      integer new_sched(1),num,n,call_num
      integer used(1),j,k,m

c     On entry, array new_sched is an itinerary of
c     num cities, the first num stops on the
c     salesman's route. new_sched(1) = 1. There are
c     a total of n cities. Generate a new schedule in new_sched.
```

```
c       If no more schedules are possible, return
c       new_sched(1) = 0. call_num should be initialized to 1
c       on the first call. It is incremented, and used in the
c       section to detect duplicates.
c       used(i) — a temporary array used to detect duplicates.
c       This routine generates the next schedule by first
c       incrementing new_sched(num). if new_sched(num) > n,
c       it sets new_sched(num) = 2, and increments
c       new_sched(num - 1). if new_sched(num - 1) > n,
c       it sets new_sched(num - 1) = 2 and increments
c       new_sched(num - 2), and so forth. When the algorithm
c       proceeds to the point where new_sched(1) must be
c       incremented, then all possible schedules have been
c       generated. Once a tentative schedule is generated, then
c       new_sched(2)...new_sched(num) are checked for
c       duplicates (i.e., if new_sched(i) = new_sched(j)).
c       If a duplicate is found, the procedure is repeated
c       until there are no duplicates.


        k = num
        if (call_num .eq. 1) then
c               initialize and return
                do 2 j = 1,n
                    used(j) = 0
                    new_sched(j) = j
2               continue
                call_num = call_num + 1
                return
        endif


100     continue
        new_sched(k) = new_sched(k) + 1
        if (new_sched(k) .gt. n) then
                new_sched(k) = 2
                k = k - 1
                if (k .eq. 1) then
c                       all schedules have been generated.
                        new_sched(1) = 0
                        return
                endif
                goto 100
        endif


c       now check for duplicates
c       if find duplicate in new_sched(j) (duplicating
```

```
c          new_sched(m), m < j), then it does not matter
c          what the values of new_sched(m) are
c          m > j).
              do 1 j = 2,num
                  if (used(new_sched(j)) .eq. call_num) then
                      used(new_sched(j)) = 0
c                     there are duplicates
                      do 5 m = 2,j
                          used(new_sched(m)) = 0
5                     continue
                      k = j
                      goto 100
                  else
                      used(new_sched(j)) = call_num
                  endif
1             continue

c          At this point, a schedule has been generated with no
c          duplicates.

              call_num = call_num + 1
              return
              end
```

The implementation of schedule_cities above is not the most efficient one possible. Its virtues are simplicity and brevity. However, it will suit our purposes nicely, and its inefficiencies will not be important. This will be discussed after the full parallel program is introduced.

To solve the traveling salesman problem in parallel, a new main program is needed. All subroutines remain the same, and one can use either the recursive or nonrecursive version of find_minimum_distance. The program is

```
c          Traveling salesman problem, parallel version.
c          assume a maximum of 30 cities.
c          n - the number of cities.
c          x(i), y(i) - the x and y positions of city number i.
c          Assume that city number 1 is always at the origin,
c          so x(1) = y(1) = 0.0.
c          itin(i) - the itinerary for the trip with the
c          minimum distance travelled. Each itin(i) is a city,
c          so the cities are visited in the order
c          itin(1),itin(2),...,itin(n), itin(1) where itin(1) = 1.
c          For any i and j, i .ne. j, itin(i) .ne. itin(j), so no
c          city is visited twice.
```

```
c       dmin - the maximum distance of all paths enumerated.
c       This is the distance travelled for the path in itin(i).
c       separation(i,j) - the distance between cities i and j.
c       Note that separation(i,j) = separation(j,i).

        real x(30),y(30),separation(30,30),dmin,dstart,dmintem
        real get_travel_distance,find_minimum_distance
        integer n,itin(30),nproc,id,num,process_fork
        integer priv_itin(30),new_sched(30)
        integer lok,lok_min,unlocked,call_num,used(30)
        integer city_buffer(30),locked
        real d_num

c       first executable statement.
c       shared variables

        call shared(itin,120)
        call shared(new_sched,120)
        call shared(dmin,4)
        call shared(lok,4)
        call shared(lok_min,4)
        call shared(used,120)
        call shared(call_num,4)

c       initialize
        (enter n,x(i),y(i))
        (enter num,nproc)
        unlocked = 0
        locked = 1
        call_num = 1
        do 1 i = 1,n
            itin(i) = i
            new_sched(i) = i
            city_buffer(i) = 0
    1   continue
        priv_itin(1) = 1

        call spin_lock_init(lok,unlocked)
        call spin_lock_init(lok_min,unlocked)

c       form separation(i,j)
        do 10 i = 1,n
            do 11 j = i,n
                if (i .eq. j) then
                    separation(i,j) = 0.
                else
                  separation(i,j) =
```

```
       s                           sqrt((x(i) - x(j))**2 + (y(i) - y(j))**2)
                           separation(j,i) = separation(i,j)
                       endif
 11            continue
 10        continue


 c     dmin - travel distance for the path in itin(i)
           dmin = get_travel_distance(itin,n,separation)


 c     create nproc - 1 additional processes
           id = process_fork(nproc)


 c     In the following loop, the first num cities on the
 c     itinerary for each process are generated.
 c     The locked region below is the essence of the
 c     parallel program. It schedules the first num visits
 c     for each process. Each process gets a different
 c     sequence of num cities.

 100       continue
           call spin_lock(lok)
               if (new_sched(1) .eq. 0) then
                       call spin_unlock(lok)
                       goto 150
               endif
               call schedule_cities(new_sched,num,n,
       s       call_ num,used)
               if (new_sched(1) .eq. 0) then
                       call spin_unlock(lok)
                       goto 150
               endif


 c             now get private itinerary for the process.
 c             the first num cities are obtained in locked region.
               do 30 i = 2,num
                       priv_itin(i) = new_sched(i)
 30            continue
           call spin_unlock(lok)


 c     Now generate the rest of the itinerary. This consists of
 c     cities not already in priv_itin. city_buffer(j) = 1 if
 c     city number j is in priv_itin, and 0 otherwise. All
 c     statements below use private variables.
 c
 c     prepare city_buffer
           do 31 i = 2,num
                   city_buffer(priv_itin(i)) = 1
```

```
31        continue
c      create the rest of the initial itinerary
          j = num + 1
          do 32 i = 2,n
              if (city_buffer(i) .eq. 0) then
                  priv_itin(j) = i
                  j = j + 1
              endif
32        continue
c      reinitialize city_buffer
          do 33 i = 2,num
              city_buffer(priv_itin(i)) = 0
33        continue

c      Find the travel distance for this itinerary.
c      first the travel distance for the first num cities
c      i.e., for the visits 1 - priv_itin(1) - priv_itin(2)....
c      priv_itin(num)
          d_num = get_travel_distance(priv_itin,num,separation)
     s            - separation(priv_itin(num),1)

c      next the travel distance for starting at priv_itin(num) and
c      then visiting priv_itin(num + 1) - priv_itin(num + 2)...
c      priv_itin(n) - 1.
          dstart = get_travel_distance(priv_itin(num),
     s            n - num + 1,separation)

c      Find the minimum travel distance for the itineraries
c      which start at priv_itin(num) and
c      then visits priv_itin(num + 1) - priv_itin(num + 2)...
c      priv_itin(n) - 1 in any order. (The trip must always
c      start at priv_itin(num)).
          dmintem = find_minimum_distance(priv_itin(num),
     s            n - num + 1,dstart,separation)

c      get total travel distance
          dmintem = dmintem + d_num

c      If this is less than dmin, then replace itin(i) with the
c      itinerary in priv_itin(i)
          call spin_lock(lok_min)
              if (dmin .gt. dmintem) then
                  do 40 i = 2,n
                      itin(i) = priv_itin(i)
40                continue
                  dmin = dmintem
              endif
```

```
          call spin_unlock(lok_min)

c       cycle back to get next itinerary
          goto 100

c       -------------  FINISHED  --------------------------
150       continue
C       ------------------------------------------------------

          call process_join()
c       output result
          print *, 'minimum travel distance = ',dmin
          print *, 'path of least travel distance is'
          print *, 'stop #      city #'
          do 2 i = 1,n
          print *, i, itin(i)
2         continue

          end
```

In general, the value of num is expected to be between 2 and 4. To see why num is so small, note that the total number of itineraries that must be explored is $n!$, which is

$$n! = n * (n - 1) * (n - 2) * (n - 3) * \ldots * 3 * 2 * 1$$

There are n choices for the first city of an itinerary, $n - 1$ choices for the second, $n - 2$ choices for the third, and so forth, and all these choices are independent.

The value of $n!$ increases very rapidly with n, as is seen in the chart below.

n	n!
2	2
4	24
6	720
8	40,320
10	3,628,800
12	479,001,600

The number of different sets of itineraries to be scheduled among the processes is given by n!/(n − num)! If, for example, n = 10, then using num = 2 means that there are 90 different *sets* of itineraries to be apportioned among the processes. If there are 10 processes, then on the average each process will explore nine sets of itineraries. For each set, the first two stops are fixed and the next eight stops will be explored in all possible orders. Thus *for each set*, a process must explore 8! = 40,320 possible itineraries, and each process does nine sets. The amount of time to explore 8! different paths is so much larger than the time required for scheduling that it is not necessary to streamline or parallelize the scheduling algorithm itself.

Problem: The traveling salesman problem, when solved by complete enumeration, becomes inordinately time-consuming for 15 or more cities. In applications (such as laying out communication networks), it frequently happens that the cities are clustered. In this case, one can carry out the minimization among clusters, and among cities within each cluster, thus keeping the number of trips between clusters to a minimum. Write a parallel algorithm to approximate the solution of the traveling salesman problem using the clustering approach. The formation of the clusters should also be executed in parallel.

13.7   General Gaussian Elimination

Gaussian elimination is an algorithm for solving a set of simultaneous linear algebraic equations. It is one of the most frequently used numerical algorithms, finding particular applicability in differential equations solvers and optimization problems. In this section, the basic algorithm is presented and a simple parallelization described. In Section 13.9, a variant of the algorithm is described which is applicable to simultaneous equations in which each equation has, at most, three terms.

The set of simultaneous equations is

$$a(1,1)x(1) + a(1,2)x(2) + a(1,3)x(3) + \ldots + a(1,n)x(n) - b(1) = 0$$
$$a(2,1)x(1) + a(2,2)x(2) + a(2,3)x(3) + \ldots + a(2,n)x(n) - b(2) = 0$$

.

.

.

$$a(n,1)x(1) + a(n,2)x(2) + a(n,3)x(3) + \ldots + a(n,n)x(n) - b(n) = 0$$

$$(13\text{-}1)$$

The a(i,j) and b(i) are all known initially, and the problem is to solve for the b unknowns x(1), x(2), ..., x(n).

These equations are usually written in the matrix form

Ax = b

where **A** is the n x n matrix with elements a(i,j), x is the vector of unknowns with elements x(1), ..., x(n) and b is the vector of known constants b(1), ..., b(n).

First, the general algorithm for solving the set of equations (13-1) will be described, along with an illustrative example. Then the single-stream computer program implementing the algorithm will be presented. Following this, the parallelization of the algorithm will be given and the ideal and actual speedups described.

Before beginning, it is most efficient to incorporate the b(i) into the array **A**, so that **A** has n rows and n + 1 columns. Let

$$a(1, n + 1) = -b(1)$$
$$a(2, n + 1) = -b(2)$$
.
.
.
$$a(n, n + 1) = -b(n).$$

Equations (13-1) become

$$a(1,1)x(1) + a(1,2)x(2) + a(1,3)x(3) + \ldots$$
$$+ a(1,n)x(n) + a(1,n + 1) = 0$$
$$a(2,1)x(1) + a(2,2)x(2) + a(2,3)x(3) + \ldots$$
$$+ a(2,n)x(n) + a(2,n + 1) = 0$$
.
.
.
$$a(n,1)x(1) + a(n,2)x(2) + a(n,3)x(3) + \ldots$$
$$+ a(n,n)x(n) + a(n, n + 1) = 0$$
$$(13\text{-}2)$$

The reason for writing the equations in this manner will become clear after the algorithm is described.

The algorithm consists of two parts: an elimination part and a back-substitution part. To illustrate the elimination step, consider the set of three simultaneous equations below:

$$2x(1) - 4x(2) + 24x(3) - 12 = 0 \qquad (13\text{-}3a)$$
$$6x(1) + 18x(2) + 12x(3) + 24 = 0 \qquad (13\text{-}3b)$$
$$3x(1) + 7x(2) - 2x(3) - 4 = 0 \qquad (13\text{-}3c)$$

First, eliminate $x(1)$ from two of the three equations. As will be seen, all the coefficients $a(i,j)$ of that equation from which $x(1)$ is *not* eliminated must be divided by the coefficient of $x(1)$ in that equation. Thus we eliminate $x(1)$ from all the equations *except* that equation for which the coefficient of $x(1)$ has the largest magnitude (regardless of sign). This means that $x(1)$ is eliminated from equations (13-3a) and (13-3c).

It is convenient to reorder the equations, so that equation (13-3b) is on top. (This is an *interchange step*, in which equations (13-3a) and (13-3b) are interchanged.) The equations above are the same as

$$6x(1) + 18x(2) + 12x(3) + 24 = 0 \qquad (13\text{-}4a)$$
$$2x(1) - 4x(2) + 24x(3) - 12 = 0 \qquad (13\text{-}4b)$$
$$3x(1) + 7x(2) - 2x(3) - 4 = 0 \qquad (13\text{-}4c)$$

Now eliminate $x(1)$ from all but equation (13-4a). Equation (13-4a) is called the *pivot equation* and the coefficient of $x(1)$, 6 is called the *pivot element*. To eliminate $x(1)$ from equation (13-4b), multiply (13-4a) by 2/6, subtract (13-4b) from (13-4a), and the result is the new (13-4b). That is, after multiplying, equations (13-4a) and (13-4b) become

$$2x(1) + 6x(2) + 4x(3) + 8 = 0$$
$$2x(1) - 4x(2) + 24x(3) - 12 = 0$$

Subtracting these two, the resulting equation is

$$10x(2) - 20x(3) + 20 = 0$$

Equations (13-4a)–(13-4c) are now

$$6x(1) + 18x(2) + 12x(3) + 24 = 0 \qquad (13\text{-}5a)$$
$$10x(2) - 20x(3) + 20 = 0 \qquad (13\text{-}5b)$$
$$3x(1) + 7x(2) - 2x(3) - 4 = 0 \qquad (13\text{-}5c)$$

Repeat this procedure, this time multiplying (13-5a) by 3/6 and subtracting the result from equation (13-5c). This results in the three equations

$$6x(1) + 18x(2) + 12x(3) + 24 = 0 \qquad \text{(13-6a)}$$
$$10x(2) - 20x(3) + 20 = 0 \qquad \text{(13-6b)}$$
$$2x(2) + 8x(3) + 16 = 0 \qquad \text{(13-6c)}$$

The next step is to eliminate $x(2)$ from one of the equations (13-6b) or (13-6c). Since equation (13-6b) has the largest coefficient of $x(2)$, then $x(2)$ will be eliminated from equation (13-6c). Thus equation (13-6b) is the pivot equation. To do the elimination, multiply (13-6b) by 2/10 and subtract equation (13-6c) from the result. This gives

$$6x(1) + 18x(2) + 12x(3) + 24 = 0 \qquad \text{(13-7a)}$$
$$10x(2) - 20x(3) + 20 = 0 \qquad \text{(13-7b)}$$
$$- 12x(3) - 12 = 0 \qquad \text{(13-7c)}$$

The elimination phase is now complete. The last row is an equation in only a single unknown.

For the general case, the algorithm for the elimination step is

```
c       Part 1 - elimination step
c       sum over all rows irow of matrix A.
        do irow = 1,n - 1
           icol = irow
           For column icol, find the maximum |a(jrow,icol)|,for all
              jrow between irow and n inclusive. |...| means
              absolute value.
           If irow .ne. jrow, interchange the elements of rows irow
              and jrow, so that, now, row irow has those elements
              that used to be in row jrow, and row jrow has the
              elements that used to be in row irow.
              Row irow is now the pivot row.
           do jrow = irow + 1,n
              Multiply each a(irow,kcol), by
                 a(jrow,irow)/a(irow,irow), for all kcol >= irow.
              Subtract row jrow from row irow. The result becomes
                 the new row jrow.
           endo
        endo
```

At the end of the elimination step, the set of equations can be written in the form

$$\mathbf{W}x = 0$$

which looks like

$$w(1,1)x(1) + w(1,2)x(2) + w(1,3)x(3) + \ldots + w(1,n)x(n) + w(1,n+1) = 0 \quad (13\text{-}8a)$$

$$w(2,2)x(2) + w(2,3)x(3) + \ldots + w(2,n)x(n) + w(2,n+1) = 0 \quad (13\text{-}8b)$$

$$w(3,3)x(3) + \ldots + w(3,n)x(n) + w(3,n+1) = 0 \quad (13\text{-}8c)$$

$$w(n-1,n)x(n-1) + w(n-1,n)x(n) + w(n-1,n+1) = 0 \quad (13\text{-}8y)$$

$$w(n,n)x(n) + w(n,n+1) = 0 \quad (13\text{-}8z)$$

where, for row i, all $w(i,k) = 0$ if $k < i$. Thus for equation i (row i), all variables $x(j)$, $j < i$, have been *eliminated*. It is this elimination process which accounts for the name of the algorithm: Gaussian elimination.

Equations (13-7a) – (13-7c) provide an example of equations (13-8a) through (13-8z).

The second stage then solves equations (13-8a) – (13-8z). Since row n (eq. (13-8z)) has only one unknown, $x(n)$, it may be found directly. Then the value of $x(n)$ is substituted in rows 1 to n – 1 inclusive. Then, since $x(n)$ is known, $x(n-1)$ may be determined from row n – 1 (eq. (13-8y)), and so forth. This step is called *back substitution*, because one is finding an unknown and substituting backwards (from the bottom up) for it.

The back substitution may be illustrated by solving the equations (13-7a) – (13-7c). First, solve for $x(3)$ in (13-7c). This gives

$$x(3) = -1,$$

while the other two equations remain

$$6x(1) + 18x(2) + 12x(3) + 24 = 0 \qquad (13\text{-}9a)$$
$$10x(2) - 20x(3) + 20 = 0 \qquad (13\text{-}9b)$$

Now substitute $x(3)$ into these equations (the so-called *back-substitution* step). This gives

$$6x(1) + 18x(2) + 12 = 0 \qquad (13\text{-}10a)$$
$$10x(2) + 40 = 0 \qquad (13\text{-}10b)$$

Now equation (13-10b) has only one unknown. This gives

$$x(2) = -4$$

Substituting this in (13-10a),

$$6x(1) - 60 = 0$$

resulting in

$$x(1) = 10$$

The three equations have been solved.
The general algorithm for the back substitution step is

```
c       Step 2 - backward substitution
        do icol = n,1, -1
            x(icol) = -w(icol,n + 1)/w(icol,icol)
            do jrow = 1,icol - 1
                w(jrow,n + 1) = w(jrow, n + 1) +
      s             a(jrow,icol)x(icol),
            endo
        endo
```

The single-stream program is

```
c           subroutine gaus_elim(a,x,n,row)

c       The LOGICAL action of this routine is
c       Gaussian elimination to solve n x n set of equations
c                   Ax = b
c       array b(i) is incorporated into a, so that
c                   a(i,n + 1) = b(i)
c       On entry, arrays a,x are passed. On return, x(i)
c       contains the unknowns.
c       However, the implementation is as follows:
c       It is assumed that array A is stored by rows, rather
c       than by columns. That is, a is passed as a linear array,
c       and
c           a(row(irow) + j - 1) <-> a(irow,j).
c       That is, a(row(irow))is the first matrix element of row
c       irow, a(row(irow)) <-> a(irow,1).
```

```
c       Note that
c           b(i) <-> a(row(i) + n)
c       Single-stream version

        real a(l),x(l),t,amul
        integer irow,jrow,icol,jcol,n,row(l),item

c       sum over all rows.
        do 1 irow = 1,n - 1

c               find the pivot row.
                call find_pivot_row(a(row(irow) + irow - 1),
                irow,n + 1,jrow)

c               interchange rows irow and jrow if necessary
                if (irow .ne. jrow) then
                        item = row(jrow)
                        row(jrow) = row(irow)
                        row(irow) = item
                endif

c               eliminate x(irow) from rows irow + 1,irow + 2, ..., n
c               For each row jrow, multiply each element of row
c               irow by a(jrow,irow)/a(irow,irow), and subtract
c               equations irow and jrow. Do this for elements
c               from irow + 1 to n + 1 inclusive.
                t = -1./a(row(irow) + irow - 1)
                do 2 jrow = irow + 1,n
                    amul = a(row(jrow) + irow - 1) * t
                    call elim(a(row(irow) + irow),
     s                    a(row(jrow) + irow),
     s                    n + 1 - irow, amul)
  2             continue
  1     continue

c       back substitution
        do 3 irow = n,1,-1
                x(irow) = -a(row(irow) + n)/a(row(irow) + irow - 1)
c               substitute for x(irow) in the other equations
                do 4 jrow = 1,irow - 1
                        a(row(jrow) + n) = a(row(jrow) + n)
     s                        + x(irow) * a(row(jrow) + irow - 1)
  4             continue
  3     continue

        return
        end
```

```
c       **********************************************find_pivot_row
        subroutine find_pivot_row(c,irow,num_of_elements,jmax)
        real c(1),abs,cmax
        integer irow,num_of_elements,jmax,jrow,ielem
c
c    c(1) is the matrix element a(row(irow) + irow - 1) - ie,
c    the coefficient of x(irow) in equation irow.
c    num_of_elements is the number of elements in any row.
c    num_of_elements - 1 is total number of equations.
c    Find the maximum coefficient of x(irow) for
c    all rows >= irow.
c    intrinsic function abs finds absolute value of
c    its argument.

        jmax = irow
        cmax = abs(c(1))
        ielem = 1
        do 1 jrow = irow + 1,num_of_elements - 1
            ielem = ielem + num_of_elements
            if (abs(c(ielem)) .gt. cmax) then
                jmax = jrow
                cmax = abs(c(ielem))
            endif
1       continue
        return
        end




c       ********************************************** elim
        subroutine elim(c,d,num,amul)
        real c(1),d(1),amul
        integer num,i

c    Do elimination step. If irow is the pivot row, then
c    c(1) = a(row(irow) + irow), ie, the coefficient of
c    x(irow + 1) in the pivot row. Then d(1) is the coefficient
c    of x(irow) in some other column (say jrow).
c    num = the number of elements n + 1 - (irow + 1) + 1, that is,
c    the number of elements on which to perform the
c    elimination step.

        do 1 i = 1,num
            d(i) = d(i) + amul * c(i)
1       continue
        return
        end
```

The purpose of writing the program in this way will become clear after the following discussion.

Problem: Would it be more or less efficient to replace the call to subroutine elim with in-line code?

This program will be parallelized in the simplest possible way. It is left as a programming project to make a more complex parallelization, which is appropriate for small problems (Chapter 15). The parallelization in this section will be reasonable for n large.

The first step in parallelization is to determine where the above program spends all its time. There are three major sections:

1. find_pivot_row
2. Do elimination step
3. Back substitution

To find the pivot row, the statements

```
ielem = ielem + num_of_elements
if (abs(c(ielem)) .gt. cmax) then
      jmax = jrow
      cmax = abs(c(ielem))
endif
```

must be executed a total of n − irow + 1 times when the pivot row is irow. The total number of execution steps is

$$n + n - 1 + n - 2 + \ldots + 2 = n(n + 1)/2 + 1.$$

The elimination step executes the statement

```
d(i) = d(i) + amul * c(i)
```

a total of n + 1 − irow times for each pair of rows irow, jrow, where irow is the pivot row and jrow goes from irow + 1 to n inclusive. Thus the total number of times this statement is executed is

$$sum(irow = 1, n - 1) \, sum(jrow = irow + 1, n) \, (n + 1 - irow)$$
$$= n(n - 1)(n + 1)/3.$$

The back substitution step executes the statement

```
         a(row(jrow) + n) = a(row(jrow) + n)
   s                      + x(irow) * a(row(jrow) + irow - 1)
```

a total of `irow - 1` times for each `irow`, where `irow` goes from n − 1 to 1 inclusive. Thus this statement is executed a total of

$$(n - 2)(n - 1)/2$$

times.

For various values of n, these expressions are

n	find_pivot_row	elim	back_substitution
10	54	330	36
20	209	2660	171
30	464	8990	406
50	1274	41650	1176
100	5049	333300	4851
200	20099	$2.67 \times 10^{**}6$	19701
300	45149	$9 \times 10^{**}6$	44551

The elimination step goes as approximately n**3, while the other two go as n**2. For larger n, the elimination step takes up by far the largest amount of time. Therefore, the biggest bang for the buck is obtained by doing the elimination step in parallel, leaving the rest of the program single-stream. Parallelizing the elimination step can be done by making a few simple changes in subroutine gaus_elim. The parallel program is

```
         subroutine gaus_elim(a,x,n,row,nproc,id,bar)

c        The LOGICAL action of this routine is
c        Gaussian elimination to solve n x n set of equations
c                     Ax = b
c        array b(i) is incorporated into a, so that
c                     a(i,n + 1) = b(i)
c        On entry, arrays a,n are passed. On return, x(i)
c        contains the unknowns.
```

```
c       However, the implementation is as follows:
c       It is assumed that array A is stored by rows, rather
c       than by columns. That is, a is passed as a linear array,
c       and
c          a(row(irow) + j - 1) <-> a(irow,j).
c       That is, a(row(irow))is the first matrix element of row
c       irow,
c                a(row(irow)) <-> a(irow,1).
c       Note that
c          b(i) <-> a(row(i) + n)
c
c       PARALLEL VERSION
c       It is assumed that each process calls this routine
c       separately. nproc is the total number of processes, and
c       id is the process id of the calling process.
c       bar is shared array for a barrier. The barrier is
c       presumed initialized for nproc processes
c       a,x must be shared.

        real a(1),x(1),t,amul
        integer irow,jrow,icol,jcol,n,row(1),item
        integer bar(1),nproc,id

c    sum over all rows.
        do 1 irow = 1,n - 1

c           find the pivot row. This is done by a
c           single process.
            if (id .eq. 0) then
                call find_pivot_row(a(row(irow) + irow - 1),
     s               irow,n + 1,jrow)

c               interchange rows irow and jrow if necessary.
                if (irow .ne. jrow) then
                    item = row(jrow)
                    row(jrow) = row(irow)
                    row(irow) = item
                endif
            endif

            call barrier(bar)

c           eliminate x(irow) from rows irow + 1, irow + 2,..., n
c           For each row jrow, multiply each element of row
c           irow by a(jrow,irow)/a(irow,irow), and subtract
c           equations irow and jrow. Do this for elements
c           from irow + 1 to n + 1 inclusive.
```

```
                     t = -1./a(row(irow) + irow - 1)
        c            Parallelize the loop below
                     do 2 jrow = n - id,irow + 1,- nproc
                        amul = a(row(jrow) + irow - 1) * t
                        call elim(a(row(irow) + irow),
     s                            a(row(jrow) + irow),
     s                            n + 1 - irow,amul)
        2            continue
                     call barrier(bar)
        1       continue
             call barrier(bar)

        c       back substitution. This is done by a single process.
                if (id .eq. 0) then
                   do 3 irow = n,1,-1
                      x(irow) = -a(row(irow) + n)
     s                         /a(row(irow) + irow - 1)
        c             substitute for x(irow) in the other equations
                      do 4 jrow = 1,irow - 1
                         a(row(jrow) + n) = a(row(jrow) + n) +
     s                            x(irow) * a(row)jrow) + irow - 1)
        4             continue
        3          continue
                endif

             call barrier(bar)

             return
             end
```

Apart from the barrier calls, all that is done is to parallelize the do 2 loop, so that each process carries out the elimination step for all elements of row jrow. Note that the iteration is from bottom up. This maximizes the effectiveness of cache, as was discussed in Section 11.5.

Problem: Explain the function of all the barrier calls in the parallel program above. Can any of these barrier calls be removed? Do you expect the barrier call directly following the 2 continue statement will produce significant overhead?

It is of interest to determine the ideal speedup of the above algorithm. The ideal speedup is the speedup determined by assuming that all the time is spent in the elimination step, while the find_pivot_row and back substitution steps take negligible time. This is a valid approximation for large n.

For pivot row `irow`, each process carries out the substitution step for $n - $ `irow` $+ 1$ elements. Suppose that T is the time required to execute a single

```
d(i) = d(i) + amul * c(i).
```

Then the time required for the parallel case is

$$[(n - irow)/nproc] (n - irow + 1) T$$

where $[$`i/j`$] = $`i/j` if `j` divides `i` evenly, and $($`i/j`$) + 1$ if `j` does not divide `i` evenly. The expression in brackets is the maximum number of rows that can be executed by a single process.

The total time for the parallel algorithm is, then,

$$sum(irow = 1, n - 1)\{[(n - irow)/nproc] (n - irow + 1) T\}.$$

The ideal speedup is, then,

$$\frac{ideal}{speedup} = \frac{n(n-1)(n+1)/3}{sum(\texttt{irow} = 1, n - 1)\{[(n - \texttt{irow})/nproc] (n - \texttt{irow} + 1) T\}}.$$

For the case n = 100, the ideal speedup is

nproc	ideal speedup
2	1.98
4	3.91
6	5.78
8	7.59
10	9.37
12	11.07
14	12.78
16	14.37
18	15.89
20	17.59

Note that the ideal speedup is less than the number of processors. In general, as n/nproc becomes smaller, the ideal speedup decreases. The reason is that, during elimination for each row, some processes are idle while others are computing, and the fraction of idle time becomes greater as the number of processes increase, for given n.

Problem: Using the techniques of Chapter 7, try alternative parallelizations of the elimination step to increase the ideal speedup.

Problem: What is the purpose of writing the equations in the form (2) rather than the form (1), so that, in the algorithm, b(i) would be carried explicitly as a separate one-dimensional array?

An optimized version of this routine, useful for small n/nproc, is left as a programming project (see Chapter 15).

13.8   Gaussian Elimination for Tridiagonal Matrix

In this section, an algorithm for parallel Gaussian elimination of a tridiagonal matrix is described. The algorithm formulates the problem as a set of linear recurrence relations, which may be executed in parallel as described in Chapter 10. Because the resulting program is complex and introduces nothing essentially new, implementing the algorithm is left as one of the programming projects, along with generalizing the algorithm to the case of other banded matrices.

A tridiagonal matrix $a(i,j)$ has the property that

$$a(i,j) = 0 \text{ if } |i - j| > 1.$$

That is, the only nonzero elements are the diagonal and one-off-diagonal elements. The equation to be solved is the same as for Section 13.7, namely

$$\mathbf{A}x = b$$

where $\mathbf{A}$ is an n x n array with elements $a(i,j)$, b is a known linear array, and x is the linear array of unknowns.

The equations to solve are

$$a(1,1)x(1) + a(1,2)x(2) \qquad\qquad\qquad\qquad\qquad\qquad = b(1) \qquad \text{(13-11a)}$$

$$a(2,1)x(1) + a(2,2)x(2) + a(2,3)\ x(3) \qquad\qquad\qquad\qquad = b(2) \qquad \text{(13-11b)}$$

$$a(3,2)x(2) + a(3,3)\ x(3) + a(3,4)x(4) \qquad\qquad\quad = b(3) \qquad \text{(13-11c)}$$

$$a(4,3)\ x(3) + a(4,4)x(4) + a(4,5)x(5) \quad = b(4) \qquad \text{(13-11d)}$$

$$\vdots$$

$$a(n,n-1)x(n-1) + a(n,n)x(n) = b(n) \qquad \text{(13-11z)}$$

In solving these equations, it is normally the case that the diagonal elements $a(i,i)$ are always suitable as pivot elements. This will be assumed, so there is no search for the pivots. The method is to eliminate $x(i)$ from *row* i (except for the first row), so that $x(2)$ is eliminated from row 2, equation (13-11b), $x(3)$ is eliminated from row 3, equation (13-11c), and so forth. The resulting equations have the following form:

$$h(1,1)x(1) + \ h(1,2)x(2) \qquad\qquad\qquad\qquad\qquad\qquad = \quad c(1) \qquad \text{(13-12a)}$$

$$h(2,1)x(1) \qquad\qquad\qquad + h(2,3)x(3) \qquad\qquad\quad = \quad c(2) \qquad \text{(13-12b)}$$

$$h(3,2)x(2) \qquad\qquad\qquad\quad + h(3,4)x(4) = \quad c(3) \qquad \text{(13-12c)}$$

$$h(4,3)x(3) \ + h(4,5)x(5) = \quad c(4) \qquad \text{(13-12d)}$$

$$\vdots$$

$$h(n-1,n-2)x\ (n-2) \qquad + h(n-1,n)x(n) = \quad c(n-1)$$

$$h(n,n-1)x(n-1) \qquad\quad = \quad c(n) \qquad \text{(13-12z)}$$

For back substitution, find $x(n-1)$ from equation (13-12z). Then use equation (13-11z) to find $x(n)$. After this, $x(n-2)$ may be found from equation (13-12y), and so forth.

The first stage is to compute the values of $h(i,j)$ and $c(i)$. First, eliminate $x(2)$ from equation (13-11b). To do this, multiply eq. (13-11b) by

$$-a(1,2)/a(2,2)$$

and add the resulting equation to equation (13-11a). This gives the new coefficients $h(2,i)$ as

$$h(2,3) = -a(1,2)a(2,3)/a(2,2) \qquad\qquad\qquad\qquad\qquad \text{(13-13a)}$$
$$h(2,1) = a(1,1) - a(1,2)a(2,1)/a(2,2) \qquad\qquad\qquad\qquad \text{(13-13b)}$$
$$c(2) \ \ = -a(1,2)b(2)/a(2,2) + b(1) \qquad\qquad\qquad\qquad \text{(13-13c)}$$

To eliminate $x(3)$ from equation (13-11c), equations (13-12b) and (13-11c) must be combined. These equations are

$$h(2,1)x(1) \qquad\qquad + h(2,3)x(3) \qquad\qquad\qquad = c(2) \qquad\qquad \text{(13-12b)}$$
$$a(3,2)x(2) + a(3,3)x(3) + a(3,4)x(4) = b(3) \qquad\qquad \text{(13-11c)}$$

Multiplying equation (13-11c) by $-h(2,3)/a(3,3)$ and adding the result to equation (13-12b) gives

$$h(3,2) = -h(2,3)a(3,2)/a(3,3) \qquad\qquad\qquad \text{(13-14a)}$$
$$h(3,4) = -h(2,3)a(3,4)/a(3,3) \qquad\qquad\qquad \text{(13-14b)}$$
$$c(3) \quad = -h(2,3)b(3)/a(3,3) + c(2) \qquad\qquad \text{(13-14c)}$$

Continuing in this vein, the general equations for $h(i,j)$ are

$$h(i,i-1) = -h(i-1,i)a(i,i-1)/a(i,i) \qquad\qquad \text{(13-15a)}$$
$$h(i,i+1) = -h(i-1,i)a(i,i+1)/a(i,i) \qquad\qquad \text{(13-15b)}$$
$$c(i) \qquad = -h(i-1,i)b(i)/a(i,i) + c(i-1) \qquad \text{(13-15c)}$$

These equations are valid for $i = 3, 4, ..., n-1$. For $i = 2$, equation (13-15b) is still valid, but the other two must be replaced by equations (13-13b) and (13-13c). For $i = n$, equation (13-15b) is not needed, and the other two equations are valid.

For the back substitution phase, the algorithm is as follows: First find $x(n-1)$ from

$$\text{(13-16a)}$$
$$x(n-1) = c(n)/h(n,n-1).$$

Next find $x(n)$ from

$$\text{(13-16b)}$$
$$x(n) = (b(n) - a(n,n-1)x(n-1))/a(n,n).$$

Finally find $x(n-2), x(n-3), ..., x(1)$ from

$$x(i-1) = (b(i) - a(i,i+1)x(i+1) - a(i,i)x(i))/a(i,i-1) \qquad \text{(13-16c)}$$

for $i = n-1, n-2, ..., 2$.

To parallelize this algorithm, we note that equations (13-15b), (13-15c) and (13-16c) are recurrence relations. For example, for equation (13-15b), if we use the notation $z(i) = h(i,i + 1)$, then equation (13-15b) has the form

$$z(i) = -z(i - 1) * a(i,i + 1)/a(i,i).$$

Once $h(i,i + 1)$ are known, then $h(i,i - 1)$ may be determined from eq. (13-15a) by direct substitution.

The parallel algorithm is now the following:

1. Find $h(i,i + 1)$ from the recurrence relation (13-15b).
2. Find $h(i,i - 1)$ by substituting $h(i,i + 1)$ into (13-15a).
3. Find $c(i)$ from the recurrence relation (13-15c).
4. Find $x(i)$ from the recurrence relation (13-16c).

Note that this solution may potentially have a numerical problem. If the diagonal $a(i,i)$ are larger than the off-diagonal elements $a(i,i - 1)$ and $a(i,i + 1)$, the equations (13-15a) and (13-15b) indicate that $h(i,i + 1)$ and $h(i,i - 1)$ will decrease as i increases. The behavior of $c(i)$ is not known. Then equation (13-16a) for $x(n - 1)$ may potentially contain a division by a very small number. Whether this is a problem or not depends on the situation, but it is a good idea to check the residuals when using the algorithm.

The problem below suggests another way of formulating this problem.

Problem: Write the single-stream and parallel program to implement the algorithm described above.

Problem: A different algorithm may be generated as follows: For every step, eliminate $x(i - 1)$ from row i, starting with row 2. To do this, multiply the equation i by

$$-h(i - 1,i - 1)/a(i,i - 1)$$

and add equations i - 1 and i to produce the new equation i. The set of equations is now

$$
\begin{aligned}
h(1,1)x(1) + h(1,2)x(2) &= & c(1) \\
h(2,2)x(2) + h(2,3)x(3) &= & c(2) \\
h(3,3)x(3) + h(3,4)x(4) &= c(3)
\end{aligned}
$$

Formulate the recurrence relations for this algorithm.

CHAPTER 14

Semaphores and Events

14.1 Introduction

Up to this point, the parallel programming examples have used just two synchronization functions—barriers and spin-locks. In this chapter, two more common synchronization functions are described—events and semaphores.

Not all four functions are logically independent. All of them may be constructed, in software, from the spin-lock, and many other synchronization functions, for specific purposes, may also be constructed. Which functions are used in a particular situation depends on the required functionality, on performance issues, and on the style of the programmer. For example, it will be seen that a binary semaphore is logically equivalent to a spin-lock. If, on a particular computer system, the spin-lock is implemented in hardware while the semaphore is implemented in software, then the spin-lock will be used if performance is an important issue. On the other hand, a semaphore allows one to create a protected region where more than one process is allowed at any time. Whether one uses the semaphore, or constructs a similar functionality from the spin-lock or event, depends on the details of the problem and the programmer's inclination.

14.2   Semaphores

14.2.1   Description of Semaphores

The semaphore is a generalization of a spin-lock, to provide a more complex kind of mutual exclusion. (Historically, the semaphore came first.) Unlike the spin-lock, the semaphore can provide mutual exclusion in a protected region for *groups* of processes, not just one process at a time. That is, it can protect regions in which groups of processes may enter at any one time.

The following functions provide basic semaphore functionality:

```
integer sem,new_count,sem_value
call shared(sem,4)

call semaphore_init(sem,set_count)
call semaphore_wait(sem)
call semaphore_send(sem)
call semaphore_reset(sem,new_count)
```

The semaphore is initialized by calling the subroutine `semaphore_init`. The shared integer `sem` holds the semaphore identifier and is analogous to similar variables used for barriers and spin-locks. It may be that, in a particular implementation of a semaphore, `sem` will be an array rather than a scalar. (An integer was chosen because, in Unix system V, the semaphore identifier is an integer, and the operating system holds the other information required by the semaphore, such as the counter described below. Different implementations may put this information in a `sem` array.) The value of `sem` is initialized by the subroutine `semaphore_init`.

A semaphore has an internal counter, which is part of the state of the semaphore and which is an integer greater than or equal to 0. When the semaphore is initialized with `semaphore_init`, the value of the counter is set to `set_count`.

The above function and subroutine calls may be used in the following way:

```
integer sem,set_count
integer id,nproc
call shared(sem,4)
    .
    .
    .
```

```
call semaphore_init(sem,5)
   .
   .
   .
id = process_fork(nproc)
   .
   .
   .
call semaphore_wait(sem)
            (statements in the
            protected region)
call semaphore_send(sem)
   .
   .
   .
call process_join()
   .
   .
   .
end
```

Program 14-1

When a process calls semaphore_wait, the following action occurs. If the internal counter of the semaphore is greater than zero, then the internal counter is decremented by 1, and the process is allowed to proceed into the protected region. The decrementing is an atomic operation. If the internal counter is 0 when the process calls semaphore_wait, then the counter remains zero, and the process is blocked within the semaphore_wait function until the internal counter is incremented, at which time it may return from the subroutine and proceed with the statement following semaphore_wait.

Note that a semaphore allows more than one process at a time into a protected region, whereas a spin-lock allows only a single process into the protected region. In Program 14-1, up to five processes may be in the protected region at any one time. After five processes have called semaphore_wait (and if no process has yet called semaphore_send), the internal counter is 0 and no other process may proceed into the protected region.

When a process calls semaphore_send, the counter is incremented by 1, and the calling process is allowed to continue. In Program 14-1, when a process leaves the protected region, it calls semaphore_send, which increments the counter. If the counter is 0 before the call, and any processes are waiting at the semaphore_wait, then when the counter is incremented to 1, *one* of the waiting processes may cause the counter to be decremented by 1 and that process may enter the protected region.

Incrementing the counter is an atomic operation. The counter may be incremented as often as desired. There is no upper limit imposed by the semaphore itself. (This is a common behavior. Of course, in a different implementation, the semaphore could impose a limit.)

The subroutine `semaphore_reset` resets the internal counter to the value `new_count`. It will be assumed that `semaphore_reset` is an atomic operation.

14.2.2 Implementation of Spin-Locks Using Semaphores

The relation between a semaphor and a spin-lock is the following: *A binary semaphore is equivalent to a spin-lock.* A *binary semaphore* is a semaphore whose internal counter can be only 0 or 1. A binary semaphore allows only a single process at a time into the protected region, which is exactly the functionality of the spin-lock. Therefore, if one has a system which only provides semaphores, one may implement spin-locks based on the semaphores, and vice versa.

The following is an implementation of the spin-lock from the binary semaphore. Note that the spin-lock identifier `lok` and the semaphore identifier `sem` are both integers in the implementation assumed here. This may not be the case for the user's own system.

The subroutine to initialize the spin-lock is

```
subroutine spin_lock_init(lok,condition)
integer lok,condition,locked,unlocked

locked = 1
unlocked = 0

if (condition .eq. locked) then
    call semaphore_init(lok,0)
else
    call semaphore_init(lok,1)
endif

return
end
```

Program 14-2

The initialization of the spin-lock creates a binary semaphore. If the spin-lock is initialized as unlocked, then the internal counter of the semaphore is set to 1. This means that, when a process calls semaphore_wait, the counter will be decremented to 0 and the process will be allowed into the protected region. Clearly, then, the call to spin_lock is implemented using semaphore_wait.

```
subroutine spin_lock(lok)
integer lok

call semaphore_wait(lok)

return
end
```

Program 14-3

In order to unlock a locked lock, the internal counter (which is 0) must be incremented. Therefore, the spin_unlock is implemented using semaphore_send.

```
subroutine spin_unlock(lok)
integer lok

call semaphore_send(lok)

return
end
```

Program 14-4

Problem: Show that the implementation of the spin-lock described above provides all the functionality of spin-locks as outlined in Section 5.4.

14.2.3 Implementation of Barriers Using Semaphores

The following routines implement the barrier from a binary semaphore. Note that, in this implementation, the variable bar is an integer array of dimension 4.

```
              subroutine barrier_init(bar,blocking_number)
              integer bar(4),blocking_number

c     The following information is stored in bar(i):
c     bar(1) - the blocking number
c     bar(2) - the number of processes waiting at the barrier.
c             This is an internal counter for the barrier, not for
c             the semaphore.
c     bar(3) - used for releasing processes. When fewer than
c             blocking number of processes are waiting at the
c             barrier, and the barrier is waiting for more,
c             then bar(3) = 0. However, when processes
c             are being released from the barrier, bar(3) = the
c             number of processes that remain to be released.
c     bar(4) - the semaphore identification number.
c     The binary semaphore is initialized so the internal counter
c     is 1 (that is, the lock is unlocked).
c     array bar must be shared.

          call semaphore_init(bar(4),1)
          bar(1) = blocking_number
          bar(2) = 0
          bar(3) = 0

          return
          end

c     **************************************************barrier

          subroutine barrier(bar)
          integer bar(1),incremented

c     Variable incremented is set to 1 when this process
c     increments the internal barrier counter bar(2).
c     bar must be shared.

          incremented = 0

 95       continue

c     It is possible for q processes to be here
c     but bar(2) + q > blocking number.
c     Any process that has already incremented the counter
c     has incremented = 1, and such a process is already
c     blocked by the barrier. If incremented = 0, and bar(3) > 0,
c     it means the barrier is in release mode but
c     this particular process has not yet been blocked by the
```

```
c      barrier. The process musut spin until all the blocked
c      processes are released, and then it becomes part of
c      the next group of processes to be blocked by the barrier.

       call semaphore_wait(bar(4))
c          check for nonblocked process in release mode
           if ((incremented .eq. 0) .and.
     s         (bar(3) .gt. 0)) then
                call semaphore_send(bar(4))
                goto 95
           endif
c                                            point B***
           if (increment .eq. 0) then
c              increment internal counter
               bar(2) = bar(2) + 1
               incremented = 1
           endif
c                                            point C***
           if ((bar(2) .lt. bar(1)) .and.
     s         (bar(3) .eq. 0)) then
c              fewer than blocking number of processes
c              have arrived at the barrier
               call semaphore_send(bar(4))
               goto 95
           else
c              Release mode.
c              first process.
               if (bar(3) .eq. 0) then
                   bar(3) = bar(1) - 1
c                  reset the barrier
                   bar(2) = 0
                   call semaphore_send(bar(4))
                   return
               else
c                  release next process
                   bar(3) = bar(3) - 1
                   call semaphore_send(bar(4))
                   return
               endif
           endif
c      if arrive at this point, is an error
       call semaphore_send(bar(4))
       print *,'ERROR,barrier,abort'
       call exit(-1)

       return
       end
```

Program 14-5

Problem: In Program 14-5, why is `semaphore_send` always called just before the gotos?

Problem: What would happen if the protected region ended at point B and was restarted at point C in Program 14-5?

Problem: In Program 14-5, if a process (say process A) calls the barrier while the barrier is in release mode but before all processes which are blocked have been released, then process A will wait until the barrier has released all the originally blocked processes. Then process A itself will become part of the next group to be blocked at the barrier. A different alternative is to allow process A to pass through the barrier. Why is this alternative not logically valid? (Hint: consider the situation

```
        call barrier(bar)
        .

        .

        .
        call barrier (bar)
        .

        .

        .
```

where the blocking number equals the total number of processes.)

14.2.4 Producer-Consumer Problems

Semaphores are frequently discussed in the context of the producer-consumer problem, a version of which is as follows: One process, called a producer, creates and stores data in shared memory for the benefit of other processes (consumers) which want to access the data.

For example, consider a division of a corporation whose purpose it is to repair equipment. There is a central office to which reports of broken equipment are sent. The people in this office have access to a computer system, and each time a report comes in, it is entered into a database. At any time, repairmen at other locations, who also have access to the database, can examine the list of problems and select those which are relevant for their own purposes.

The central office logging the reports is the *producer*, while the repair departments are the *consumers*. The producers create data while the consumers read the data. The consumers can also modify or delete data, for example, to indicate the status of a job.

The producer-consumer problem is a model of simultaneous access to data, and as such it is a paradigm of parallel data base management systems, linked-list managers, and so forth.

In the traditional solution of the problem, the producing and consuming of data must be done in a protected manner. That is, while the producer is adding data to the database, the consumers cannot be allowed either to read it (because in general the data is incomplete) or to alter it (because reports may be updated by the producer as well). Alternatively, while the consumer is reading the reports, and perhaps modifying them, the producer cannot be allowed to either add more data or modify the data that is already there. This type of solution will be illustrated in the examples below.

In fact, there are ways of protecting portions of the data, so that producing and consuming can proceed simultaneously. This desirable type of solution will be solicited in the problems.

First, consider the very simple situation in which there is a single producer and a single consumer. The producer fills an array data(i) with integers, then the consumer reads the numbers in the array, adds them up, prints the sum, and indicates to the producer that it has read the data. The consumer can then add more data, and so forth. Here is the program:

```
c       Illustrate producer-consumer. This is not
c       a realistic program.
c       a single producer and a single consumer.
c       process 0 is producer, process 1 the consumer
c       n = amount of data

        integer sem_prod,sem_cons
        integer data(1000),n,id,process_fork,i,j,sum

        call shared(sem_prod,4)
        call shared(sem_cons,4)
        call shared(data,4000)

c       initialize two binary semaphores
        call semaphore_init(sem_prod,1)
        call semaphore_init(sem_cons,0)

        n = 1000

c       fork another process.
        id = process_fork(2)
```

```
c       Producer and consumer come back to here after
c       each cycle, to produce or consume more data

        do 90 j = 1,10

        if (id .eq. 0) then

c               PRODUCE DATA
                call semaphore_wait(sem_prod)
                    do 1 i = 1,n
                        data(i) = i * j
 1                  continue
c               signal consumer that data is ready
                call semaphore_send(sem_cons)

        else
c               CONSUME DATA
                call semaphore_wait(sem_cons)
                    sum = 0
                    do 2 i = 1,n
                        sum = sum + data(i)
 2                  continue
                    print *,'sum is ',sum
c               signal producer that it can produce more data
                call semaphore_send(sem_prod)

        endif
 90     continue

        call process_join()
        end
```

Program 14-6

This program works as follows. There are two binary semaphores, which are used to protect two different regions. Only a single process can be in each region at any time. The semaphore sem_prod protects the code executed by the producer, while sem_cons protects the code executed by the consumer.

The semaphores are initialized so that the producer is allowed into his region, while the consumer must block. (Data must first be produced before it can be consumed.) After the producer is finished, he signals to the consumer that the data is ready by calling semaphore_send, which increments the internal counter of the *consumer's* semaphore sem_cons. The consumer can now enter his protected region, to form the sum.

While the consumer is proceeding, the producer cycles back and calls his own semaphore sem_prod. But the producer has not incremented his own internal counter (only the internal counter of the consumer). The internal counter of the producer's own semaphore is 0. In other words, *the producer has locked himself out of his own region.*

The net effect of this is that, while the consumer is consuming the data, the producer is waiting and cannot produce more. This is exactly the effect we intended. Either the producer is producing, or the consumer is consuming, but not both at the same time.

After the consumer has finished using the data, he increments the internal counter of sem_prod, for the producer. The producer can now enter his protected region and create more data. The consumer, on the other hand, cycles back and tries to enter his own protected region again. But his internal counter is 0 (he set it to 0 himself on the previous cycle), so the region is locked, and he must wait until the producer signals him to continue.

Problem: Rewrite Program 14-6 using spin-locks instead of semaphores. How does this use compare with the use of spin-locks in previous chapters?

Program 14-6 is, of course, sequential, and there is no reason why the same process can't be, first the producer, and then the consumer, in which case no semaphores are needed, no forks, and no illustrative Program 14-6. In more realistic situations, the producer might be doing calculations, or accumulating data at the same time that the consumer is reading it, and the consumer might be creating reports or doing calculations at the same time that the producer is updating the data. In this case, Program 14-6 provides a simplified version of the actual situation.

In addition, it is possible to have many consumers. In such a case, the internal counter of the consumer semaphore would be initialized to the maximum number of readers allowed into the consumer region at any one time.

The above program is now rewritten for this case. It is more structured to have two subroutines, one of which is called by the producer (and named, appropriately enough, producer), and another which is called by all consumers (and which is called consumer). The program is

```
c     producer-consumer.
c     a single producer and a many consumers.
c     process 0 is producer, other processes are consumers.
c     num_cons = number of consumers. In this program, =10.
c     num_in_region - number of consumers in the protected
```

```
c       region.
c       n = amount of data
        integer sem_prod,sem_cons,lok_sem
        integer data(1000),n,id,process_fork,num_cons
        integer locked,unlocked,num_in_region,j

        call shared(sem_prod,4)
        call shared(sem_cons,4)
        call shared(lok_sem,4)
        call shared(data,4000)
        call shared(num_in_region,4)

        num_cons = 10
        locked = 1
        unlocked = 0

c     initialize two binary semaphores.
c     consumer semaphore initialized to num_cons.
        call semaphore_init(sem_prod,1)
        call semaphore_init(sem_cons,0)

c     initialize a spin-lock
        call spin_lock_init(lok_sem,unlocked)

        n = 1000

c     fork the consumers.
        id = process_fork(num_cons + 1)

c     producers and consumers come back to here after
c     each cycle, to produce or consume more data

        do 90 j = 1,10
        if (id .eq. 0) then
            call producer(sem_prod,num_cons,lok_sem,data,n,
     s            num_in_region,sem_cons,j)
        else
            call consumer(sem_prod,num_cons,lok_sem,data,n,
     s            num_in_region,sem_cons)
        endif

90      continue
        call process_join()
        end

c     ********************************************************producer
        subroutine producer(sem_prod,num_cons,lok_sem,data,n,
```

```
     s                num_in_region,sem_cons,j)

           integer sem_prod,num_cons,lok_sem,sem_cons
           integer data(1),n,num_in_region,j,i

c              PRODUCE DATA
               call semaphore_wait(sem_prod)

c       ------------------------------------------------------------
c              do work of producer
               do 1 i = 1,n
                   data(i) = i * j
  1            continue
c       ------------------------------------------------------------
c              signal consumer that data is ready
               call spin_lock(lok_sem)
                   num_in_region = 0
               call spin_unlock(lok_sem)
               call semaphore_reset(sem_cons, num_cons)

               return
               end

c    *****************************************************consumer
        subroutine consumer(sem_prod,num_cons,lok_sem,data,n,
     s              num_in_region,sem_cons)

           integer sem_cons,sem_prod,lok_sem
           integer data(1),n,num_in_region,num_cons,sum,i

c              CONSUME DATA
               call semaphore_wait(sem_cons)
c                                              ***** point A

c       ------------------------------------------------------------
c              do work of consumer
               sum = 0
               do 2 i = 1,n
                   sum = sum + data(i)
  2            continue
               print *,'sum is ',sum
c       ------------------------------------------------------------

               call spin_lock(lok_sem)
                   num_in_region = num_in_region + 1
                   if (num_in_region .eq. num_cons) then
c                       num_cons processes have now consumed
```

```
c                                  the data.
c                                  signal producer that it can produce
c                                  more data.
                                   call semaphore_send(sem_prod)
                           endif
                     call spin_unlock(lok_sem)

             return
             end
```

Program 14-7

Problem: In Program 14-7, what would happen if `num_in_region` were incremented at point A? What would happen if this variable were not incremented in a region protected by a spin-lock?

This program allows exactly `num_cons` processes into the consumer region. The problem with the program as written is that exactly `num_cons` processes must pass through the consumer region before the producer can produce more data. Moreover, the variable `num_in_region`, which is used by the consumer for synchronization, *must* be reset by the producer. This is not satisfactory so far as data hiding is concerned.

The use of semaphores in Program 14-7 is artificial, and additional synchronization is needed to make the program run correctly. These include spin-locks and the variable `num_in_region`, making the synchronization rather diffuse. A better approach is to construct a new synchronization primitive which has the desired functionality, as in the problem below.

Problem: Create a synchronization function called by both the producer and consumer, which protects both the producer and consumer work areas and which enforces the following kind of exclusiveness:

(a) It allows any number of consumer processes to enter the consumer work area and allows one producer to enter the producer work area at any time.

(b) It can be "turned off" by a producer. That is, its state can be set so that it will not allow more consumer processes into the consumer work area.

(c) It will "signal" the producer when the protected region is empty.

(d) The function can protect portions of the shared data, so that producers can be updating some data and consumers reading other data simultaneously.

Use this function in a producer-consumer problem, with arbitrary numbers of consumers. Make up a data structure to hold the appropriate information. How does your synchronization function have to be tailored for the particular data structure you use?

14.3   Events

Events are a way of blocking an *arbitrary* number of processes until some action takes place, in which case the block is cleared and the processes can continue. It is a kind of traffic light. The number of processes is not predetermined.

There are routines to initialize, post, clear, and wait at events. These are (all are subroutines)

```
integer event,condition

call event_init(event,condition)
call event_post(event)
call event_wait(event)
call event_clear(event)
```

The event is first initialized with the subroutine `event_init`. An event has exactly two states—*posted* or *cleared*. The variable `condition` is either 0 or 1, for the event initialized as posted or cleared, respectively. This terminology is explained below.

When a process calls `event_wait`, one of two things happens. If the state of the event is posted, it means that the event does *not* act as a block, and the process can continue executing at the statement following `event_wait`. In the traffic light analogy, an event which is posted means the light is green, and processes may proceed. There is no limit on the number of processes that can call, and then pass through, a posted event.

On the other hand, if the state of the event is cleared, then the event is acting as a block and the process cannot continue. It is a red light, blocking all processes. There is no limit to the number of processes that are blocked at the `event_wait` function because the event is "cleared." When the event becomes posted, *all* the processes that are waiting may proceed.

The terminology used with an event is this: If processes are waiting at a cleared event, so they cannot proceed, it is said that the processes are *waiting on the event*.

The subroutine `event_post` causes an event to become posted. The event will remain posted no matter how many processes call `event_wait` or `event_post`, and for an indeterminate amount of time, until the event is cleared. The entire time that the event is posted, it does not block processes. A call to `event_clear` clears the event, causing all processes which subsequently call `event_wait` to block until the event is posted again.

The release is atomic, in the following sense. If an event is posted and then cleared soon after, it is possible that, when the event becomes cleared, some processes that were waiting on the event were not yet physically released, in the sense that they had not yet returned from the `event_wait` function. (They could have been idled.) The clearing of the event should have no effect on the physical release of processes that were already logically released following the posting of the event. In addition, any process that calls `event_wait` after the event has been cleared, but before all waiting processes have been physically released, should be blocked at the event until the event is posted the next time.

Events can be used for the producer-consumer problem for the case where there are an indeterminate number of consumers, and where, when the producer is ready, no more consumers are allowed in the protected region. Furthermore, the producer will not produce while there are consumers in the protected region. Instead of the entire program, we present the two subroutines, `producer` and `consumer`.

Before these subroutines are called the first time, the producer event should be initialized as posted, the consumer event should be initialized as cleared.

```
          subroutine producer(prod_event,cons_event,
    s                producer_waiting,num_in_region,lok_event)

          integer prod_event,cons_event,lok_event
          integer producer_waiting,num_in_region
c     all arguments must be shared.

c     stop other consumers from entering the locked
c     consumer region
          call event_clear(cons_event)

c     set variable producer_waiting to indicate that the
c     producer is ready to produce data. This must be
c     done after the consumer event is cleared.
          call spin_lock(lok_event)
              producer_waiting = 1
```

```
      call spin_unlock(lok_event)

c     The producer won't continue
c     unless there are no consumers in the consumer work region.
      call event_wait(prod_event)

c     ------------------------------------------------
      (producer work)
c     ------------------------------------------------

c     reinitialize producer_waiting
c     zero the counter which counts number of consumers
c     in the consuming region.
c                                             ****** point D
      call spin_lock(lok_event)
          producer_waiting = 0
          num_in_region = 0
      call spin_unlock(lok_event)

c     producer locks itself out of producing region
c     and opens up the consumers region
      call event_clear(prod_event)
      call event_post(cons_event)

      return
      end

c     **************************************************consumer
      subroutine consumer(prod_event,cons_event,
     s            producer_waiting,num_in_region,lok_event)

      integer prod_event,cons_event,lok_event
      integer producer_waiting,num_in_region

c     all arguments must be shared.

c     many consumers can do work
c     check if region is unlocked
 100     continue
      call event_wait(cons_event)

c         if the producer is ready, the consumer cannot
c         proceed
      call spin_lock(lok_event)
c                                             ***** Point B
          if (producer_waiting .eq. 0) then
              num_in_region = num_in_region + 1
```

```
            else
                call spin_unlock(lok_event)
                goto 100
            endif
        call spin_unlock(lok_event)

c       ---------------------------------------------
        (consumer work)
c       ---------------------------------------------

c       check if producer is waiting. If so, make sure all
c       consumers have finished, then post producer event.
c       The producer will have cleared the cons_event already.

        call spin_lock(lok_event)
c                                               ***** Point C
            num_in_region = num_in_region - 1
            if ((producer_waiting .eq. 1) .and.
     s          (num_in_region .eq. 0)) then
                    call event_post(prod_event)
            endif
        call spin_unlock(lok_event)

        return
        end
```

Program 14-8

Problem: Suppose the protected region, point B, contained only the statement

```
        num_in_region = num_in_region + 1
```

and did not check `producer_waiting`. What might go wrong? (Hint: consider the following possible sequence of events:

1. Consumer process (say process A) calls `event_wait(cons_event)`, then is idled.
2. The producer clears event `cons_event`.
3. The producer sets `producer_waiting` to 1.
4. A different consumer process decrements the variable `num_in_region` at point C, and in so doing sets `num_in_region` to 0.
5. Process A recommences executing.

Problem: Show how it is possible for a consumer process to be in the consumer work area before the producer clears the cons_event event. Is this an error?

Problem: Could there be a problem if the producer set producer_waiting to 0 at point D, not in a protected region?

Problem: Could the two protected regions in the consumer subroutine be protected by different spin-locks?

Problem: Implement the final problem of Section 14.2.4 using events.

Problem: Why should event_wait not be called in a region locked by a spin-lock.

Events can also be used in the parallelization of 8-23, which appeared in Section 8.8. The fragment 8-23 is repeated below (where m(i,j) replaces c(i) * a(i,j)):

```
            .
            .
            .
      do 1 j = 1,n
          do 2 i = j + 1,n
              x(i) = x(i) + m(i,j) * x(j)
2         continue
1     continue
```

Program 8-23

One parallelized version of this loop is given in Program 8-25. The idea was to halt processes until done(j) attained a certain value, at which time the processes could be released. The loop

```
90        continue
          if (done(j) .ne. j) goto 90
```

can be replaced by an event, as is done in the following program:

```
            real x(50),m(50,50)
            integer done(50),n,process_fork,locked,unlocked
            integer lok_x(50),lok,event(50),i,j
```

```
            integer cleared,posted,next_index,bar(4),id,nproc

            call shared(done,200)
            call shared(lok_x,200)
            call shared(lok,4)
            call shared(event,200)
            call shared(done,200)
            call shared(x,200)
            call shared(next_index,4)
            call shared(bar,16)

            (initialize m(,j),x(1),nproc,n)

            cleared = 1
            posted = 0
            locked = 1
            unlocked = 0

c       initialize events,locks,barrier
            do 30 i = 1,n
                call event_init(event(i),cleared)
 30         continue
            do 35 i = 1,n
                 call spin_init(lok_x(i),unlocked)
 35         continue
            call spin_init(lok,unlocked)
            call barrier_init(bar,nproc)

c      other initialization
            call event_post(event(1))
            next_index = 1

            id = process_fork(nproc)
c      initialize done in parallel
            do 5 j = 1 + id,n,nproc
                 done(j) = 1
  5         continue

            call barrier(bar)

 10    continue
            call spin_lock(lok)
                j = next_index
                next_index = next_index + 1
            call spin_unlock(lok)
            if (j .gt. n) goto 20
c           Now compute the contribution of m(i,j) * x(j)to
```

```
c           x(j + 1),...,x(n). Wait until x(j) has attained its
c           new value
c
c           The following event replaces the 90 continue loop
            call event_wait(event(j))
c
c           update x(i) with x(j)
            do 2 i = j + 1,n
                call spin_lock(lok_x(i))
                    x(i) = x(i) + m(i,j) * x(j)
                    done(i) = done(i) + 1
                    if (done(i) .eq. i) call event_post(event(i))
                call spin_unlock(lok_x(i))
     2      continue
            goto 10
    20      continue
            call proc_join()
            (store results)
            end
```

Program 14-9

Comparison of Program 14-9 with 8-25 reveals three changes:

(a) Event_init is called n times.
(b) An additional statement

```
        if (done(i) .ge. j) call event_post(event(i))
```

has been added to a locked region. This statement will be executed once for every multiplication.
(c) The loop on 90 continue has been replaced by a call to event_wait.

While Program 14-9 is more elegant than 8-25, due to the use of a synchronization primitive rather than a tight spinning loop in the program, the use of the event has added considerable overhead to the program. First, calling event_init is likely to be time consuming. And secondly, the conditional (b) is executed once for each multiply, which is considerable overhead. This illustrates the trade-off between high-level and low-level synchronization (8-25 is low level, 14-9 is high-level).

Problem: Implement the event functions based on spin-locks.

Problem: Create a synchronization function with the following properties:

(a) It contains two integers, a *threshold* and a *counter*. Upon initialization, both integers can be set to arbitrary values.

(b) Like an event, the function can be initialized to *cleared* or *posted*.

(c) There is a operation which can increment or decrement the counter.

(d) When the counter becomes greater than or equal to the threshold, the state of the event is altered. If the event was originally posted, it is then cleared. If the event was originally cleared, it is then posted. The function can also be posted or cleared at will.

(e) The event can be reset at any time, as an atomic operation.

Use this function to rewrite Program 14-9.

14.4   Summary

Four basic synchronization mechanism have been introduced in this book:

1. spin-locks,
2. barriers,
3. semaphores
4. events.

They serve four different functions. The spin-lock allows only a single process at a time into a particular region. The semaphore allows up to some maximum number into the region at one time. The spin-lock is equivalent to a binary semaphore.

The barrier and the event both block processes from continuing. The barrier blocks up to a preset number of processes, while the event blocks an arbitrary number of processes. The barrier cannot be "lowered" by any process, while the event may be posted by any process which is not waiting on the event. The event functions as a signal from one process to another.

Apart from the binary semaphore (which is an important synchronization function), the semaphore is not by itself very useful. Its primary function is to allow more than one process into a protected region, while keeping out others. Generally, the functionality needed is more than the semaphore can provide, so that special-purpose synchronization functions should be devised.

CHAPTER 15

Programming Projects

Stars (*) denote large projects.

1. Write a parallel version of the fast Fourier transform.
2. Write a parallel program to generate Fibonnacci numbers.
3. Write a parallel program to find prime numbers using the Sieve of Eratosthenes.
4. (*) Write a linear algebra package in which the subroutines execute in parallel. Such a package would include matrix and vector manipulations, such as: matrix-matrix and matrix-vector multiply, dot product, multiplication of a vector by a scalar, matrix inversion, matrix diagonalization (eigenvalues and eigenvectors), Gaussian elimination, and determinants.
5. (*) Do as above, but for sparse matrices. It is difficult to obtain high performance for sparse matrix manipulations from vector processors. Parallelization, however, should provide a considerable performance advantage.
6. (*) Write a simple, flat-file database management system (DBMS) using separate processes to perform various aspects of database management. Possible functions are parsing the query, inputting data from disk, searching data to satisfy the query, updating the table, deleting rows

from the table, inserting into the table, writing altered data back to disk, and rollback. A flat-file DBMS is one where all the data is in a single table. Your DBMS should not lock the entire table, otherwise only a single user could access the database at any one time. Try record or even entry locking.

7. Write a parallel program to count the number of partitions of a number. (A partition of a number is the different ways of writing that number as sums of unlike smaller numbers. For example, a partition of 5 is $1 + 4, 2 + 3$.)

8. (*) Write a computer "dungeon" game, in which individual characters and monsters are each controlled by separate processes.

9. Write a parallel program to integrate a set of ordinary differential equations, using an implicit algorithm.

10. Write a parallel program to generate a fractal image using affine transformations.

11. (*) Write a parallel linked-list manager for an indexed or unindexed singly or doubly linked list, where unused list members are maintained on a free list. The free list can be singly linked. The manager can be callable by many processes simultaneously and should provide functionality to search the list, remove elements from the list and add elements to the list. Any of these functions can be invoked by an arbitrary number of processes at any time. Processes trying to access the list should not be blocked for long times waiting for other processes to finish.

12. (*) Write a parallel program to explore a real maze—that is, one with continuous corridors. One algorithm that is particularly effective is the right-hand rule—walk so as to keep a wall always on the right and mark corridors which have already been entered.

13. (*) Write a discrete event simulator to model a factory, including assembly lines, inventory delivery and use, product packaging and shipment, quality control, and so forth. Or write one to simulate a computer.

14. (*) Write a parallel neural net simulator, using your favorite neural net algorithm.

15. Implement the parallel algorithm for Gaussian elimination of a tridiagonal matrix, Section 13.9.

16. (*) Devise algorithms for Gaussian elimination for matrices of any bandwidth. Implement the algorithms.

APPENDIX A

Equivalent C and Fortran Constructs

A.1 Program Structure

This section describes those differences between Fortran and C which will aid C programmers to follow the programs in this book.

C is statement oriented, while Fortran is line oriented. In Fortran, there is, normally, one statement per line. Each statement must start in column 7 or greater. To indicate that a statement is continued on one or more lines, column 6 of the continuation lines must contain any nonblank character. Columns 1–5 are reserved for statement labels. A statement may be broken up anywhere to be continued, even in the middle of an identifier. Statements are not terminated by any particular character but rather by whatever serves as the linefeed character. Fortran comments must occupy an entire line, and a c must appear in the first column of a comment line.

Fortran is not block structured. Standard Fortran77 is nonrecursive, although some implementations allow recursion. Fortran does not have pointer data types or structures. The examples in this book do not use global variables or character strings.

A.2   Loops

The only loop construct in Fortran is the do-loop:

```
      do 1 i = a,b,c
      (work)
    1 continue
```

The analogous loop in C is

```
      for (i = a;i <= b;i += c)
          {
          (work)
          }
```

In C, variables a. b, c can be any expression. In Fortran, the expressions must result in a noncomplex number. In the case of C, the logical action is that, first the expression

```
      i = a
```

is evaluated before the start of the loop. The expression

```
      i <= b
```

is evaluated before each iteration (including the first) and checked for being true (nonzero) or false (0). If it is false, the loop is terminated. The expression

```
      i += c
```

is reevaluated on every iteration. These expressions are arbitrary, in that expressions a, b, c may contain the variable i and each may contain variables appearing in any of the other expressions. The variable i and all variables appearing in a, b, c may be assigned arbitrarily during any iteration. (The for-expression above is not the most general one possible in C, but it is the one analogous to the Fortran do-loop.)

In the case of Fortran, each expression a, b, c is evaluated once, before the start of the loop, the results converted to the same type as i if necessary, and i assigned the (converted) value of a. The variable i is incremented by c for each iteration except the first, and the loop terminates the first time that i becomes greater than b. (This assumes c is positive. A corresponding behavior occurs if c is negative.) The (converted) values of a, b, c may not change during the course of the loop, even if the expressions a, b, c contain variables that are reassigned during the course of the loop. The (converted) value of c cannot be 0. The expressions a, b, c may not contain the variable i, because the order of evaluation of a, b, c and the initialization of i is arbitrary. The value of i may not be altered during the course of the iterations (except when it is incremented by c, automatically, for the next iteration.) If b < a initially, the loop is not executed even once.

A.3   Conditionals

In the C conditional

```
if (exp)
     {
     (work)
     }
```

the work is done if exp is nonzero, and it is not done if exp is zero. The equivalent Fortran construct is

```
if (exp) then
      (work)
endif
```

If the work is a single statement, this can be contracted to

```
if (exp) statement
```

In the Fortran case, exp must result in a logical data type, where the two values are .true. and .false.. This is discussed in Chapter 2.

The Fortran if-then-endif block has the form

```
if (exp1) then
      s1
else
      s2
endif
```

where s1 and s2 are any arbitrary sequence of statements. The equivalent C form is

```
if (exp1)
      {s1}
else
      {s2}
```

The Fortran if-then-elseif-endif block

```
if (exp1) then
      s1
elseif (exp2) then
      s2
elseif (exp3) then
      s3
else
      s4
endif
```

is, in C,

```
if (exp1)
      {s1}
else
      if (exp2)
            {s2}
      else
            if (exp3)
                  {s3}
            else
                  {s4}
```

Note that, in C, the if-else combination is a single statement (unless the if-clause is set off by brackets) so in the above example, the else is associated with the if directly above it.

One important difference concerns expressions made up of logical expressions connected by the logical connectives .and. and .or.. In Fortran, the individual subexpressions are evaluated in any order, so that

```
if((x .ne.0.) .and. (a/x < 1.)) then ...
```

may *not* work, because the second subexpression may be evaluated first. In C, the equivalent

```
if ((x != 0.) && (a/x < 1.)) ...
```

will work as expected. It may be that, for a particular Fortran implementation, the subexpressions will be evaluated in order. Depending on an order of evaluation will result in nonportable code.

The Fortran syntax is certainly more readable. Chapter 2 gives a more detailed explanation of the Fortran conditionals.

A.4   Branches

In Fortran, statement labels appear anywhere in columns 1–5. Thus, a branch

```
1   continue
    .
    .
    .
    goto 1
```

directs control back to statement with label 1, when the `goto` statement is executed, and `continue` is a null, executable statement.

In C, labels can be any identifier, followed by a colon. The label must be followed by a statement, which can be null. Thus, the C fragment corresponding to the above Fortran fragment is

```
one: ;
    .
    .
    .
    goto one;
```

A.5   Functions and Subroutines

Fortran subroutines are equivalent to C `void` functions.

```
void foo(x,y)
int *x;
```

```
real *y;
{
        *x = ...
        *y = ...
}
```

is equivalent to

```
subroutine foo(x,y)
integer x
real y
x = ...
y = ...
return
end
```

In Fortran, all variables are passed as pointers, and so by reference. Thus, in the Fortran routine above, x and y are altered in the calling program. There is *no* Fortran equivalent to the C function

```
foo_1(x,y)
int x;
real y;
{
        x = ...
        y = ...
}
```

where x and y are not altered in the calling program.

In Fortran, subroutines are called using

```
call foo(...)
```

while in C, no `call` keyword is necessary.

Fortran functions are defined as follows:

```
integer function foo(...)
real function bar(...)
double precision function foo_bar(...)
```

and so forth. This is similar to the declarations in C. Fortran functions are used in the same way as C functions, that is, as terms in expressions. However, Fortran functions must be a term in an expression, where the returned value is actually used. The function cannot stand alone on a line. Thus, the following Fortran fragment is not valid. (In the following, foo is the integer function defined above).

```
c       Fortran invalid fragment. foo is integer function
        .
        .
        .
        x = 3
        foo(x,y)
        z = y**2
        .
        .
        .
```

For this case, a subroutine call must be used.

In both C and Fortran, the arguments of functions and subroutines may be evaluated in any order, so that including functions with side effects as part of the argument list can be dangerous.

APPENDIX B

EPF: Fortran77 for Parallel Programming

B.1 Introduction

Encore Parallel Fortran (EPF) is a parallel programming computer language developed and distributed by Encore Computer Corporation. EPF enhances standard Fortran77 with program statements that allow any portions of a program to be executed in parallel. EPF is a superset of Fortran77, so that standard Fortran programs may be compiled with the EPF compiler. At present, the EPF compiler runs only on the Encore Multimax line of multiprocessors. EPF contains features which are characteristic of other parallel programming languages.

Parallel programming with EPF provides a convenient alternative to using a parallel programming library. A major advantage is that processes may be started up and halted freely, so that programs tend to be more structured and so are easier to maintain and modify. The drawback of using EPF is that the program is written in a nonstandard (but almost standard) language.

In this appendix, most of the elements of EPF are described, and several programs written in EPF are presented.

B.2   Parallel Regions and the Structure of an EPF Module

The highest-level structure of an EPF program is the same as that of Fortran77—it is a collection of modules. One module must be a main program, and the rest can be subroutines, functions, and a single block-data subroutine.

The structure of a module is

```
module name (if not main)
declarations
single-stream region
[parallel region]
[single-stream region]
[parallel region]
etc etc
[return]
end
```

A single-stream region is a sequence of Fortran77 statements which are executed by a single process only. A parallel region is a sequence of EPF statements which are executed by many processes in parallel.

A parallel region is created with the `parallel` statement and terminated at the `end parallel` statement, as

```
parallel
        .

        .
        (EPF statements)
        .
end parallel
```

(Indentations are optional).

Upon encountering the `parallel` statement, a number of additional processes are started up. These execute in parallel with the original one on the available processors. The number of additional processes that are created is determined by the environment variable EPR_PROCS. (An environment variable is a named storage area maintained by the operating system.) If EPR_PROCS = 10, for example, then 9 additional processes are created when the `parallel` statement is executed.

When the end parallel statement is executed, the additional processes are stopped.

As an example of the use of the parallel–end parallel construct, consider a parallel version of the simple, nonparallel program below.

```
print *,'starting'
print *,'in the middle'
print *,'the end'
end
```

The output of this program is

```
starting
in the middle
the end
```

One parallel version of this program is

```
print *,'starting'
PARALLEL
      print *,'in the middle'
END PARALLEL
print *,'the end'
end
```

The parallel and end parallel statements are capitalized for presentation purposes. Indentation is used for readability. Neither capitalization nor indentation is required.

If EPR_PROCS is 3, then the output of the parallel program is

```
starting
in the middle
in the middle
in the middle
the end
```

When the program is started, only a single process is executing, which prints out the first message, "starting." Upon encountering the parallel statement, two child processes are started up, which are copies of the original. There are now three processes running the same code. The two children begin executing at the statement following the parallel statement. All three processes print the message in the middle. When the processes encounter the end parallel statement, the two children are stopped, so that only the parent process executes the statement following the end parallel statement.

There is no automatic barrier at the end parallel statement. The parent does not wait at the end parallel statement for the children to be destroyed. Therefore it is possible that the "the end" output line may appear before one or two of the "in the middle" output statements. (Why can't it appear before all three?)

The *logical* action of the program, when executing the parallel statement, is the same as for the process_fork, as described in Section 11.3. That is, a number of child processes are "started up." In implementing EPF, the parallel statement does not invoke a Unix-like fork, in which the parent is copied. Rather, its action is more like waking up preexisting processes which have been dormant up to that point. This start-up can be quite efficient (tens of microseconds, or less), meaning that the parallel region can be created and terminated many times without undo performance penalty.

There can be any number of parallel regions in a module. Parallel regions cannot be nested.

B.3   Sharing Memory—Private

EPF assumes that, in the absence of any declarations to the contrary, all variables are shared among all processes. This includes variables in common blocks, dummy subroutine arguments, and automatic and save variables (variables which are local to the module). It is frequently necessary for each process to have its own, private copy of some variables. The private statement is used to allow each process in a parallel region to have its own copy of one or more variable.

The basic idea is illustrated in the following main program:

```
integer i10,j20
i10 = 10
j20 = 20
print *,'i10 = ',i10,',j20 = ',j20
PARALLEL
      PRIVATE i10
      i10 = 555
      print *,'i10 = ',i10,',j20 = ',j20
      j20 = 0
END PARALLEL
```

```
print *,'i10 = ',i10,',j20 = ',j20
end
```

If `EPR_PROCS = 3`, one output of this program is

```
i10 = 10 , j20 = 20
i10 = 555 , j20 = 20
i10 = 555 , j20 = 20
i10 = 555 , j20 = 0
i10 = 10 , j20 = 0
```

Altering j20 to 0 within the parallel region also changes it outside, because j20 is shared. On the other hand, i10 is private within the parallel region, so that changing its value within the parallel region does not alter it outside.

A parallel region is analogous to a separate program module. (Strictly speaking, it is like a block in C or Pascal.) A variable that is declared private within a parallel region acts in the same way as a local variable declared within a subroutine. It is not visible outside the parallel region and, in addition, each process has its own copy of this variable. Therefore, from the logical point of view, the variable i10 which is used in the parallel region refers to a different memory location than does the i10 appearing outside the parallel region.

The data types of all variables declared within a parallel region must also be declared in the declaration section (following the module name) of the module in which the parallel region appears.

This constraint of EPF will probably be relaxed in the future, so that the type declarations of private variables can be made in the private region only. (They can be declared in the private region now but should also be declared in the declaration section of the module.) This alteration would be more consistent with the blocklike behavior of the parallel region.

Consider the following fragment, in which a function is called from within a parallel region.

```
integer i,k
real a(100)
.

.

.
PARALLEL
     PRIVATE i
     .

     .

     .
```

```
            call foo(i,k,a)
            .

            .

            .
      END PARALLEL
      .

      .

      .
      end

      subroutine foo(n,m,b)
      integer n,m
      real b(1)
      .

      .

      .
      return
      end
```

Each process calls foo. In the course of executing foo, the variable n will be private to each process, while m and b will be shared.

B.4 doall—end doall

The doall—end doall statements are used within a parallel region to execute a loop in parallel—i.e., to apportion the work of the loop among the different processes. For example, consider the simple array assignment:

```
      real a(1000),b(1000)
      integer i
      .

      .

      .
      do 1 i = 1,1000
            a(i) = b(i)
    1     continue
      .

      .

      .
      end
```

This loop may be parallelized as

```
real a(1000),b(1000)
integer i
.

.

.
PARALLEL
    PRIVATE i
    DO ALL (i = 1:1000)
        a(i) = b(i)
    END DOALL
END PARALLEL
.

.

.
end
```

First a parallel region is created, at the parallel statement. Following this, the do is replaced by the do all. The do all currently does loop splitting. It is likely that various scheduling methods will be available in the future.

The general form of the do all statement is

```
doall (i = a:b:c)
```

where a is the initial value of i, b is the maximum value, and c is the increment. There is no barrierlike behavior at the end doall statement.

Suppose that EPR_PROCS = 5, so there are 5 processes executing in the parallel region. Then the do all directs process 1 to execute

```
a(1) = b(1)
```

while process 2 will execute

```
a(2) = b(2)
```

etc, and process 5 executes

```
a(5) = b(5).
```

When process 1 completes its work, it then does

```
a(6) = b(6)
```

while process 2, the second time around, executes

```
a(7) = b(7)
```

and so forth, process 5 in its second pass executing

```
a(10) = b(10).
```

On the third round, process 1 executes

```
a(11) = b(11)
```

and so forth.

In the above example, each process has its own, private copy of the variable i. A graphic example of shared and private memory is obtained by considering the output of the following program (assume EPR_PROCS = 10):

```
integer i,k,m
k = 50
i = 20
PARALLEL
      PRIVATE i
      DO ALL (i = 1:10)
            print *,'i = ',i,',k = ',k
      END DOALL
END PARALLEL
print *,'end,i = ',i
end
```

One possible output of this program is

```
i = 4 , k = 50
i = 2 , k = 50
i = 6 , k = 50
i = 1 , k = 50
i = 7 , k = 50
i = 3 , k = 50
i = 10 , k = 50
i = 5 , k = 50
i = 8 , k = 50
i = 9 , k = 50
end, i = 20
```

In the parallel region, the variable k is shared by all processes, but each process has its own private value of i. Note that the values of i are not output in numerical order, because the scheduling of processes on processors is subject to the vagaries of time-sharing. Note also that the declaration of i within the parallel region does not affect the value of i outside the parallel region. Thus the variable i seen outside the parallel region is different from the i used by the parent within the parallel region.

B.5   critical section–end critical section

A *critical section* is a group of statements which can be executed by only one process at a time. It is equivalent to a region protected by a spin-lock, but the critical section "variable" (analogous to the variable used as the argument to the spin-lock call) is not explicitly used. The critical section is delineated by critical section–end critical section statements and is illustrated by the parallelization of the familiar program to sum the elements of an array.

```
c       sum 1000 elements of array a(i)
        real a(1000), sum
        integer i
        .
        .
        .
        sum = 0.
        do 1 i = 1,1000
             sum = sum + a(i)
1       continue
        .
        .
        .
```

This fragment is parallelized as follows:

```
c       sum 1000 elements of array a(i)
c       Illustrate the use of the critical section
c       variable sum holds final result.
        real a(1000),sum,temsum
```

```
            integer i
            .
            .
            .
            sum = 0.
            PARALLEL
                PRIVATE i,temsum
c               each process creates a partial sum
                DO ALL (i = 1:1000)
                    temsum = temsum + a(i)
                END DOALL
c       accumulate the partial sums into final value
c       only one process at a time is allowed in the
c       critical section.
                CRITICAL SECTION
                    sum = sum + temsum
                END CRITICAL SECTION
            END PARALLEL
            .
            .
            .
            end
```

This program is equivalent to Program 5-9 of Section 5.4.

In the parallel region, each process accumulates a partial sum in its private variable temsum. The critical section is delineated by the statements critical section–end critical section. A process within the critical section is executing the statements delineated by the critical section–end critical section statements. Variable sum is shared by all processes.

When a process (say A) arrives at the critical section statement, and if there is a process executing within the critical section (say process B, which in this case would be executing the statement sum = sum + temsum), then process A must wait until B leaves the critical section. (A process leaves the critical section by executing the statement end critical section.) After B leaves the critical section, A may enter. If process A arrives at the critical section statement, and there is no process within the critical section, then it may enter the critical section and execute the statements there.

There can be only one process at a time within the critical section. There can be many processes waiting at the critical section statement, because there is a single process within the critical section. When the critical section becomes empty, only one of the waiting processes is chosen to enter the critical section. So far as the user is concerned, the choice of which particular process enters the critical section is random.

In the fragment above, each process updates the value of sum separately. We are assured that, when process accesses sum, no other process can be updating sum at the same time. Thus, after all processes pass through the critical section, sum contains the complete sum of a(1) through a(1000).

B.6 barrier

The barrier statement sets up a barrier for all the processes executing in the parallel region. When a process arrives at the barrier statement within a parallel region, it must wait until *all* the processes have arrived at the barrier. When all processes have executed the barrier statement, then they may all proceed. At present, it is not possible to create a barrier for a subset of the processes executing in the parallel region.

An example of the use of the barrier statement is given below:

```
c       Execute two loops, where the second loop depends on
c       the results of the first.
        real x(1000),y(1000),z(1000)
        integer i
        .
        .
        .
        do 1 i = 1,1000
            x(i) = x(i) + y(i)
1       continue
        do 2 i = 2,999
            z(i) = x(i - 1) + x(i) + x(i + 1)
2       continue
        .
        .
        .
```

The parallel version is

```
c       Use barrier to ensure that the first loop is complete
c       before commencing the second loop.
        real x(1000),y(1000),z(1000)
```

```
            integer i
                .
                .

                .
            PARALLEL
                PRIVATE i
                DOALL (i = 1:1000)
                    x(i) = x(i) + y(i)
                END DOALL

c       Make sure everyone is done before continuing.
                BARRIER

                DOALL (i = 2:999)
                    z(i) = x(i - 1) + x(i) + x(i + 1)
                END DOALL

c       Make sure everyone is done before parent can
c       execute in single-stream region.
                BARRIER
            END PARALLEL
                .

                .

                .
```

In this example, the barrier statement makes sure that all the x(i) have been calculated before proceeding with the calculation of the z(i). If the barrier were not there, then, for example, a process may race ahead, finish calculating its share of x(i), and then start calculating z(i) before the required x(i) computed by other processes, have been updated.

B.7 barrier begin—end barrier

When a process executes the barrier begin statement, it must wait until all processes have arrived. In this, it is like a barrier. After all processes have arrived at the barrier begin statement, then *only one* process is allowed to execute the statements located between the barrier begin and the end barrier. When that process executes the end barrier statement, then all waiting processes begin executing the first statement following the end barrier statement. The user has no control over which process actually executes the statements in the protected region.

The barrier begin—end barrier construct is used to update a shared variable within a parallel region. It ensures that the shared variable is updated only once, by a single process. In the following fragment, the average of a(i) is found. First, all elements of a(i) are summed, and then the sum is divided by 1000 in a protected region to form the average.

```
real a(1000),sum
integer i
  .
  .
  .
sum = 0.
do 1 i = 1,1000
     sum = sum + a(i)
1    continue
sum = sum/1000.
```

This program is parallelized as follows:

```
real a(1000),sum,temsum
integer i
  .
  .
  .
sum = 0.
PARALLEL
     PRIVATE i,temsum
     temsum = 0.
     DO ALL (i = 1:1000)
          temsum = temsum + a(i)
     END DOALL

     CRITICAL SECTION
          sum = sum + temsum
     END CRITICAL SECTION

     BARRIER BEGIN
          sum = sum/1000.
     END BARRIER
       .
       .
       .
          (other statements within the parallel region)
     END PARALLEL
```

It may not be desired to end the parallel region after the critical section, and so the `barrier begin—end barrier` construct is used to make sure that sum is divided by 1000 only once. If it were not there, each process would divide sum by 1000, producing the incorrect result.

B.8   Spin-Locks

The spin-lock in EPF is identical to that described in the library approach, Section 5.4, except that the function calls are replaced by language statements. The statements are

```
lock var1,var2,...

var = value

wait lock(var)
send lock(var)
```

The `lock` statement is an EPF declaration, and appears in the declaration section of the module. It is used like a Fortran declaration; `var1`, `var2`,... are variable or array names. The array can be dimensioned in the `lock` statement or in a separate dimension statement. The `lock` declarations declare `var1`, `var2`,... to be variables of type `lock`.

Variables of type lock can have only one of two possible values: `.unlocked.` or `.locked.`. These values initialize the lock represented by the variable to be in the unlocked or locked state respectively.

The `wait lock(var)` statement is equivalent to the call to `spin_lock(lok)`. The `send lock(var)` statement is equivalent to the call to `spin_unlock(lok)`, where `lok` is the appropriate integer variable, while `var` is a variable of type `lock`. The use of these statements is illustrated in the histogram program, Section B.11.3.

B.9   Events

The statements for events are

```
event var1,var2,...

var = value
```

```
wait sync(var)
send sync(var)
```

The `event` statement is a declaration and declares `var1`, `var2`, . . . to be of type event; `var1`, `var2`, . . . can be variable or array names. Arrays can be dimensioned in the `event` declaration or in a separate dimension statement.

A variable of type event can have one of two values: `.wait.` and `.go.`, which initialize the event to the cleared or posted states respectively.

The `wait sync(var)` statement is equivalent to the call to `event_wait(event)`, while the statement `send sync(var)` is equivalent to the `event_post(event)` statement.

B.10   Built-in Functions

EPF has several built-in functions which return information about the processes executing in the parallel region.

1. `condlock`

```
logical result
lock var

result = condlock(var)
```

If the lock represented by `var` is locked when the statement is executed, then `result` is `.false.`. If the lock was not locked, then it is locked and result is `.true.`.

2. `ntasks`

```
integer ntasks,num

num = ntasks()
```

The function `ntasks` returns the number of processes executing in the parallel region.

3. `taskid`

```
integer taskid(),id

id = taskid()
```

The function `taskid` returns the process-id for the particular process
which executes the statement. Process-ids are integers in the range of 0
to `ntasks()` − 1. The parent has process-id = 0.

B.11   Some Subroutines Written in EPF

B.11.1   Find Minimum and Maximum Value of an Array

```
      subroutine find_min_max(a,n,shr_amin,shr_amax)
      real a(n),amin,amax,shr_amin,shr_amax
      integer n,l

c
c     **************************************************************
c     Find mimimum and maximum value of a(i), i <= l <= n.
c     EPF version.
c     shr_amax is the maximum value.
c     shr_amin is minimum value.
c     Parent only calls this routine. The additional processes
c     are created below, in the "parallel" region.
c     Variables declared above are automatically shared
c     among all the processes.
c     **************************************************************

c     initialize shared variables
      shr_amax = a(1)
      shr_amin = a(1)

c     ------------------------------------------------------------
c     start parallel region. If the environment variable
c     EPR_PROCS is nproc, then the "parallel" statement creates
c     nproc - 1 additional processes. All processes share the
c     variables declared above, but the variables declared
c     within the parallel region are private to each process.
c     ------------------------------------------------------------
      parallel
      private amin,amax,i

c     initialize private variables
      amax = a(1)
      amin = a(1)

c     Each process finds the min and max of a subset of
```

```
c       array elements. The scheduling is left up to
c       the compiler.
        doall(i = 1:n)
            if (a(i) .gt. amax) then
                amax = a(i)
            endif
            if (a(i) .lt. amin) then
                amin = a(i)
            endif
        end doall
```

```
c       ----------------------------------------------------------
c       maximum of partial maxima (and minima) is found
c       in critical section. Only one process at a
c       time is allowed in the critical section. Each process
c       checks its own partial max (min) against the
c       global value.
c       ----------------------------------------------------------
        critical section
            if (amax .gt. shr_amax) then
                shr_amax = amax
            endif
            if (amin .lt. shr_amin) then
                shr_amin = amin
            endif
        end critical section
```

```
c       barrier makes sure all processes have finished,
c       before continuing
        barrier
```

```
c       end parallel region. Parent only continues following
c       the statement below.
        end parallel
```

```
        return
        end
```

B.11.2 Matrix-Vector Multiply

```
        subroutine matvec(a,v,n,c)
        real a(1000,n),v(n),c(n),sum
        integer n,i,j
```

```
c       ********************************************************
c       matrix vector multiply
c          c(i) = a(i,j) * v(j), sum over j
```

```
c     EPF version.
c     v(i) and c(i) cannot be the same array.
c     Parent only calls this routine. The additional processes
c     are created below, in the "parallel" region.
c     Variables declared above are automatically shared
c     among all the processes.
c     **********************************************************

c     ----------------------------------------------------------
c     start parallel region. If the environment variable
c     EPR_PROCS is nproc, then the "parallel" statement creates
c     nproc - 1 additional processes. All processes share the
c     variables declared above, but the variables declared
c     within the parallel region are private to each process.
c     ----------------------------------------------------------
      parallel
      private i,j,sum
c     Each process computes a different element of c(i).
c     scheduling is up to compiler
      doall (i = 1:n)
          sum = 0.
          do 2 j = 1,n
              sum = sum + a(i,j) * v(j)
  2       continue
          c(i) = sum
      end doall

c     barrier makes sure all processes have finished
c     before proceeding.
      barrier

c     end parallel region. Parent only continues
c     following the statement below.
      end parallel

      return
      end
```

B.11.3 Histogram

```
      subroutine hist(a,n,histogram,num_bins,bin_size,amin)
      real a(n),amin,bin_size
      integer num_bins,histogram(1),i,n,bin,temhist(50)
      lock lok_hist(50)
```

```
c     *********************************************************
c     compute histogram of a(i), 1 <= i <= n
c     num_bins = number of bins in histogram.
c     bin_size = size of each bin
c     amin - smallest value of a(i)
c     EPF version.
c     Parent only calls this routine. The additional processes
c     are created below, in the "parallel" region.
c     Variables declared above are automatically shared
c     among all the processes.
c     *********************************************************

c     initialize locks (lok_hist is shared).
          do 30 j = 1,num_bins
              lok_hist(j) = .unlocked.
  30      continue

c     initialize global variable
          do 20 j = 1,num_bins
              histogram(j) = 0
  20      continue

c     ---------------------------------------------------------
c     start parallel region. If the environment variable
c     EPR_PROCS is nproc, then the "parallel" statement creates
c     nproc - 1 additional processes. All processes share the
c     variables declared above, but the variables declared
c     within the parallel region are private to each process.
c     ---------------------------------------------------------
          parallel
          integer temhist(50)
          private temhist,i,bin

c     initialize private variables. Each process has its
c     private copy of array temhist(i).
          do 1 i = 1,num_bins
              temhist(i) = 0
   1      continue

c     ---------------------------------------------------------
c     compute histogram in parallel.
c     Each process computes contribution of a different a(i)
c     to the histogram. First each process updates
c     a partial histogram, using private array temhist(i).
c     Then, each element of histogram(i) is locked separately for
c     update, so different array elements can be
c     updated simultaneously by different processes.
c     ---------------------------------------------------------
```

```
                      doall(i = 1:n)
                          bin = int((a(i) - amin)/bin_size) + 1
                          temhist(bin) = temhist(bin) + 1
                      end doall

c        now accumulate partial results into histogram
c        each process does part of accumulation.
                      do 50 i = 1,num_bins
                          wait lock(lok_hist(i))
                             histogram(i) = histogram(i) + temhist(i)
                          send lock(lok_hist(i))
    50                continue

c        barrier makes sure all processes have finished
c        before continuing.
                      barrier

c        end parallel region. Parent only executes
c        after statement below.
                      end parallel

                      return
                      end
```

B.11.4   Numerical Integration

```
                      subroutine integrate(n,sum,step)
                      integer n,i
                      real step,funct,sum,temsum

c        ***********************************************************
c        numerical integration of funct(x) using Simpson's rule.
c        integrate over interval 0 → n * step, n even
c        value of integral returned in "sum."
c        EPF version.
c        funct - user supplied function to be integrated
c        Parent only calls this routine. The additional processes
c        are created below, in the "parallel" region.
c        Variables declared above are automatically shared
c        among all the processes.
c        ***********************************************************

c        initialize shared variable
                      sum = 0.

c        _____
c        start parallel region. If the environment variable
c        EPR_PROCS is nproc, then the "parallel" statement creates
```

```
c       nproc - 1 additional processes. All processes share the
c       variables declared above, but the variables declared
c       within the parallel region are private to each process.
c       ------------------------------------------------------------
        parallel
        private i,temsum

c       do integration. Each process computes a portion of
c       the sum.
        temsum = 0.
        doall(i = 1:n - 3:2)
            temsum = temsum + 4. * funct(i * step)
            temsum = temsum + 2. * funct((i + 1) * step)
        end doall

c       accumulate the partial sums into the final integral
c       "sum." Only one process at a time is allowed in
c       a critical section.
        critical section
            sum = sum + temsum
        end critical section

c       barrier makes sure all processes have finished
c       before continuing.
        barrier

c       end parallel region. Parent only executes
c       after statement below.
        end parallel
c       now the final points
        sum = (step/3.) * (funct(0.) + sum
     s           + 4. * funct((n - 1) * step) + funct(n * step))

        return
        end
```

APPENDIX C

Parallel Programming on a Uniprocessor Under Unix

C.1 Introduction

A parallel program subdivides the work done by the program among a number of processes. It is not necessary to execute the different processes of a parallel program on different processors. It is possible to have all the processes execute on a single processor, which is the case when a parallel program is run on a uniprocessor computer. The advantage of being able to create parallel programs on a uniprocessor is that one can develop parallel programs, or practice parallel programming, without requiring access to a multiprocessor computer. At present, uniprocessor computers are far more common than multiprocessor computers. A parallel program running on a uniprocessor will in general run slower than the equivalent single-stream program, because of the extra overhead involved in creating processes, because of synchronization, and because of the extra computation that is not found in the single-stream version.

This appendix describes how parallel programs may be executed on uniprocessor computers which run the Unix system V operating system or its equivalent. (There are two widespread versions of Unix, one called system V, which is the official AT&T version, and the other called BSD which is supported by the University of California at Berkeley. Xenix is a version of system V commonly found on PCs.) Unix V provides a set of functions, callable from a C program, which allow the program to do such things as create and destroy processes, allocate and share memory and create a lock. From the user's point of view, these functions are used much like any library of functions. The following calls from Standard Unix V can be used to implement the parallel-programming functions described in this book:

1. `fork`—The `fork` system call allows the parent to fork a single child. The `process_fork` function is based on the `fork`.
2. `exit,wait`—the `exit` function terminates the process calling it. The parent calls `wait` to wait for the children to terminate before continuing. These functions are used to implement the `process_join`.
3. `shared memory`—There are several functions to share memory among processes. These are used to implement the functionality of the `shared` call. The `shared` function itself cannot be implemented in a Fortran program, because of Fortran's static memory allocation, but a simple workaround is described.
4. `semaphore`—There are several functions to implement the semaphore, which is the fundamental synchronization mechanism in Unix. From it, the `spin_lock` is constructed. The `barrier` is then based on the spin-lock.

It is beyond the scope of this book to provide an introduction to Unix and to C programming. Rather, this appendix explains how Unix V functions may be used to implement the parallel-programming subroutines and functions described in this book, assuming that the user has the required background in Unix.

C.2   Calling C Programs from Fortran and Vice Versa

The Unix system calls are functions which are normally called from within C programs. For a particular Unix implementation, there may exist a Fortran interface to these functions. However, one should not count on this. If there is no explicit Fortran interface, then there is still a *de facto* standard by which Fortran programs may call a C program, which then makes the required system call.

To illustrate what is involved, consider the following toy example. A Fortran program sets a scalar variable and the elements of an array, then calls a C program which prints out the values. The Fortran program is

```
c       Fortran main calls C function cfunct.
c       File test.f
        integer i,a(0:10),j
        i = 200
        do 1 j = 0,10
            a(j) = 2 * j
    1   continue
        call cfunct(i,a)
        end
```

The file containing the C program cfunct might be

```
void cfunct_(i,a) /* Function called by Fortran routine.
                     Note the appended underscore.
                     File cfunct.c */
int *i,a[];      /* Fortran passes pointers */
{
    int j;
    printf("i = %d\n", *i);
    for(j = 0;j <= 10;j++)
        printf("j a[j] = %d %d\n",j,a[j]);
}
```

Note the underscore in the function name. This is the standard notation for a C function which will be called from a Fortran routine.

In standard Unix, the C function is compiled as

   cc −c cfunct.c

where *cc* invokes the C compiler, *-c* instructs the compiler to produce an object program, but no executable, and *cfunct.c* is the name of the source file.

The Fortran program is compiled by

   f77 test.f cfunct.o

which produces the executable *a.out*. When this executable is run, the output is what is expected.

The important point here is that the C function which is called from a Fortran program, is defined by appending an underscore to the function name.

It is also possible to call a Fortran program from a C program. In this case, the calling C program appends an underscore when it calls the Fortran module. Fortran modules themselves never have an appended underscore. Below, a C main calls a Fortran subroutine, which then calls a C routine.

```
/* --------- c file c_prog.c -------------------*/

void fort_foo_(); /* The C main will call Fortran routine
                    fort_foo. */
main(){
     int i,a[21];

/* put code here to do something */

     fort_foo_(&i,a);    /* call fortran routine */
}


void c_foo_(i,a) /* This routine is called from the Fortran
                    routine fort_foo. */
     int *i,a[];
{
     /* put code here to do something */
}

/* --------------- end of file --------------------*/
```

```
c       -----------fortran file   f_prog.f --------------
c
        subroutine fort_foo(i,a)
        integer i,a(0:1)

c       do something useful here, then
c       call C routine.
        call c_foo(i,a)
        return
        end

c       ------------------------end of file  -------------------
```

To compile,

```
cc −c c_prog.c
f77 f_prog.f c_prog.o
```

To run,

    a.out

The reader should ascertain whether this convention is actually obeyed for his particular system, and if not, if there is an equivalent substitute.

C.3 process_fork

The `process_fork` function is created from the Unix `fork` function:

```
int fork(),proc_id;
proc_id = fork();
```

The function `fork()` creates a single additional process, and returns 0 to the child and a positive integer `proc_id`, called the process-id, to the parent. The process-id could be any number, and is used to identify the *child* process to the operating system.

    The C program which implements the `process_fork` is (note the underscore):

```
int process_fork_(nproc)
int *nproc;

/* fork *nproc - 1 additional processes, return 0
to the parent (which originally calls this routine) and
1,2,.., nproc - 1 to each of the children. */

{
    int j;
    for (j = 1; j <= (*nproc) - 1; j++)
        if(fork() == 0)
            return(j); /* child returns */

    return(0);    /* parent returns */
}
```

C.4   Spin-Locks

Spin-locks are implemented using the Unix V semaphores. (A description of a similar implementation is presented in Chapter 13). Unix V semaphores are complex. We illustrate here only those features required for our purposes.

All C program files implementing semaphore operations must have the include statements:

```
#include <sys/types.h>
#include <sys/ipc.h>
#include <sys/sem.h>
```

The system call `semget` creates a semaphore.

```
int semid;
semid = semget(IPC_PRIVATE,1,0666|IPC_CREAT);
```

The first and third arguments are flags that are defined in the include files. 0666 sets permissions. The second argument, 1, means that a single semaphore is created. (One can create arrays of semaphores.) The integer `semid` is the *semaphore identifier* and must be included in all future calls to identify the semaphore.

The function `semctl` resets the semaphore. Only a simplified version of the arguments are used.

```
int semid,control;

        semctl(semid,0,SETVAL,control);
```

This sets the internal counter of the semaphore to equal the value of `control`.

The `semaphore_send` and `semaphore_wait` operations are implemented using the function `semop`.

```
int semid;
struct sembuf operations;

        semop(semid,&operations,1);
```

The structure `sembuf` is defined in the include files:

```
struct sembuf{
                short num;
                short op;
                short flag;
                };
```

We always have num = 0, flag = 0. If the value of op is −1, then semop behaves as semaphore_wait. If op is 1, it behaves as semaphore_send.

The implementation of spin_lock_init, spin_lock, and spin_ unlock is as follows (note the appended underscore.)

```
/* ---------------------------------------------------*/

/*file to implement spin-locks from Unix V semaphores */

#include <sys/types.h>
#include <sys/ipc.h>
#include <sys/sem.h>

/***********************;**************spin_lock_init_*/
void spin_lock_init_(lok,condition)
int *lok,*condition;

/* if *condition = 0, spin-lock is unlocked. If
*condition = 1,it is locked */

{
     int control;

     *lok = semget(IPC_PRIVATE,1,0666|IPC_CREAT)

     if (*condition == 0)
         control = 1   /* unlocked */
     else
         control = 0   /* locked */

     semctl(*lok,0,SETVAL,control);
}
/*********************************************spin_lock*/
void spin_lock_(lok)
int *lok;
{
     struct {
             short num;
             short op;
```

```
                              short flag;
                              } operations;

              operations.num = 0
              operations.op = -1;
              operations.flag = 0

              semop(*lok,&operations,1)
      }
/*********************************************spin_unlock*/
void spin_unlock_(lok)
int *lok;
{
              struct {
                              short num;
                              short op;
                              short flag;
                              } operations;

              operations.num = 0
              operations.op = 1;
              operations.flag = 0

              semop(*lok,&operations,1)
      }
```

C.5   Barriers

Barriers may be implemented using the Fortran program of section 14.2.3.
No additional C programs are necessary. The barrier array is an integer of
dimension 4, so one would have

```
        integer bar_array(4),nproc,blocking_number

        call barrier_init(bar_array,blocking_number)

        call barrier(bar_array)
```

Below, the implementation of Chapter 14 is reproduced, except that spin-
locks are used instead of semaphores. Most of the comments have been removed.

```
        subroutine barrier_init(bar,blocking_number)
```

```
        integer bar(1),blocking_number

c       The following information is stored in bar(i):
c       bar(1) - the blocking number
c       bar(2) - the number of processes waiting at the barrier.
c
c       bar(3) - used for releasing processes.
c       bar(4) - the spin-lock identification integer.
c       array bar must be shared.
        call spin_lock_init(bar(4),0)
        bar(1) = blocking_number
        bar(2) = 0
        bar(3) = 0

        return
        end

c       *****************************************************barrier

        subroutine barrier(bar)
        integer bar(1),incremented

c       Private variable incremented is set to 1 when this process
c       increments the internal barrier counter bar(2).

        incremented = 0

 95       continue
c       Block processes. Check for release. Check for calls made
c       during release,and for early calls.
        call spin_lock(bar(4))
c           check for nonblocked process
            if ((incremented .eq. 0) .and.
     s          (bar(3) .gt. 0)) then
                call spin_unlock(bar(4))
                goto 95
            endif
c
            if (incremented .eq. 0) then
c               increment internal counter
                bar(2) = bar(2) + 1
                incremented = 1
            endif
c
            if ((bar(2) .lt. bar(1)) .and.
     s          (bar(3) .eq. 0)) then
c                   fewer than blocking number of processes
```

```
c                          are at the barrier
                           call spin_unlock(bar(4))
                           goto 95
                 else
c                          Release mode.
c                          first process.
                           if (bar(3) .eq. 0) then
                                bar(3) = bar(1) -1
c                                reset the barrier
                                bar(2) = 0
                                call spin_unlock(bar(4))
                                return
                           else
c                                release next process
                                bar(3) = bar(3) - 1
                                call spin_unlock(bar(4))
                                return
                           endif
                 endif
c          if arrive at this point, is an error
           call spin_unlock(bar(4))
           print *,'ERROR, barrier,abort'
           call exit(-1)

           return
           end
```

C.6 process_join

In the text, process_join is presumed to have no arguments. However, if the function is to be implemented using Unix V, then it is called with two arguments: nproc, the number of processes, and id, the process-id as returned from the function process_fork.

```
c      use of process_join in Fortran program, if the
c      subroutine is implemented with Unix system calls.

       integer nproc,id;
       .
       .

       .
       call process_fork(nproc,id)
```

The C function requires the following two Unix functions:

```
void exit();
int wait();
```

When a process calls `exit`, it is terminated. When a parent calls waits for any one of its children to be destroyed. As soon as a child is destroyed, the parent can proceed. If a child has been terminated before the call to `wait`, the parent returns from `wait` immediately. It will do this once for each child that has been terminated before the first call to `wait`. In the function `process_join` below, the parent loops through the call to `wait` a total of nproc − 1 times.

```
void process_join_(nproc,id)
int *nproc,*id;

/* When a child calls this, it is terminated. When a parent
calls, it waits for all children to be terminated before
returning. */

{
    int i;
    if (*id == 0)
        for (i = 1;i <= (*nproc) − 1;i++)
            wait(0);/* parent waits */

    else        /* child terminates */
        exit(0);
}
```

C.7   Shared Memory

Implementing shared memory in Fortran programs using Unix V involves a bit of a workaround. The problem will become clear once the workings of shared memory are revealed.

Any C file that includes functions which call the shared memory functions must include the files

```
#include <sys/types.h>
#include <sys/ipc.h>
#include <sys/shm.h>
```

In order for a process to access shared memory, first it must allocate a region of physical memory and inform the operating system that the memory will be shared among processes. This is done using `shmget`:

```
int shmid,size;
shmid = shmget(IPC_PRIVATE,size,0666|IPC_CREAT);
```

where `size` is the number of bytes to be allocated. The variable `shmid` is the *shared memory identifier*. After allocating the memory, one sets a pointer to point to it, using `shmat`.

```
char *shmat(),*tem;
int shmid;
tem = shmat(shmid,0,0);
```

where `shmid` is the identifier that was returned from `shmget`. The pointer `tem` points to the block of shared memory of `size` bytes.

The C routine which allocates `size` bytes of shared memory is

```
char *sshared(size,shmid)
int size,*shmid;

/* allocate size bytes of shared memory, return a pointer to
char which points to the start of the shared memory
segment. shmid is a pointer to the shared memory identifier.
This routine is to be called by another C module.   */
{
    *shmid = shmget(IPC_PRIVATE,size,0666|IPC_CREAT);
    return(shmat(*shmid,0,0));
}
```

To use this mechanism for sharing memory, the calling C module must declare a pointer of any data type and then coerce the pointer to point to the shared memory. For example, to allocate 12 integers of shared memory:

```
int *ptr,shmid,size;
size = 48;
ptr = (int *)sshared(size,&shmid);

/* assign values to shared memory */
*ptr = 1
*(ptr + 1) = 2
.
.
.
```

One could use the same variable `ptr` in several different allocations.

This assigning of pointers is not possible in Fortran. Even though Fortran passes pointers in function calls, the called function only uses the pointer to alter the contents of the memory locations, not the position of the location itself. That is, Fortran has statically allocated memory, while C has dynamically allocated memory.

The way to work around this is to have the parallel Fortran program be a subroutine whose arguments include all the shared-memory variables. The shared memory is allocated by a C routine, which then calls the Fortran program. Section 18.9 gives an example of how this is done.

C.8   Cleanup

The shared memory identifier shmid and semaphore identifier semid are allocated by the Unix operating system and maintained by the operating system in a table. These identifiers are meant to be used by unrelated processes, so that the same shared memory can be accessed by many users. One use of such shared memory is for databases. The identifiers are not released by the system when a process is finished with them, since other processes may start up later and use the same shared memory. There is a maximum number of such identifiers that can be allocated to all the users, and once this maximum is attained, no more shared memory or semaphores can be allocated by anyone.

It is therefore necessary to explicitly release the identifiers after a parallel program has used them. This should be done by the parent, before it exits, and can be done using the routines below. If the parent exits abnormally, before it has had a chance to release the identifiers, you will have to release them "manually." Ask your system administrator for the appropriate utilities.

```
void cleanup_memory_(shmid)
int *shmid ;
/* release shared memory identifier *shmid. This routine is
called from a Fortran program. */
{
    struct shmid_ds *buf;
    shmctl(*shmid,IPC_RMID,buf);
}

void cleanup_semaphore_(semid)
int *semid;
```

```
/* release semaphore identifier *semid. This routine is
called from a Fortran program */


{
    semctl(*semid,IPC_RMID,0);
}
```

C.9   An Example

The following example shows how to use a C main program to allocate shared memory, then call a Fortran routine which does a calculation in parallel. Using the functions described in this chapter, this program is ready to run on a Unix V system.

```
/* ---------------    C main-------------- */

#include <sys/types.h>
#include <sys/ipc.h>
#include <sys/shm.h>

void maxval_();

/*************************************************main*/
main()
/* C routine which allocates 4 integers, then calls a
Fortran routine maxval() to find maximum value of an
array in parallel.*/

  {
    struct shmid_ds *buf;
    int *ptr,shmid;

    ptr = (int *)sshared(16,&shmid);
    maxval_(ptr,ptr + 1,ptr + 2,ptr + 3);   /* call Fortran
                                        subroutine with 4
                                        integer arguments */

    shmctl(shmid,IPC_RMID,buf);   /* cleanup */
}

/* -------------- end of C main ----------------*/
```

```
c      -------------------    Fortran function ------------------

c      Fortran routine which finds maximum value. The arguments
c      are shared.
c      *******************************************************maxval
          subroutine maxval(final_amax,lokl,lok2,next_index)

c      Compute the maximum value of array a(i) using nproc
c      processes and self-scheduling
c      and spin-locks for the calculation of the maximum of all the
c      partial maxima.
c      Assume <= 50 processes.
c      final_amax - the final maximum.
c      amax is private to each process.

          integer id,nproc,process_fork,i,locked,unlocked
          integer lokl,lok2,next_index,n
          real final_amax
          real a(1000),amax

c      comment out shared statements. Shared variables
c      are dummy arguments to this function.
c          call shared(final_amax,4)
c          call shared(lokl,4)
c          call shared(lok2,4)
c          call shared(next_index,4)

          print *,'enter nproc'
          read *,nproc

          unlocked = 0
          locked = 1
          n = 1000
          next_index = n

c      initialize a(i)
          do 10 i = 1,n
              a(i) = i
 10       continue

          amax = a(1)
          final_amax = a(1)

c      initialize spin lock
          call spin_lock_init(lokl,unlocked)
          call spin_lock_init(lok2,unlocked)
```

```
c       create nproc - 1 children.
            id = process_fork(nproc)

c       loop splitting, each child calculates the maximum
c       value of a subset of the elements of a(i)

 20        continue

c          self-scheduling section
           call spin_lock(lok1)
               i = next_index
               next_index = next_index - 1
           call spin_unlock(lok1)
c       end of self-scheduling section

           if (i .le. 0) goto 1
           if (a(i) .gt. amax) then
               amax = a(i)
           endif
           goto 20
  1        continuue

c       now each child updates the shared variable
c       final_amax.
           call spin_lock(lok2)
               if (amax .gt. final_amax) then
                   final_amax = amax
               endif
           call spin_unlock(lok2)

c       destroy children
           call process_join(nproc,id)

           print *,' max value of a(i) is ',final_amax

c       cleanup spin-locks - Unix semaphores
           cleanup_semaphore(lok1)
           cleanup_semaphore(lok2)

           return
           end
```

Bibliography

There is not a lot of non-technical literature on tightly-coupled parallel programming. The book by Boyle et al. has a chapter on shared-memory parallel programming, and the book edited by Schultz has several very technical articles on this subject.

There are a number of books on Unix system programming, which is an example of loosely-coupled parallel programming. The books by Haviland and Salama, and by Rochkind describe in detail the use of Unix system calls for process creation and destruction, synchronization, and shared memory. Bach details Unix system V internals, including the way in which processes and multiprocessing are implemented, while Peterson and Silberschatz review modern operating system concepts. Finally, the book by Fortier is a nice introduction to the operating systems of distributed systems, such as shared-memory multiprocessors, and contains an extensive discussion of the concept of the process.

James Boyle, Ralph Butler, Terrernce Disz, Barnett Glickfeld, Ewing Lusk, Ross Overbeek, James Patterson, Rick Stevens, *Portable Programs for Parallel Processors*, Holt, Rinehart and Winston, NY, 1987.

Martin Schultz, ed., *Numerical Algorithms for Modern Parallel Computer Architectures*, Springer-Verlag, NY, 1988.

Marc. J. Rochkind, *Advanced Unix Programming*, Prentice-Hall, Englewood Cliffs, NJ, 1985.

Keith Haviland and Ben Salama, *Unix System Programming*, Addison-Wesley, Reading, MA, 1987.

Maurice J. Bach, *The Design of the Unix Operating System*, Prentice-Hall, Englewood Cliffs, NJ, 1986.

James L. Peterson and Abraham Silberschatz, *Operating System Concepts*, Addison-Wesley, Reading, MA, 1985.

Paul J. Fortier, *Design of Distributed Operating Systems*, McGraw Hill, NY, 1986.

Index

Order Form for Parallel Programs on Diskette

The programs in this book can be obtained on a floppy disk by using the detachable order form below. In addition, C versions of the programs are also available. Allow three to six weeks for delivery.

Send check or money order to: Steven Brawer, Parallel Program Disks, 6 Dickson Drive, Westfield, NJ 07090

Please send me

_____ diskettes of Parallel Programs in Fortran @ $15.00 each.

_____ diskettes of Parallel Programs in C @ $25.00 each.

Please check type of computer (IBM or compatible):

_____ PC, XT   _____ AT, 386

Name (please print) _____

Address _____

City _____

State _____   Zip Code _____
